LEGENDARY LOCALS

OF

JERSEY CITY

NEW JERSEY

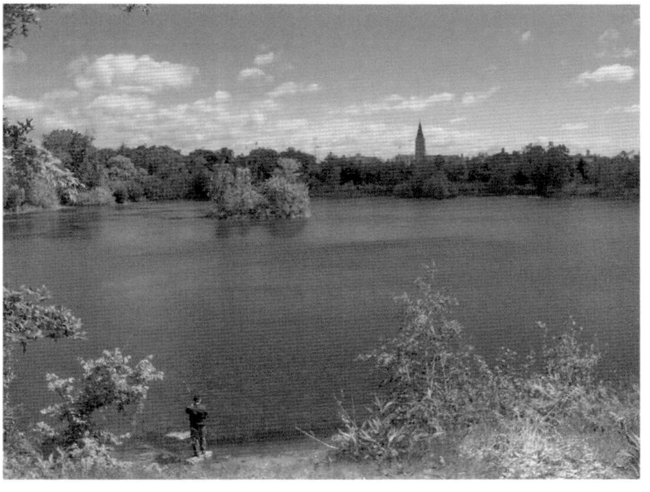

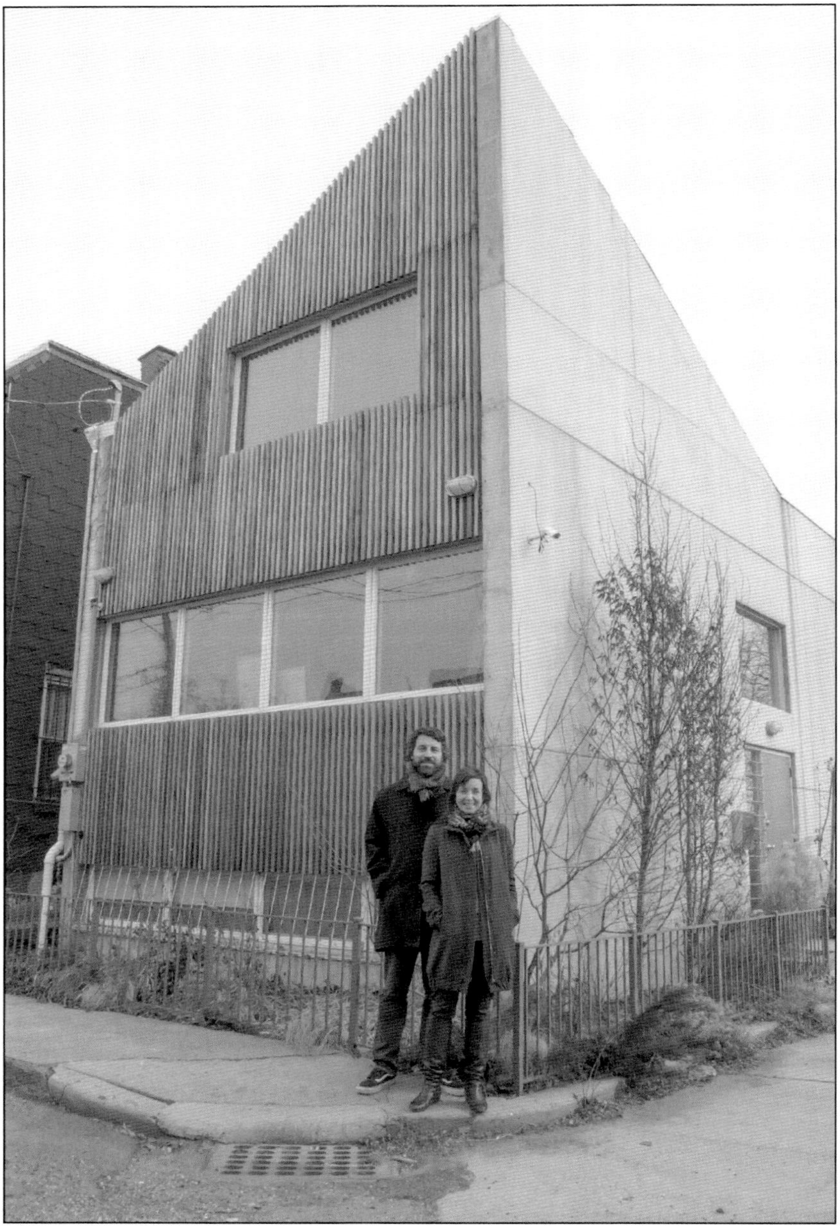

Nicole Robertson and Richard Garber
Nicole Robertson and Richard Garber of GRO Architects are making architectural history with their award-winning prefabricated housing type PREttyFAB, seen here at 1 Minerva Place in the Bergen-Lafayette section of Jersey City (see pages 110–111). (Courtesy of Andrew Doran.)

Page 1: Reservoir No. 3
If not for the tireless advocacy efforts of Steve Latham and the Jersey City Reservoir Preservation Alliance, historic Reservoir No. 3 (erected in 1871–1880) would not be the inner-city nature oasis and passive recreation attraction that it has become today (see page 97). (Courtesy of Andrew Doran.)

LEGENDARY LOCALS

OF

JERSEY CITY

NEW JERSEY

JOHN GOMEZ

LEGENDARY LOCALS

ISBN 978-1-4671-0092-2

Legendary Locals is an imprint of Arcadia Publishing
Charleston, South Carolina

Printed in the United States of America

Library of Congress Control Number: 2013932660

For all general information, please contact Arcadia Publishing:
Telephone 843-853-2070
Fax 843-853-0044
E-mail sales@arcadiapublishing.com
For customer service and orders:
Toll-Free 1-888-313-2665

Visit us on the Internet at www.arcadiapublishing.com

Dedication:
For Kenny Gomez (1943–2009)—the greatest legendary local I ever knew.

On the Front Cover: Clockwise from top left:
Paul and Eric Silverman, neighborhood builders (Courtesy of Andrew Doran; see page 91), Caroline Katz-Mount and Dr. Marshall Mount (Courtesy of Andrew Doran; see page 58), Alfred Charles Bossom, British architect (Courtesy of Avery Architectural & Fine Arts Library, Columbia University; see pages 102, 118), Erminnie Smith, prominent geologist, ethnologist, and intellectual (Courtesy of Dr. Jennifer S. Furlong; see pages 77, 78), Tris McCall, novelist (Courtesy of Andrew Doran; see page 66), A. Harry Moore, governor (Courtesy of Jersey City Free Public Library; see page 32), Laryssa Wirstiuk, short story writer (Courtesy of Andrew Doran; see page 50), Dr. Lena Edwards, prominent physician and humanitarian (Courtesy of the Afro-American Historical Society Museum; see page 29), Hugh Roberts, American Renaissance architect (Courtesy of the Newark Public Library; see pages 105, 106, 116, 122).

On the Back Cover: From left to right:
Andrzej Jerzy Lech, photographer (Courtesy of Andrew Doran; see page 68), Theodore Conrad, architect and preservationist (Courtesy of Ruth and Doris Conrad; see pages 19, 44, 75, 83, 85, 96, 99).

CONTENTS

ACKNOWLEDGMENTS

The author is indebted to the following individuals and institutions for their support, generosity, and inspiration throughout this writing: John Hallanan III, Esq., past president, and the trustees and advisors of the Jersey City Landmarks Conservancy; Cynthia Harris, manager, and the knowledgeable staff of the New Jersey Room, Jersey City Free Public Library; Neal Brunson, Esq., director, Afro-American Historical Society Museum; Avery Architectural & Fine Arts Library, Columbia University; Leon Yost, architectural photographer, preservationist, planner, author, and community visionary; Margaret Schmidt, managing editor, the *Jersey Journal*; and Michael Graves, Fellow of the American Institute of Architects (FAIA) and Karen V. Nichols, FAIA, of Michael Graves & Associates, Princeton, New Jersey.

Rightful recognition must be extended to Andrew Doran, the photographer of this book—unless otherwise noted—whose reliability, dedication, energy, creativity, and technical skills made *Legendary Locals of Jersey City* all the more exciting and enriching to work on. On many levels, his being a photographer, passionate chronicler of municipal history, and constant traveler to the monuments of the world makes him the true author.

To view extra features of *Legendary Locals of Jersey City*—including extended biographical narratives and interviews; figures, illustrations, maps, and archival images; color photographic galleries and documentary films; detailed notes and selected bibliographies; recommendations for further scholarly reading and research; locals updates, postings, and epilogues; and scheduled author readings, book signings, and special appearances and events—please visit jclandmarks.org.

INTRODUCTION

When I was very young in Jersey City, the city of my ancestors, I loved the built world so much that my dreams were inevitably invaded by the types of buildings that surrounded me and gave semblance to my distant vocation as an architectural historian. These dreams, I figured out early, were repeating reveries of the crumbling architecture I was growing up with. In my sleep—and in my city—I saw fenced-off factories, abandoned in absolution from wrecked first-floor loading docks to sky-exposed rooftops; six-story-high Gothic tenements along the narrowest streets, their decorative facades and cast-iron fire escape tiers scorched and scarred by mysterious fires; and schoolhouses so ancient that their stepped entrances and wide walls were swallowed up by strange glowing growths. Jersey City streetscapes were literally mirroring in my mind, and I could do nothing to stop the visceral proliferation—nor did I want to.

But in time, the double-architecture dreams subsided on their own, and there appeared instead the inner sanctum of my father's antiques business on Newark Avenue. At first, Village Antiques featured few items, nothing of real historical or material value. Soon, however, as my father had been studying and learning the trade and business, the shop started to swell with serious stocks of antiques and heirlooms. My father would often have me in tow in his blue Dodge Ram van to uninhabited buildings and demolition sites to get items for his shop. Suddenly, his modest storefront, which took up two addresses and featured cavernous sidewalk windows and a rear alleyway and yard, revealed its purpose and personality. Most pivotal to me, his oldest son, was the architectural atmosphere that now welcomed me every day as I entered the store after school. There was a church quality to the space and not entirely because of the stained-glass window lancets and lamps levitating from the metal ceilings. My father constantly bought and sold liturgical objects, like thick brass candelabra sticks, shining silver bowls and goblets, heavy Bible stands, and colossal crucifixes. Fragments rescued from destroyed houses of worship were not uncommon; pulled pine pews and extricated Carrera marble altars found their way into the yard. To my amazement and silent joy, architectural salvage was stationed and soldiered everywhere: cracked terra-cotta reliefs, manufacturer-stamped encaustic tiles, egg-dart moldings, caryatid statuary, ornamental wrought-iron gates, pocket doors, carved limestone pediments, wraparound porch columns, slate steps, discarded banisters, and tall mantels. In time, the lofty interior had become overcrowded with objects; labyrinthine paths and alcoves cluttered with antiques had formed. Every inch was occupied and fired by my father's passion for the past.

The store was slowly and steadily being discovered by the neighborhood; collectors started to come around and buy or sell. My father employed a few local seniors to man the store during morning and afternoon business hours while he worked at his day job; however, right after work, every weekday, he was there, all day and night, and weekends as well. And I was present with him, most times still dressed in my parochial school uniform. While my friends played wiffle ball, touch football, or bottle caps, I got lost within my father's staged showrooms and tin toy menageries. The 19th-century cuckoo clocks clinging to the walls; the Art Nouveau glassware locked inside display cabinets; the first edition books and folio parchments standing upright behind glass-door shelves; the endless array of lamps and sconces carefully suspended by hooks and cables; the maritime objects too heavy for the floor and so relegated to the back alley where they started to weather with atmospheric dust—all added to the visual majesty of the place; all became part of my father's municipal museum.

Storefronts provide access to people, who gather and mingle there, sharing urban stories that to an observant teenager seem beyond the actual. Hanging out at Village Antiques, sitting behind a buried bureau doing homework or reading an old book I had sneaked from a shelf, I was witness to locals entering and interacting with my father: politicians, police officers, barbers, butchers, artists, architects, rectors, doctors, and historians. They lingered in the store as if it were a social club, a bingo hall, or a diner.

Each one's uttered history—each disseminating purchase of a specific store item—turned, for me, into a tangible human artifact, something vertical and spatial. As more and more customers came in, bought, and revealed much about their personal lives, I came to realize that people were more interesting than the buildings I had been looking at and dreaming about ever since I was young. When they spoke, the antiques receded and were blurred. After long, I was intent on heading to my father's store to not only experience the objects of the past, but also the participants of the present. Both were inextricable.

Later in life, when I became an architectural historian, I discovered something startlingly similar: works of architecture are forever empty if the narratives of their architects and occupants are not told first. Every architectural historian must research and unearth the biography of the builder before the biography of the building. In many ways, writing *Legendary Locals of Jersey City* has been a return to my father's popular antiques atelier. With this project, I was once again able to rub shoulders with Jersey City's famous citizens—hear about their origins, discuss their career trajectories, and learn about their community triumphs. And while my father's store is long closed, this book has turned out, chapter by chapter, to be its continuation, a new gathering place, amidst a historical backdrop, for the legendary locals of Jersey City.

—John Gomez, Architectural Historian
Jersey City, New Jersey
May 2013

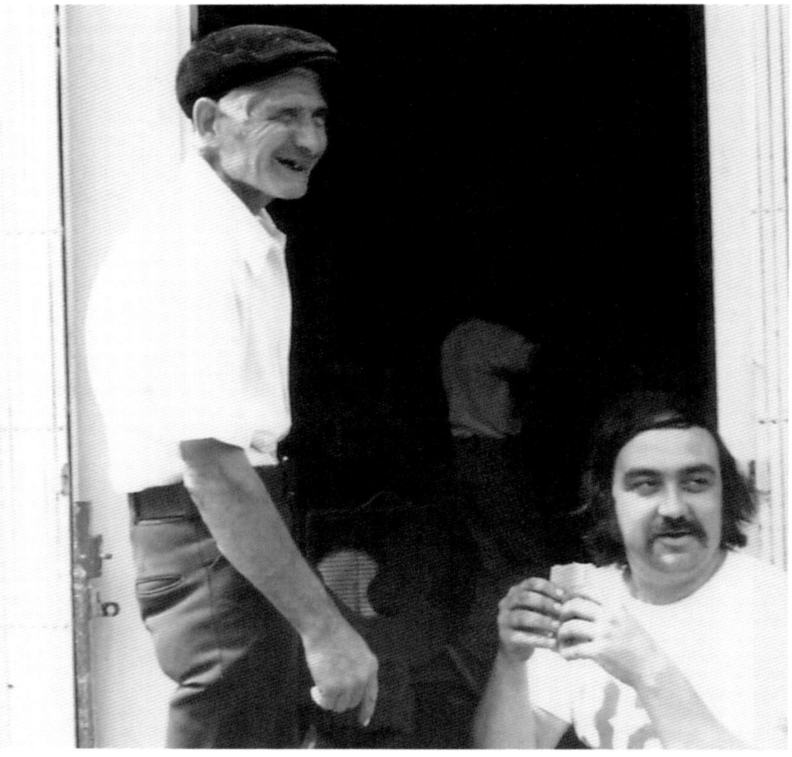

Village Antiques
For nearly 20 years, beginning in the 1970s, the author's father, Kenny Gomez (1943–2009, seated), operated a neighborhood antiques business that daily drew a host of lively locals, including collectors, dealers, architects, historians, politicians, and retired residents who were entrusted with their own set of store keys. (Collection of Anthony Nicodemo.)

CHAPTER ONE

Committed to the Community

Jersey City is a city of advocacy. It has been ever since the 19th century when groups of citizens—frustrated with the escaping fossil fuels of surrounding smokestacks and the raucous cargo railcars that overwhelmed neighborhood corridors—rose up with extraordinarily bold demands. They wanted the relocation of factories to the municipal outskirts; the elevation of freight lines onto soaring, out-of-reach steel trestles; the creation of a system of public parks bountifully highlighted with foreign flowers, shaped shrubbery, idyllic statuary, shallow moats, and turtle-filled lakes; and the wide-scale planting of shade trees along streets, turnpikes, and boulevards. The City Beautiful movement of that era, while a romantic World's Columbian Exposition ideology from which emerged great public buildings, meant nothing to the locals unless it came with wide green plazas, spouting fountains, steps leading to picturesque play fields, and comfort outlooks. A high quality of life was very important to them—their very health hung in the municipal balance.

These battles were won and still exist in the city's cherished landscapes, but only because 19th-century community trailblazers like Archibald A. Campbell, Henry Lembeck, and Mary Hudspeth-Benson fought for them relentlessly, not allowing the city to be consumed by its own destined expansion. Elected officials at the turn of the last century understood this, and shade tree commissions were formed, private lots and lands were purchased with taxpayer monies, and prominent landscape architects like John T. Withers, Charles Lowrie, and Daniel Langton were commissioned to transform former factory sites into gazebo-centered oases. Later, starting in the 1910s and lasting through the 1930s, disadvantaged groups, including African Americans with deep roots in the city and influxing European immigrants looking for basic freedoms and financial success, stood up for the right to obtain decent work for a decent wage; to own a humble home, not merely occupy a ramshackle tenement; to unionize peacefully, and vote rightfully; to form a savings and loan, start a business, attend a church service; to assemble without provocation, as the prominent African American leader Dr. George E. Cannon made clear in the Lafayette section of the city, where blacks were often harassed by the police and who he had to defend in Mayor Frank Hague's city hall. Mary Teresa Norton turned a personal tragedy, the loss of her infant son, into a crusade for mothers and babies, her mission manifesting into the majestic Margaret Hague Maternity Hospital and her long tenure in Washington as a congresswoman for the working person. From her home on Pacific Avenue, in the Lafayette district, Mary Ward grew tired of not feeling like she belonged to local Catholic churches, so she marched to Newark to demand a parish that Jersey City's African American community could call their own. In the city's Italian Village ward, mothers from every street organized in true grassroots fashion, calling for a pocket park on First Street so that neighborhood youth could have a place to play close to home.

That kind of honorable legacy and powerful spirit of advocacy—that impassioned pursuit of justice, fairness, and what is good for the community collectively—continues in this epoch. In Jersey City every district, every corner, has its prominent activists. The property owner who rises up against higher taxes; the organizers who pin up flyers on telephone poles; the block associations who meet monthly, sometimes weekly; the affordable housing advocates who broker agreements with developers and government agencies; the open space coalitions that fend off encroachments and inappropriate developments; the historic preservationists who give voice to defenseless landmarks; the gadflies who will not go away until transparency is attained—these are the locals who demand, persist, fight, attain, uphold, and selflessly commit to Jersey City. Throughout the 1960s, the Rev. Joseph Faulkner, Councilman Fred W. Martin, the Rev. Ercel F. Webb, Cornelius R. Parker Jr., the Rev. Robert W. Castle, and other community activists took on complacent, and sometimes crooked, politicians, demanding better living conditions in the city's most neglected neighborhoods. In the 1970s, giants like Eliu Rivera and the Rev. Fernando L. Colon Jr. gave voice to the city's growing Puerto Rican population, providing families with community centers and much-needed job training and housing.

Decades later, in a new millennium, local citizens and advocacy groups continue to hold high the torches of yesterday's civic legends, including Vinnie McNamara and the Heights Hope Block Association; Pankaj Kapadia and the P.S. No. 8 School Block Association; Mary Quinones, Caroline Katz-Mount, Paul Amatuzzo, Nannette Jacobs-Ali, and the Sherman Place Block Association; Laura Skolar and the Pershing Field Garden Friends; Erik Anders-Nilsson, Adela Rohena, Esther Wintner, April Kuzas, Riaz Wahid, and the Jersey City Peace Movement; Occupy Jersey City; Daoud David Williams; John Mehos; Rich Boggiano and the Hilltop Neighborhood Association; Raju Patel and the Jersey City Asian Merchants Association; and Rosalyn Browne and the Communipaw Avenue Block Association. As active participants in their city, they look back upon the visages of their community forbears and, by doing so, are teaching future advocates that the fight must always continue.

Peter Stuyvesant

Jersey City's first community advocate of record is Peter Stuyvesant (c. 1612–1672), director-general from 1647 to 1664 of the Dutch-held 17th-century colony of New Netherland, a region that included what are now the municipalities of Hudson County and the island of Manhattan. When Peter "Peg-Leg Pete" Stuyvesant (a cannonball took off one of his legs while on a Caribbean island) arrived, he found a series of half-fortified hamlets either abandoned or in total ruins, the result of bloody wars with the local Lenni Lenape natives trying to protect and hold on to their provinces. His immediate goal with surveyor general Jacques Cortelyou was to establish a permanent village protected by high pointed palisade walls, hewn from tall logs. Bergen Village, started in 1660 through charter, consisted of a simple square street grid with main and ancillary carriage roads; an octagonal edifice that served as church, schoolhouse, and prison; vernacular homesteads with great front yards, adjoining farms, and fruit tree groves; and a central artesian well. By the time the British took control of the Dutch lands in 1664, Stuyvesant had left behind the solid roots of a thriving village that soon took down its walls and expanded outward, forming, hamlet by hamlet, across the next few centuries, Jersey City. Though largely forgotten to Jersey City's citizenry today, Stuyvesant's visage is immortalized in the Bergen Monument, conceived and cast in bronze between 1910 and 1913 by master sculptor J. Massey Rhind in celebration of the 250th anniversary of the establishment of Bergen Village. (Courtesy of the Jersey City Free Public Library.)

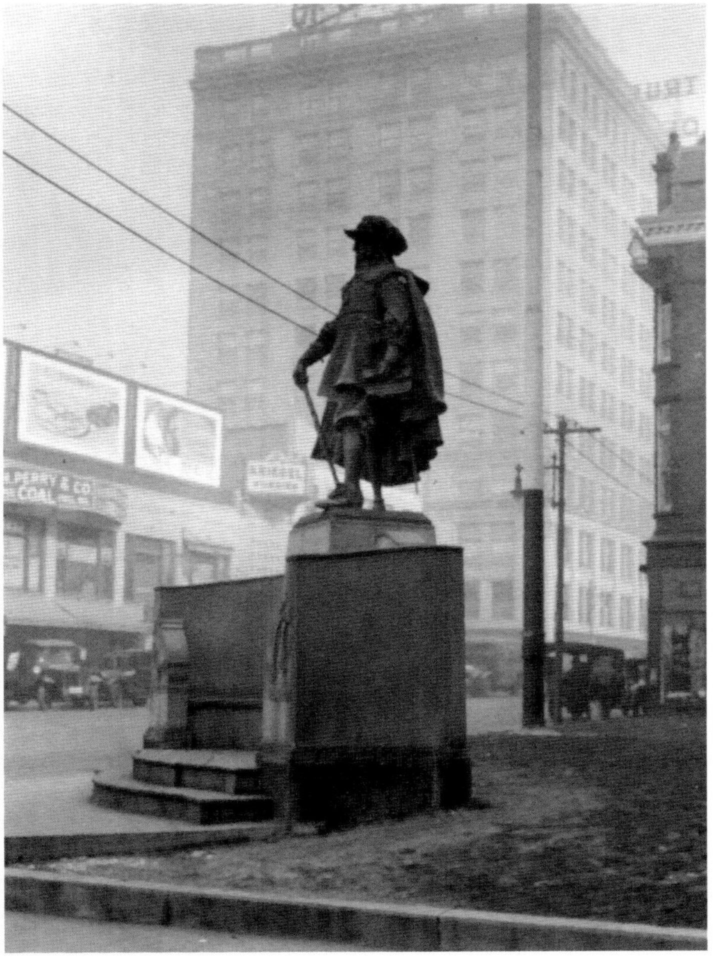

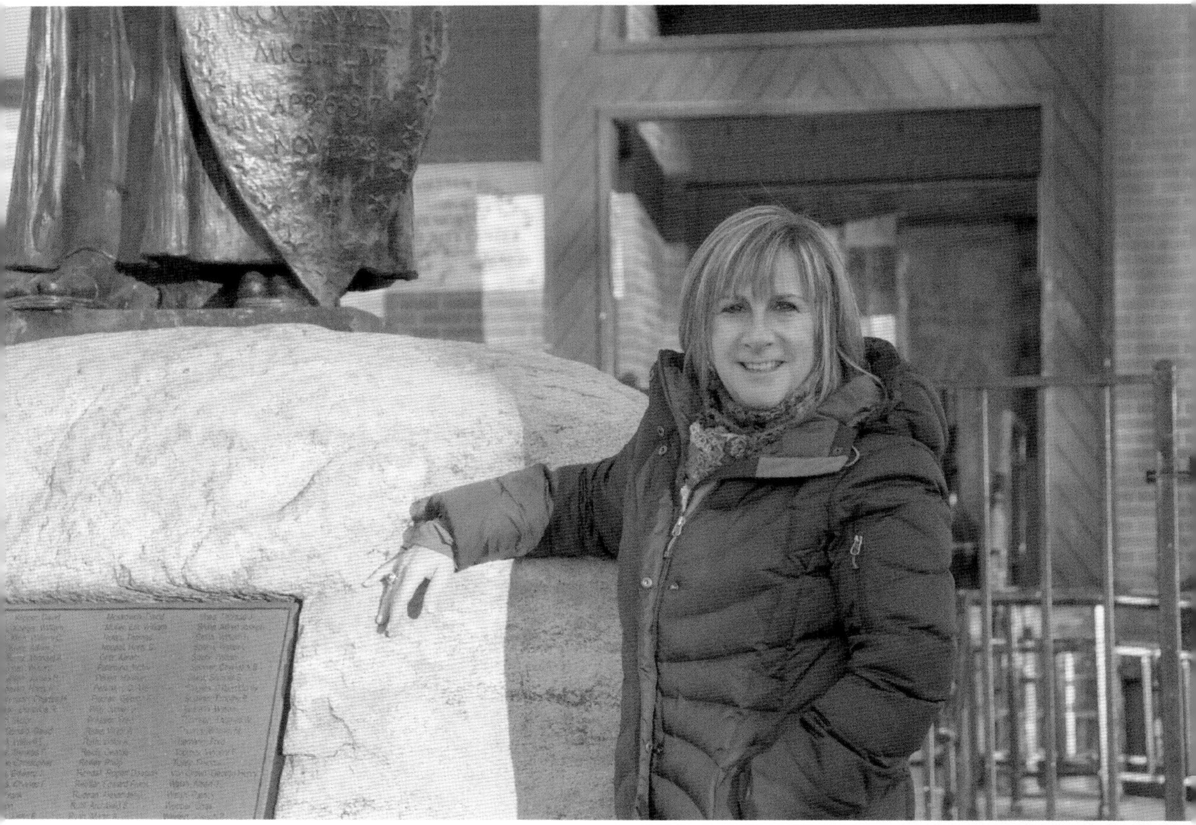

Laura Skolar

From an early age, Laura Skolar looked at things through the eyes of a free spirited person; culture and the building blocks of the city—historic architecture and family neighborhoods—interested her. Instead of going into a field that might satisfy her parents, Laura decided to study art, a destiny she attributes to her supportive Dickinson High School art teacher, Claire Warlikowski, who encouraged her to apply to the School of Visual Arts. There, in the midst of Manhattan, she met Adrienne Leban, the social activist artist who shaped who Laura would later become in the Jersey City community. Leban's curricula was, according to Laura, "based on the view that everyone has creative power which when tapped makes life more fulfilling, joyful, and healthy. Her teachings placed originality, appreciation of individual uniqueness and creativity at the center rather than the margins of society. In her words, life was simply impression; expression. That resonated with me then and even more so today." Leban's spirit can be felt in all of Laura's volunteer activities today, including the Pershing Field Garden Friends, a green group she helped found in 2002 with neighbor Eileen Green to help beautify the barren beds of the Jersey City Heights park and restore its military monuments. In 2004, the group became a founding member of the Jersey City Parks Coalition, becoming a key player in a citizen-written master parks plan.

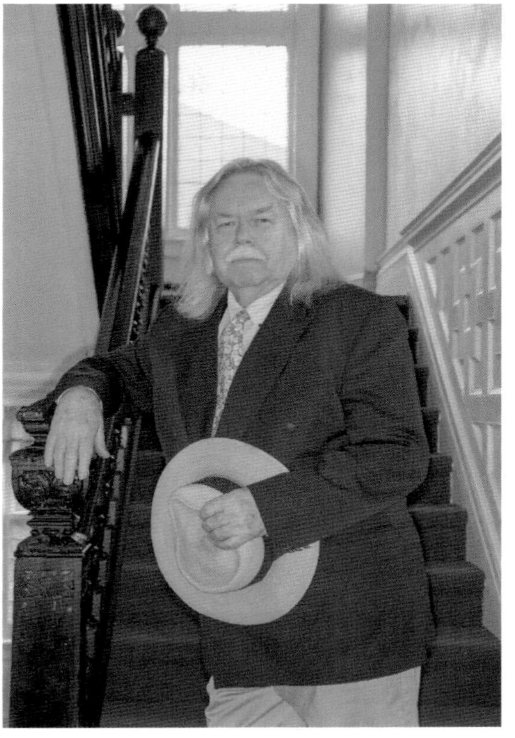

Joe Harkins
In 1994, as Gov. Christine Todd Whitman was about to decide the fate of Liberty State Park (a golf course was being proposed and pushed for the park's fragile wetlands interior), Joe Harkins took to the podium to read Sarah Norcliffe Cleghorn's famous poem "The Golf Links," which reads as follows: "The golf links lie so near the mill / That almost every day / The laboring children can look out / And see the men at play." It must have been a defining moment because Whitman ended the debate and allowed the park to remain open and green; the public outcry and Cleghorn's words were too compelling to ignore. For Joe, it was just another chapter in his long citizen advocate role.

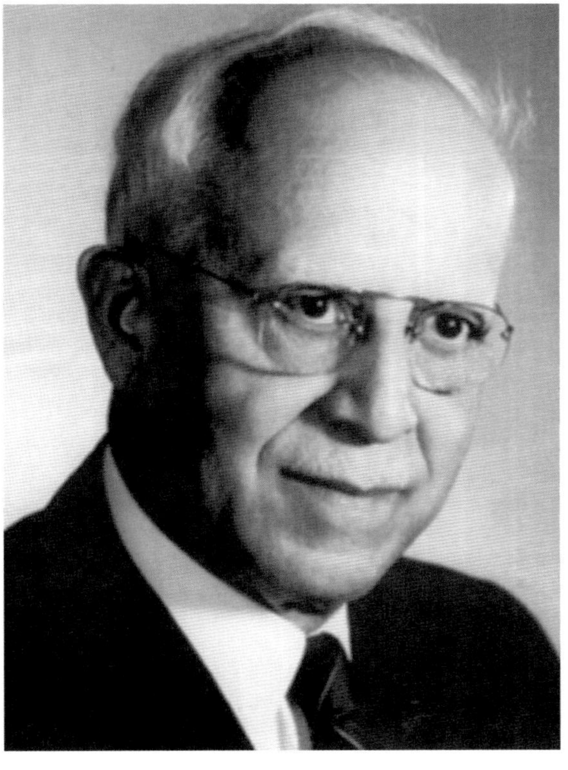

Fred W. Martin
In 1961, as soon as Jersey City had switched over from a commission to a council form of government, Fred W. Martin seized the groundbreaking moment and ran as an independent for the Bergen-Lafayette ward seat. He won in a runoff, becoming the city's first African American councilman. Throughout the next two decades, Martin, one of the first black graduates of Harvard's School of Business Administration, aligned himself with prominent local activists like Addison McLeon, Julian Robinson, Raymond Brown, Esq., Cornelius R. Parker Jr., and the Rev. Dr. Ercel F. Webb, fighting publicly for the eradication of slums and poverty, the desegregation of schools, and educational and recreational opportunities for minorities. (Courtesy of the Afro-American Historical Society Museum.)

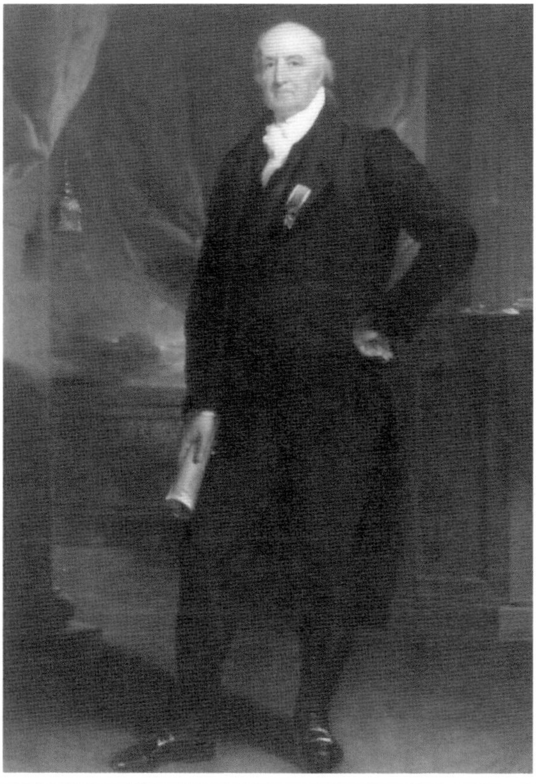

The Associates of the Jersey Company

Jersey City's first visage as a municipal entity occurred in 1804 when three visionaries, all New York lawyers, were granted by the New Jersey legislature to come together to establish the City of Jersey. Richard Varick (1752–1831, pictured at left), Anthony Dey (1776–1859), and Jacob Radcliff (1764–1842) had incorporated, in one magical municipal move, into the Associates of the Jersey Company, with Alexander Hamilton as lawyer and charter composer. Their starting point was the conveyance of Paulus Hook, a former battery used during the Revolutionary War, to the associates from Cornelius Van Vorst, followed by the wide-scale sale of lots via newspaper advertisements. Almost overnight, a community of farmers, industrialists, and builders was established and has not stopped growing ever since. (Courtesy of the Jersey City Free Public Library.)

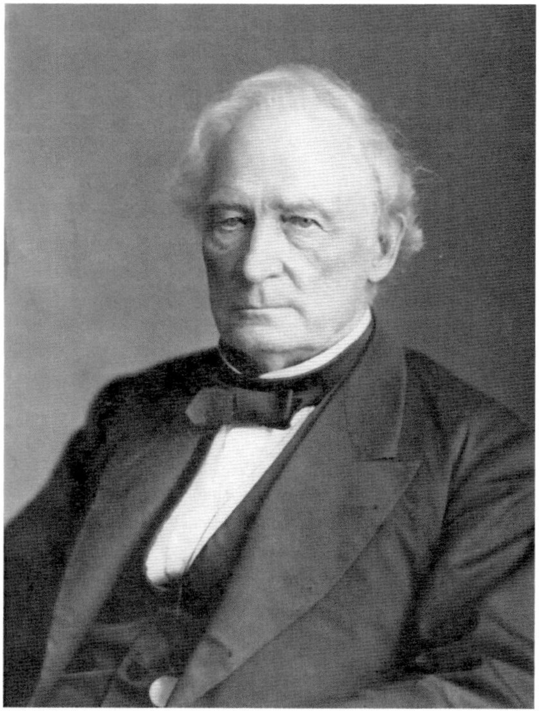

Dudley S. Gregory

Dudley S. Gregory (1800–1874) is firmly fixed in the local annals as Jersey City's first, and perhaps most important, 19th-century mayor. In 1838, after the city was chartered, Gregory was appointed mayor and went on to serve three terms (1838–1840, 1841–1842, and 1858–1860). He continued the work of the Associates of the Jersey Company in expanding the left bank province from rural Manhattan backyard and pleasure grounds to major industrial and transportation metropolis. To do that, Gregory, who also served as Hudson County freeholder and US congressman, built the earliest banking institutions, including the 1839 Provident Savings Bank; headed major infrastructure and utility companies; established the public school system; and allowed the first post office to be stationed in his Paulus Hook mansion. (Courtesy of the Jersey City Free Public Library.)

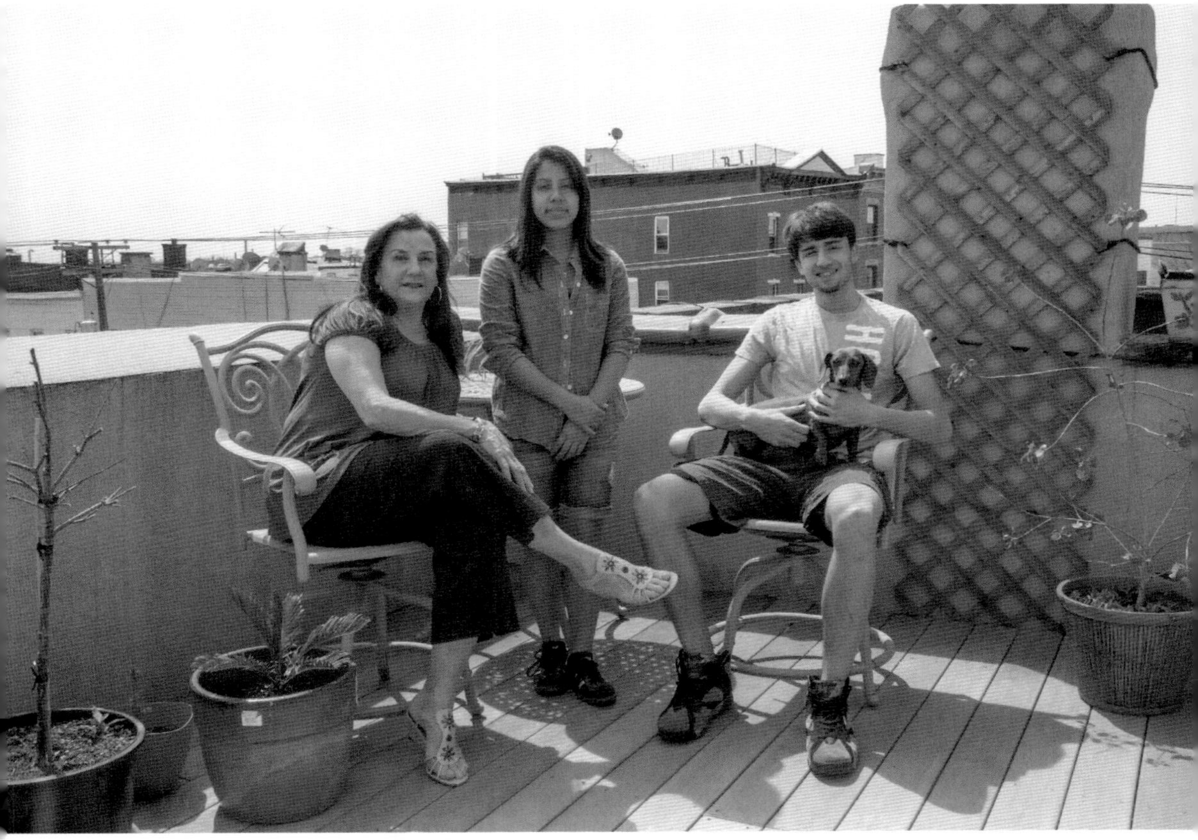

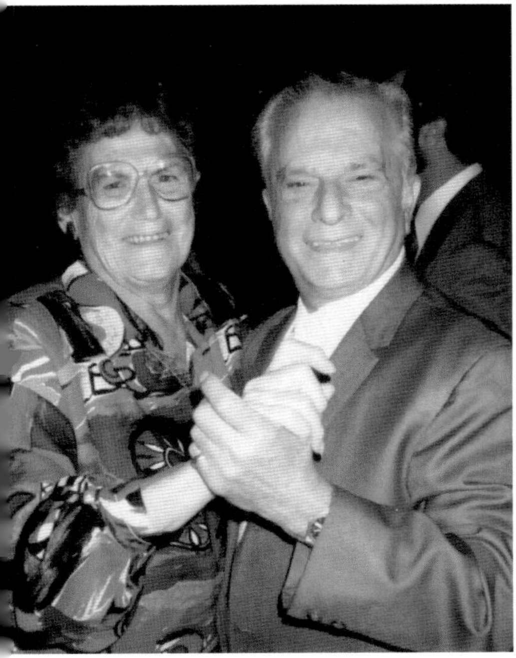

Michele La Monica-Egar

Michele La Monica-Egar has tasked herself with multiple community projects linked to her past and her strong desire for a city where her family can live and thrive. A resident of the Italian Village section of the downtown area since birth, Michele is the neighborhood's go-to person, whether it is a call for clean streets, crime prevention, or new development. An active member of the Village Neighborhood Association, Michele's Italian American heritage harks back to a not-too-long-ago time when everyone in the neighborhood knew and looked out for everyone and when the smells and scents of brick-oven bakeries, cheese and basement-pressed wine shops, and coffee bean sack emporiums lined the streets. For years, Michele's mother, Mary, and father, Francis, pictured at left, owned and operated Pinky's, a popular butcher shop on Second Street, located right next door to the Lamp Post Bar & Grille owned today by Michele and her family.

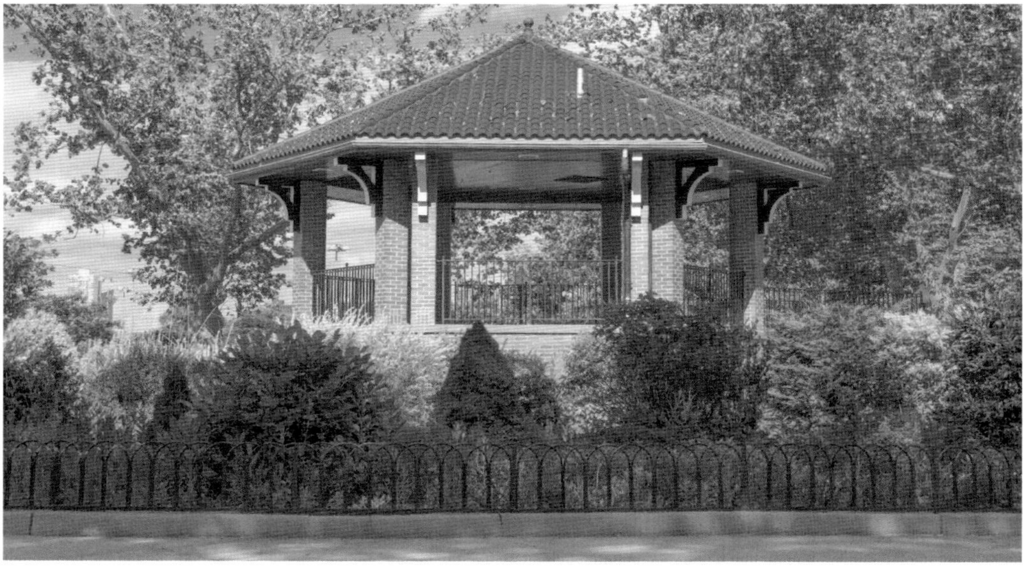

Lafayette Citizens Association

The Lafayette district of Jersey City, the city's oldest, with early Dutch settlements attempted a few years after Henry Hudson's 1609 voyage up the Hudson River, has a long legacy of community involvement and impact. Current influential citizen-led groups stand on the shoulders of the Lafayette Citizens Association, a spirited group whose work can be felt and seen in Lafayette even today. In 1887, locals disillusioned with clogged sewers, poor street pavements, stench-forming abattoirs, overwhelming industrial development, and inadequate schoolhouses formed the pioneering group to confront these issues. In 1895, it was the members' call for a "breathing spot," led by Archibald A. Campbell, who had just erected the still-extant Breadalbane Terrace tin row houses on Lafayette Street, that led to the 1904 dedication of Lafayette Park, renamed the Rev. Dr. Ercel F. Webb Park in 1994 in tribute to the late spiritual and civil rights leader. (Postcard courtesy of the Jersey City Landmarks Conservancy.)

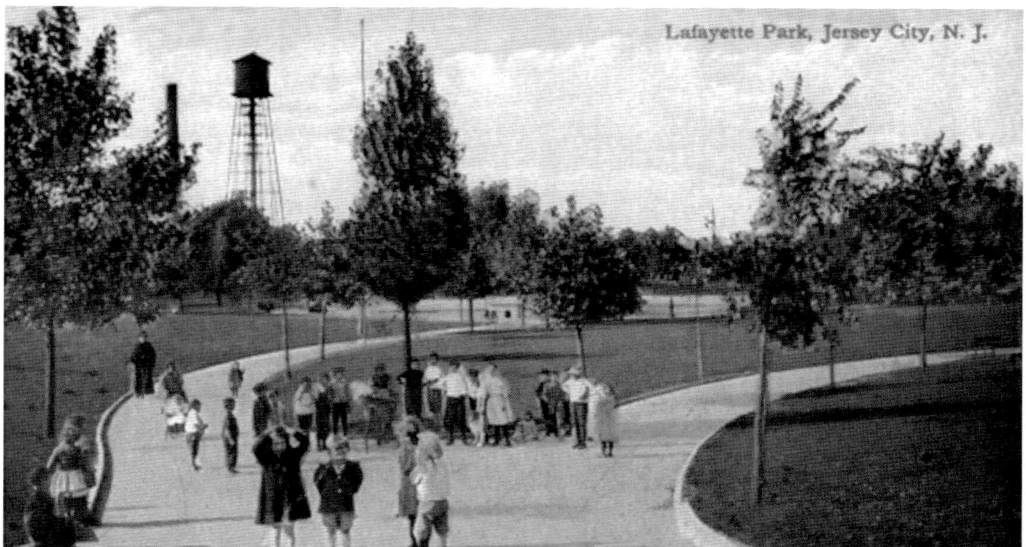

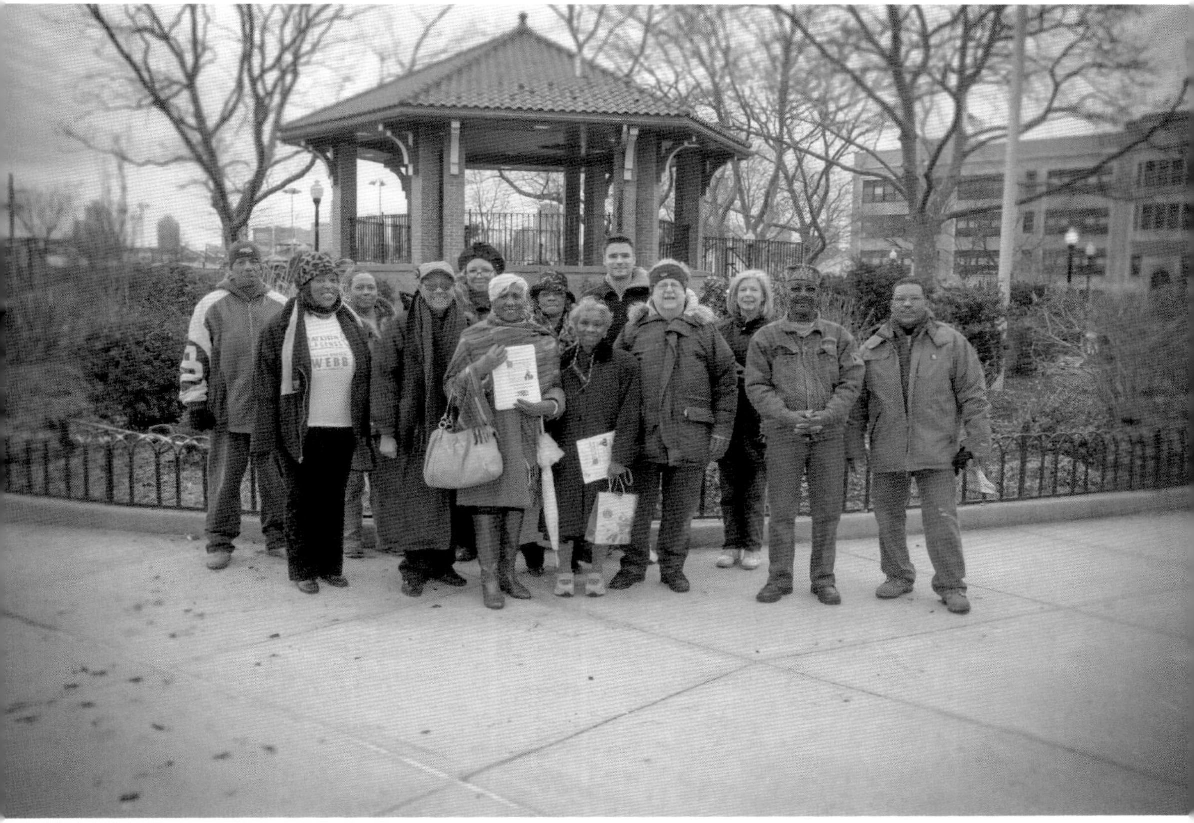

Rosalyn Browne

No one seizes the civic-duty torch more assuredly and with more sustained energy than Rosalyn Browne (back row, third from left). Always busy at the Jackson Funeral Residence on Communipaw Avenue, a dignified business founded and operated by her late parents, Herbert A. and Audrey E. Jackson, two towering legends in the Lafayette district, she somehow finds time to lead the Communipaw Avenue Block Association (CABA), a nonprofit group she established with Elizabeth Garnes, Gloria Felder, and other activists in 2000 to battle rampant crime, constant litter, lack of park space, and additional quality of life issues. CABA's communal achievements in Lafayette are numerous and paramount, but two particular projects stand out. Teaming up with the Jersey City Parks Coalition and working with municipal architects, planners, elected officials, church leaders, and the late mayor and state senator Glenn D. Cunningham, CABA had the Rev. Dr. Ercel F. Webb Park completely restored and returned as a true treasure to the community. And every year, CABA throws open Lafayette's historic gates to the public with the Lafayette History Festival & Tour in partnership with the Jersey City Landmarks Conservancy and the Afro-American Historical Society Museum. Rosalyn, a recipient of the *Jersey Journal* Everyday Hero Award for Building Better Neighborhoods, the Urban League of Hudson County Award for Community Activism, and the NAACP Madame C.J. Walker Enterprise Award for exemplary community service, credits her parents and the family business for her ardor and achievements. "If one is blessed," she says, "one should give those blessings back to the community in which one lives and works."

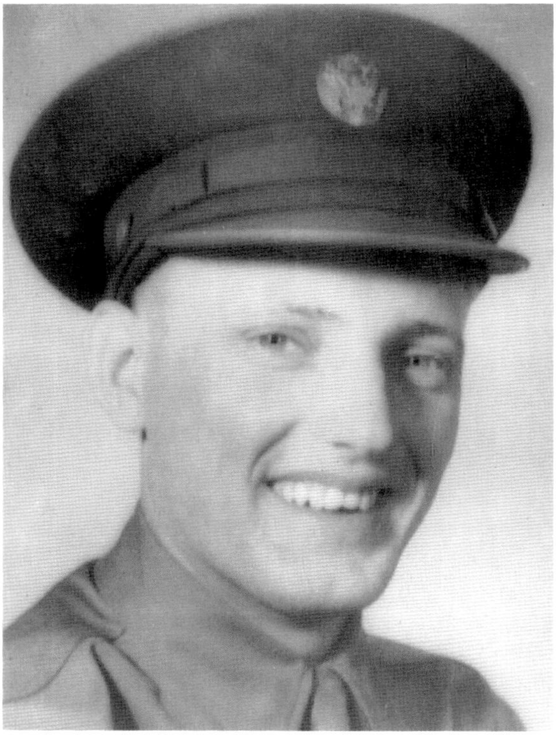

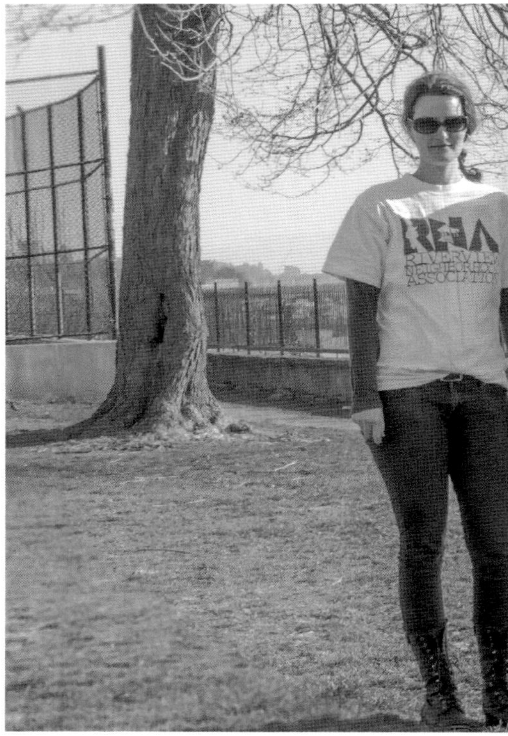

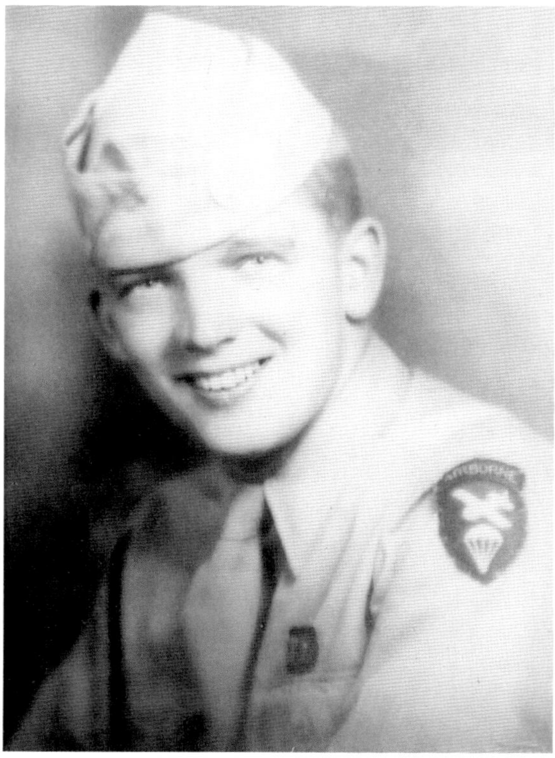

The Skinner Brothers

Dana and Douglas Sirotiak are active conservators of a special heritage alive at the intersection of Grand Street and Jersey Avenue, where a metal sign is inscribed with the names of their valorous ancestors, brothers Douglas and Arthur Skinner, World War II servicemen who perished in two different parts of the world. On January 9, 1945, 21-year-old SSgt. Douglas Skinner (above left), a tail gunner with the 5th Air Force, went missing in action over Central Luzon, Philippines. His younger brother, Pfc. Arthur Skinner (right), only 19, was a paratrooper with the 82nd Airborne Division when he died from wounds suffered in the Battle of the Bulge—on the same exact day as his brother. The brothers were temporarily interred overseas; a few years later, with full military honor, they were returned to Jersey City. It was a homecoming for the ages. (Courtesy of June, Douglas, and Dana Sirotiak.)

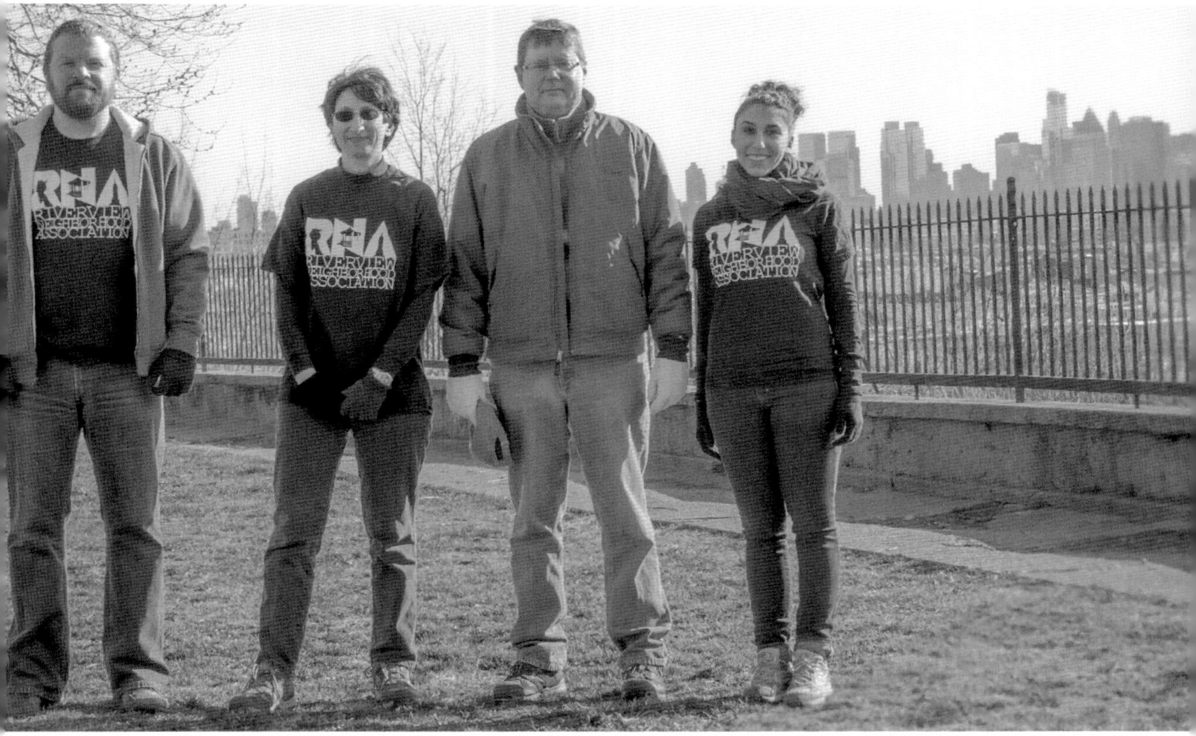

Becky Hoffman

Since 2006, when she became chair of the Riverview Neighborhood Association (RNA), Becky Hoffman (center) has had big shoes to fill. Founded in 1984 by such community giants as Theodore Conrad, Marie Tuzzo, Bob Lewis, Anne Hart, Jack Rea, and Randy Sanford, Becky has inherited an active neighborhood position held by former chairs and legends in their own right: Vito Brunetti, Ernie Quintero, Maria Tuzzo, and Cliff Steinbring. While these stalwarts laid a solid foundation for the organization as a civic powerhouse—fighting for and obtaining sensible and sensitive zoning laws; curbing inappropriate development; initiating annual flea markets, cleanups, and walking tours—Becky has brought the group into the 21st century in triumphant ways by working diligently with city officials to create an arts district overlay, attract more sidewalk restaurants, create community gardens, and initiate restoration campaigns for historical assets in the area, including the Henry Hudson Monument and a Hurricane Sandy–destroyed gazebo.

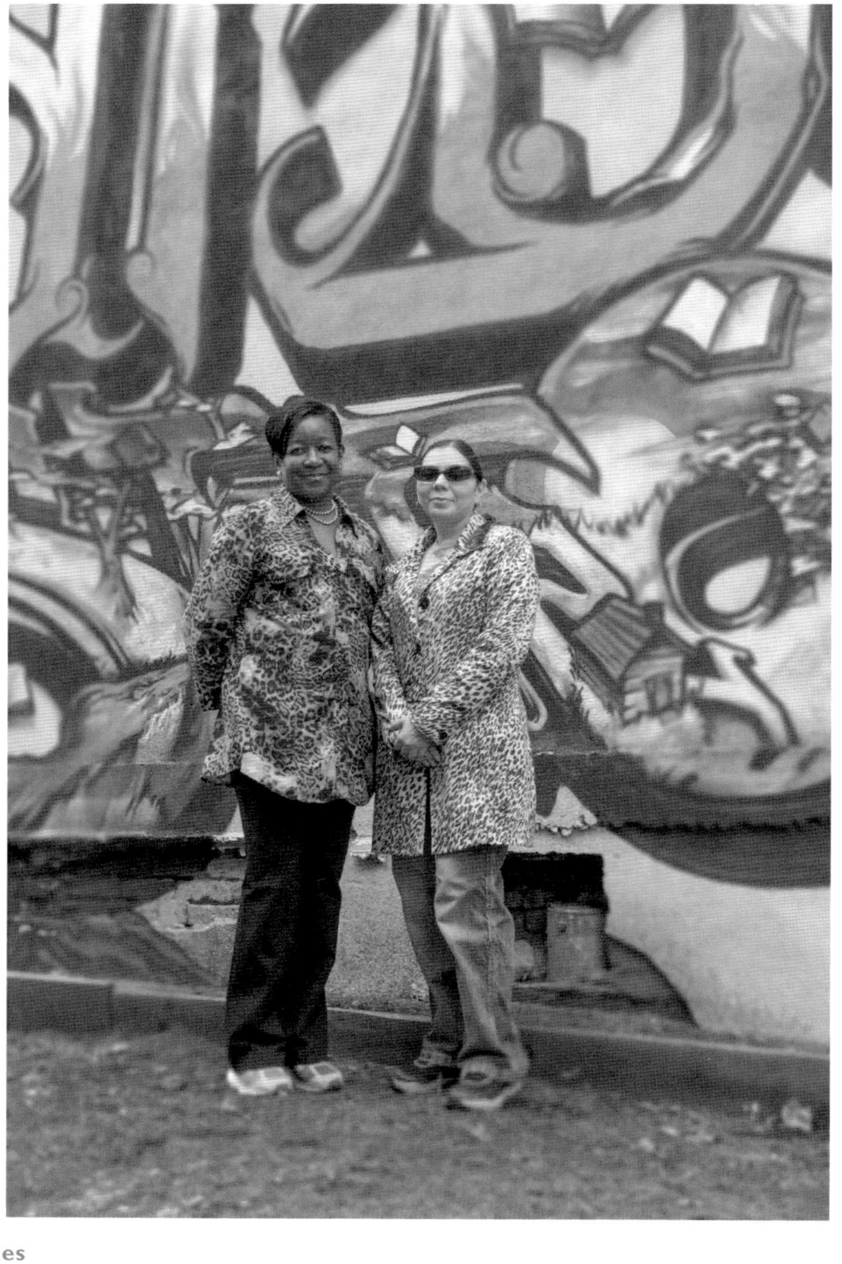

June Jones

June Jones is one of Jersey City's most active and visible community vanguards. A lifelong Lafayette resident, she is the executive director of the Morris Canal Community Development Corporation (MCCDC), an organization she helped form in 1999 with neighborhood champions Fr. Eugene Squeo and John Jayme. The MCCDC, with current members like June and Tina Senatore (left and right, respectively), ensures that architecturally sensitive bricks-and-mortar projects go up instead of eyesores; fights for affordable housing; and provides job training, employment opportunities, and other significant community services. Its most recent activity is the establishment of the Lafayette Community Learning Garden, an organic growing initiative that also provides a public gathering place for special events.

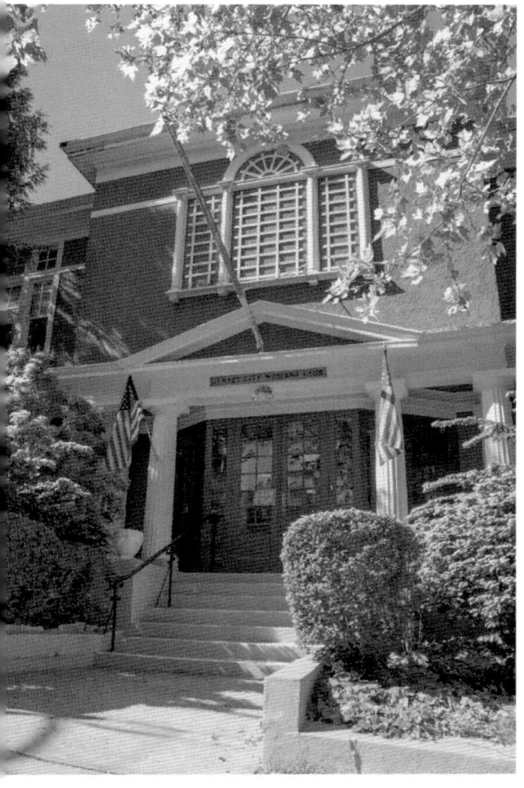

Jersey City Woman's Club

The legacy of the Jersey City Woman's Club—one of the oldest continuing civic organizations in New Jersey, having been founded in 1894 by such local pioneers as Mary Philbrook, Cecelia Gaines Holland, Cornelia F. Bradford, Harriet Phillips Eaton, and Mary Hudspeth-Benson—is kept alive through the efforts of Dorethy McGrath, the current president and an active member since 1965. When visitors step into the club's 1910 Colonial Revival headquarters, designed by local architect Charles H. Detwiller, on Fairmount Avenue in the West Bergen district of the city, Dorethy takes them through a time capsule of period parlors and up a grand staircase, lit by stained-glass windows, leading to an upper-floor auditorium. The most cherished feature of the clubhouse is a narrow side closet where preserved volumes, many capturing the club's earliest civic activities, including the campaign to preserve the Palisades, are neatly stacked. Under Dorethy's leadership, the club continues to award much-needed student scholarships and make donations to the Salvation Army. And because of her, club membership has expanded and is reflective of the increasingly diverse ethnic and sociographic backgrounds of the city, setting up the organization for another century of service.

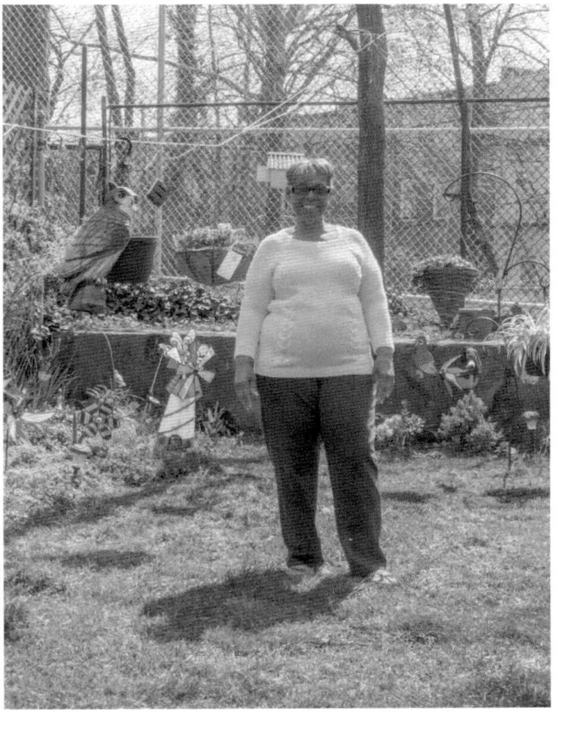

Marcia Adams

Marcia Adams is the kind of activist who will, on her own, climb steep stoops to hand out community meeting flyers; take a worn-out broom up and down the brownstone-lined lanes of a quaint 19th-century Victorian neighborhood; convince neighbors to tend to their yards, plant shade trees, and respect their precious pocket parks; and work closely with municipal offices to install new historically appropriate streetlamps. Everyone on Madison, Monticello, and Bramhall Avenues knows her; children and seniors call out her name. Working with local legends like Cornelius R. Parker Jr. and the Madison Avenue Block Association, Marcia has managed to maintain a high quality of life in the historic heart of the Bergen-Lafayette section of Jersey City.

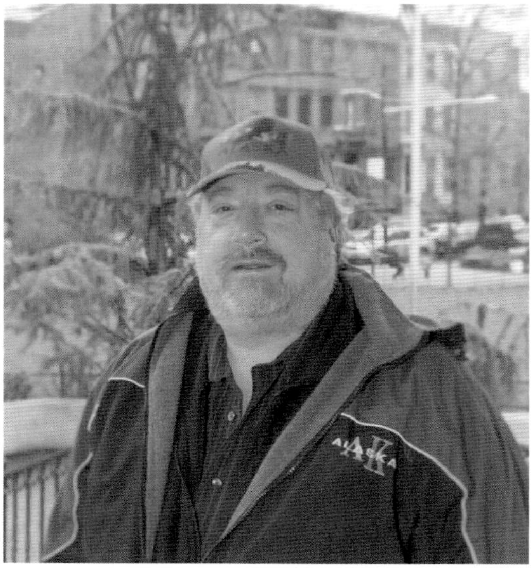

Dr. Clifford Waldman

Dr. Clifford Waldman recalls the impetus for getting involved with the communal park space initiatives that have brought him recognition and praise. In 1999, a young girl was struck down by a swerving car in front of Van Vorst Park, a brownstone-surrounded green in the downtown section of the city. Dr. Waldman, a clinical psychologist, and dozens of neighbors formed the Friends of Van Vorst Park to lobby city officials to plant a protective tree barrier along Montgomery Street where the tragedy had occurred. From that compassionate campaign came, in 2004, the wider-reaching Jersey City Parks Coalition, a consortium of over 22 local green groups, conservancies, friends-of organizations, and neighborhood associations.

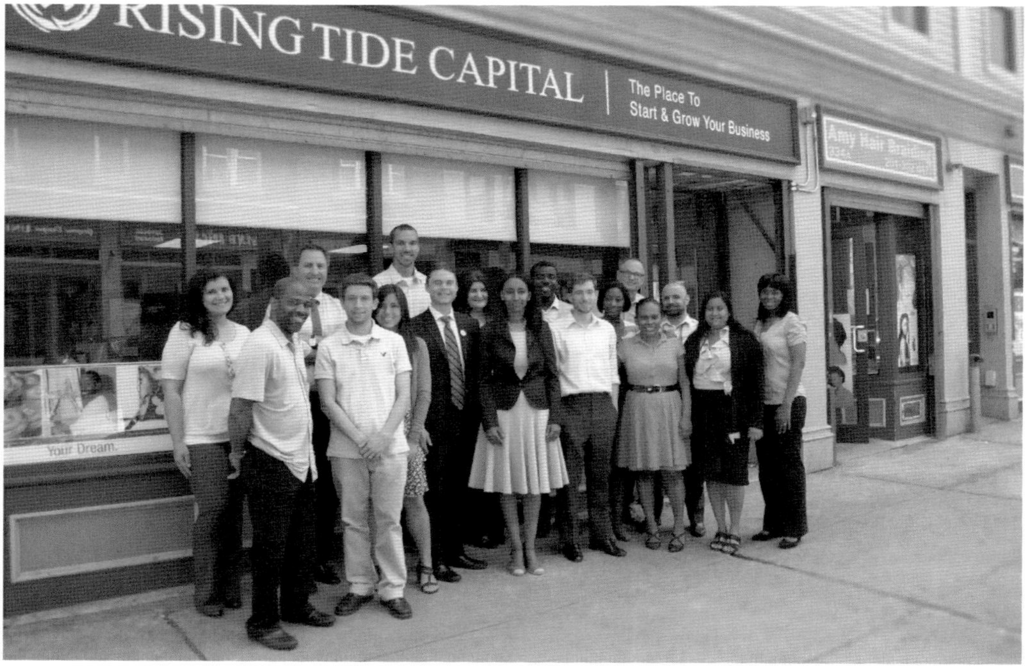

Alfa Demmellash

Alfa Demmellash's nonprofit Rising Tide Capital is situated on Martin Luther King Drive, the historical heart of Jersey City. The location is indicative of her deep dedication to her adopted hometown. An alumna of Boston Latin School and Harvard University, Alfa, along with cofounder and husband, Alex Forrester, leads an organization that provides invaluable training and mentorship to emerging minority-owned businesses. For her efforts, Alfa (front row, center) has captured major local and national honors, including the Future Global Leader Award from the World Business Forum, the 2009 Community Crusader CNN Hero Award, and, most recently, being named as one of *Forbes* Most Powerful Women Changing the World with Philanthropy.

Mary Ward

Before 1930, Mary Ward lived a quiet life on Pacific Avenue in the Lafayette district. But after feeling ignored and not entirely a part of local Catholic churches for too long, she decided to do something about it. Journeying to Newark to request a meeting with Bishop Thomas Joseph Walsh, Ward implored him to establish an African American Catholic church in the city. The Bishop was not convinced; long-established parishes properly served the black population, he argued. Ward would not stand down, and Bishop Walsh eventually changed course and ordered the official organization of Christ the King Catholic Church.

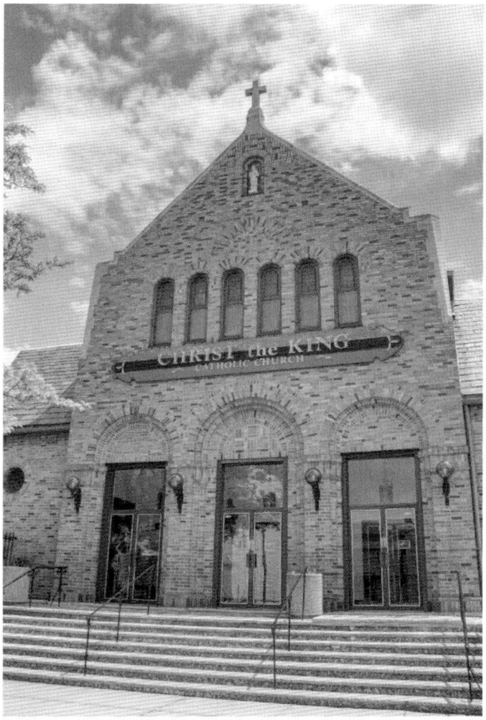

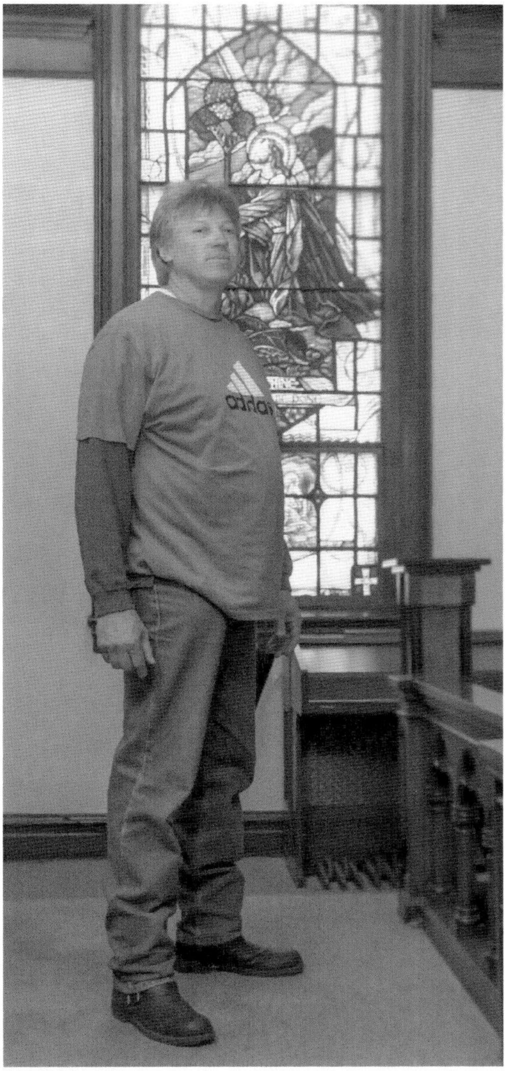

Gary Dugan

When Gary Dugan first heard about the community compassion of the Rev. Glenn L. Boisclair of Grace Lutheran Church, a small 1904 house of worship in the Jersey City Heights, he decided to experience the pastor's sermons in person. That was nearly 20 years ago. Gary, a local construction company owner, stayed for good, greatly impressed by Grace's progressive commitment to the gay community, the poor, and people struggling with substance abuse. Gary himself knows very well about the significance of giving back; for 12 years, he had been a pivotal part of Habitat for Humanity of Hudson County, participating in programs where inner city homes were chosen for free rehabilitation. "I do believe in Jersey City," he proclaims, pointing out its diversity. Speaking on behalf of the church, he adds, "You're supposed to be helping people out in this world."

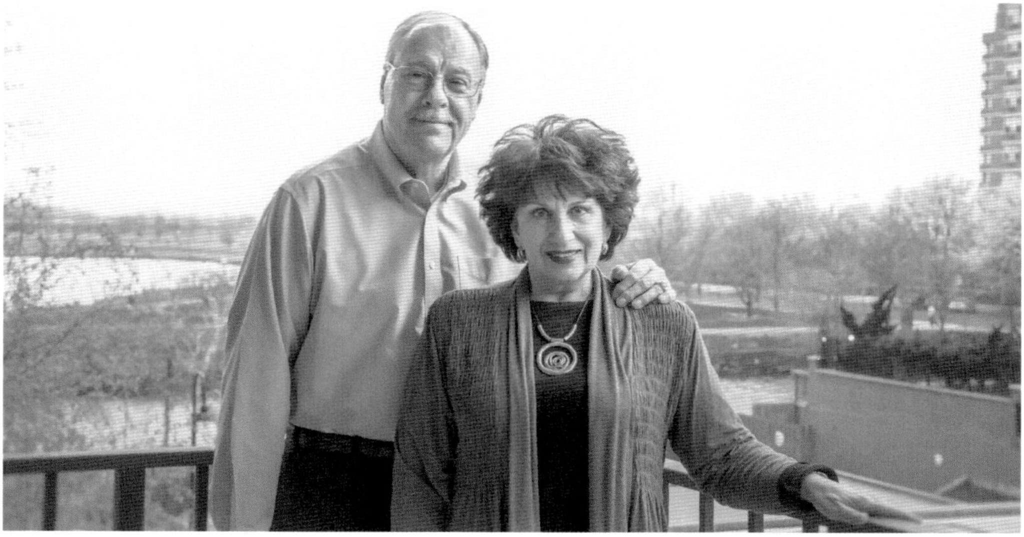

Dorcey and Richard Winant

Dorcey and Richard Winant could have blended in with the general populace when they first moved to Jersey City. Instead, as they begin their retirement over 20 years later, they look back at a legacy as some of the city's most committed, selfless citizens. Dorcey, an actress and theatrical director from the Boston area, and Rick, a former Navy reservist and dean at SUNY, were major players in the battles to preserve the Loew's Jersey Theatre and Liberty State Park. Later, they helped establish the George Washington Society of Jersey City to help preserve the Apple Tree House, a rare, surviving colonial-era homestead just outside the city's Journal Square area, and to commemorate, as Rick does most famously in full Revolutionary War–reenactment garb, the great legend's fixed place in Jersey City history.

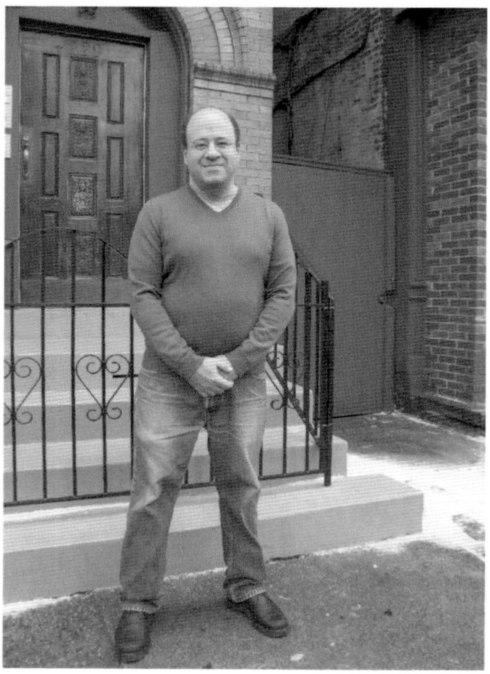

Daniel Levin

"I feel fortunate that my children have grown up around good people who do things," says good government advocate Daniel Levin. Since they were toddlers, and now approaching their teens, they have been exposed every single day to their father's extraordinary efforts in the city—from attending city council meetings calling for governmental transparency and pay-to-play reform to guiding walking tours through the abandoned Bergen Arches. As a father, husband, and resident, Dan has shared his appreciation of livable historic neighborhoods, open space amid densification, and smart transportation alternatives. His activist resume is wide-ranging and impressive; he was the founder of CivicJC, organizer of BikeJC, and grassroots campaigner for mayor and city council positions.

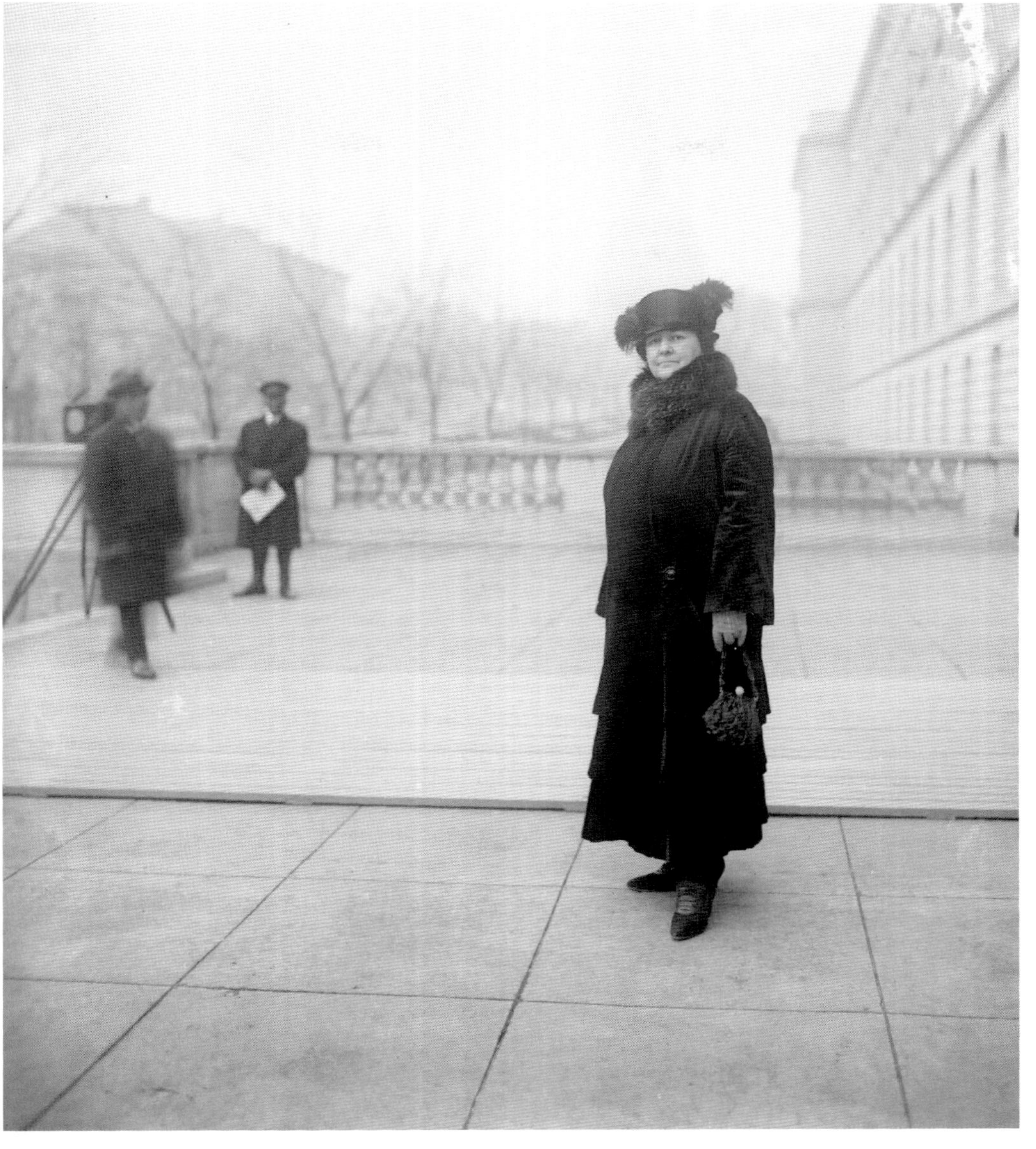

Mary Teresa Norton

Known as the working person's politician, Mary Teresa Norton (1875–1959) was a Jersey City–born congresswoman long aligned with, and staunchly dedicated to, Mayor Frank Hague. In the early 1920s, Hague was actively seeking women to join and diversify his growing administration. Norton, of the same Irish working-class background and a visible advocate for infants, having previously lost her son, was his first choice. In 1921, with Hague's help, Norton became the first woman elected to the Democratic State Committee; two years later, she was elected as Hudson County's first woman Democratic freeholder. Norton's legislative career took off from there. In 1925, she was elected to her first of 13 terms (1924–1951) in the House of Representatives and was Hague's main point person in Washington. Carving out a congressional legacy all her own, she served in high positions on labor and veterans' committees. In 2011, the Mary Norton Manor, an affordable five-story, 24-unit condominium complex, opened in her honor on Duncan Avenue. (Courtesy of the Library of Congress.)

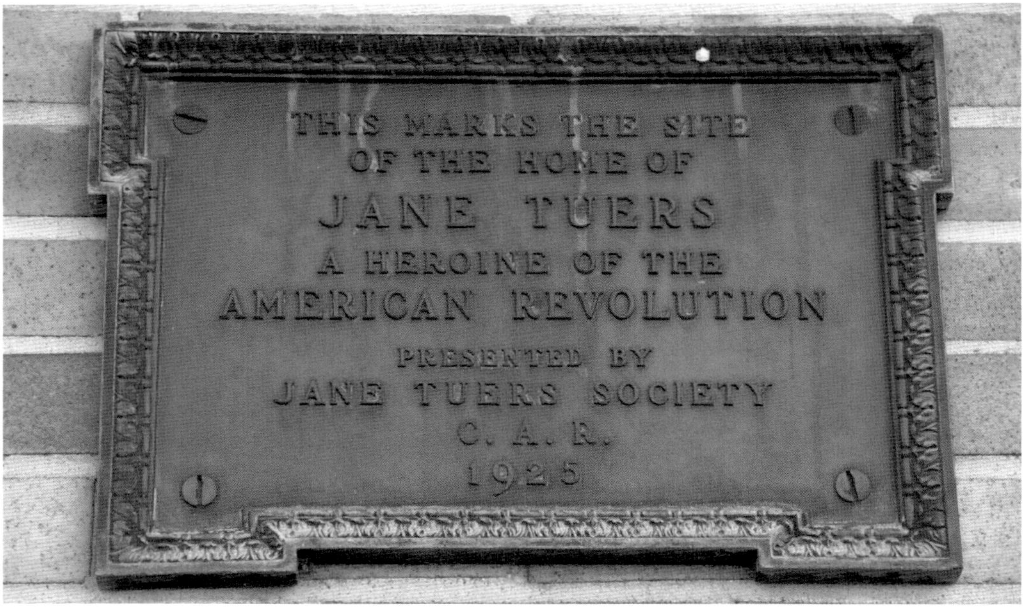

Jane Tuers

The figure of Jane Tuers as a heroine who helped save the country during the American Revolution has become folk-ridden over time. What is fact and what is fiction may never be known, but Tuers, whose house stood at the corner of Bergen Avenue and Mercer Street until 1894, when it was leveled for an armory, is thought to have overheard, or was informed of, a conversation between British soldiers inside the famed Fraunces Tavern in lower Manhattan. Apparently, a discussion about seizing West Point with the clandestine assistance of Benedict Arnold was held over a toast. Immediately, the tale goes, Tuers informed her brother Daniel Van Reypen, who then rode to Hackensack to inform Gen. Anthony Wayne. Wayne, in turn, delivered Van Reypen to share the information directly with Gen. George Washington. His plot derailed, Arnold eventually escaped, and the military stronghold, the story concludes, was saved.

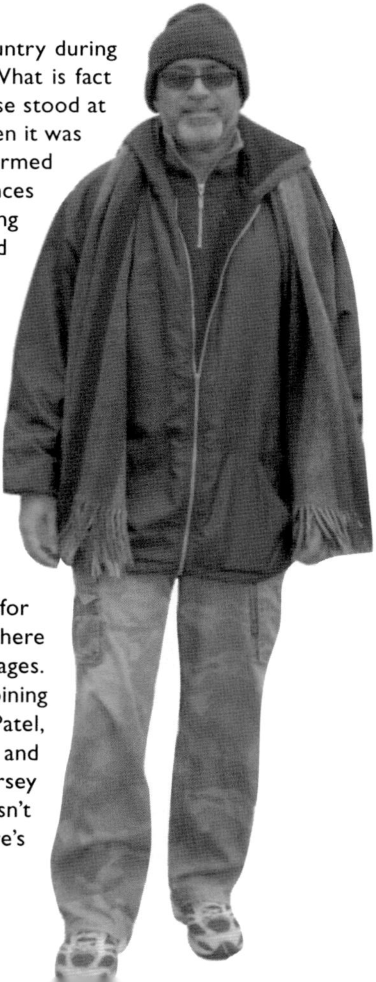

Riaz Wahid

Riaz Wahid's calling in the community as the leading advocate for the poor and the disadvantaged goes back to his youth in India where his family once financially supported and helped manage orphanages. After moving to Jersey City, Riaz immediately got involved, joining fellow advocates Esther Wintner, Eric Anders-Nilsson, Raju Patel, and Imtiaz Syed to combat homelessness, crime, high taxes, and corruption. In 2012, Riaz and Esther founded the very active Jersey City Homeless Advocacy Group. "Our life is short and there isn't much time to do everything in the world," Riaz says, "but there's enough time to do just enough."

Rob Crow

"I learned at an early age that if there is something in your environment that you don't like, you have the power to change it," says Rob Crow of the Village Neighborhood Association (VNA), an active organization in the Italian Village section of the city. Working with other VNA members like Jim Ayers, Michele La Monica-Egar, and Irene Barnaby, Rob has helped to establish bylaws and a new VNA logo; set up an active website and email list; organize historical walking tours in collaboration with preservationist Joshua Parkhurst; win funding for new sidewalks along Newark Avenue; launch art and music festival partnerships with Mike McNamara and 4th Street Arts; and guide the long redevelopment and design competition process for the Village Park on First Street. Most important to Rob, however, is the effect his community activist efforts have had on his young daughter, Adriana, who, in the third grade, formed the Village Helpers, organizing and conducting street and cemetery clean-ups with other neighborhood children. (Archival image collection of Anthony Nicodemo.)

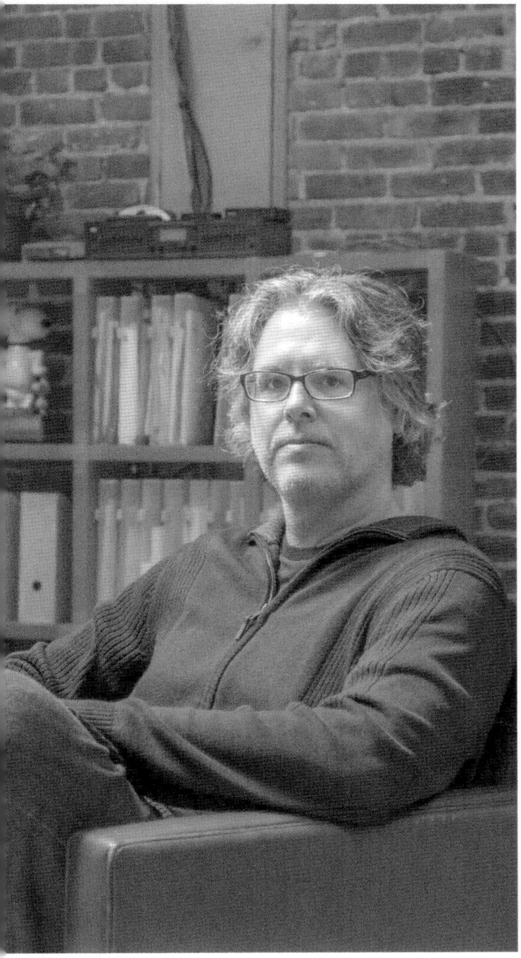

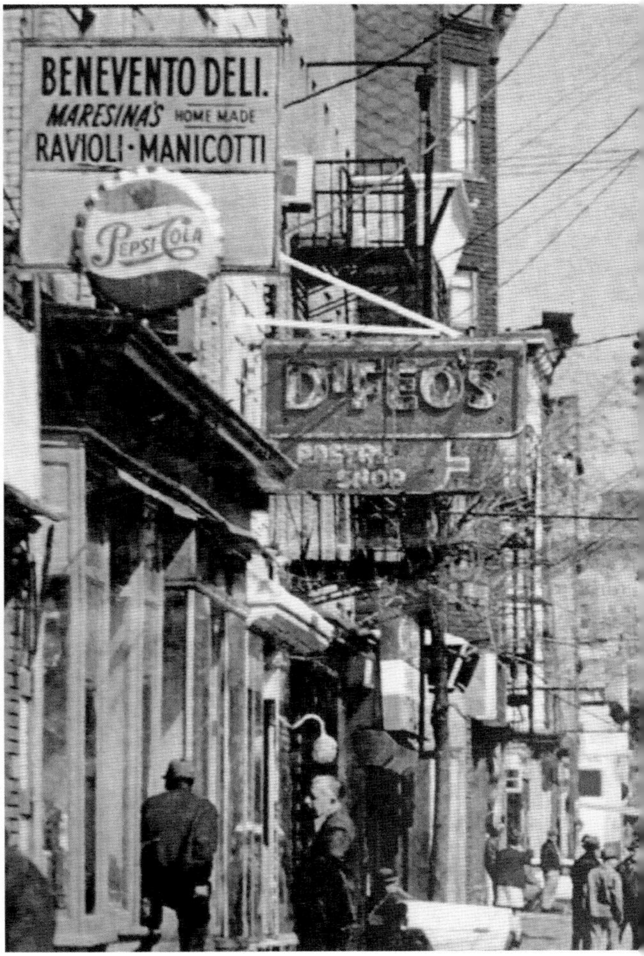

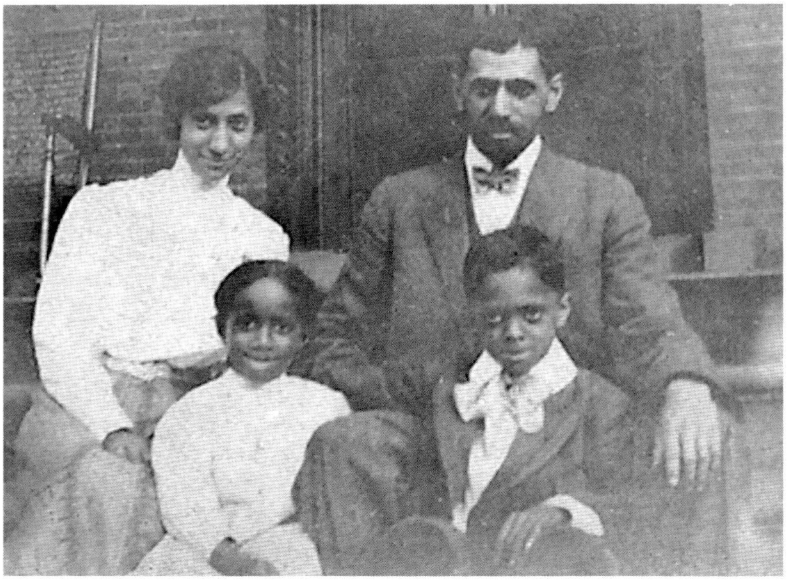

Dr. George E. Cannon

Dr. George E. Cannon (1869–1925) is locally and nationally renowned for his historical stature in the African American community. He seconded the nomination of Calvin Coolidge at the 1924 Republican National Convention, founded a savings and loan to serve Jersey City's black-owned businesses, and brokered civil rights advancements with the Frank Hague administration, but it was his pioneering film productions that loom the largest. In 1915, D.W. Griffith's racially charged *The Birth of a Nation* opened across the country, outraging leaders like Dr. Cannon. As a result, he established the Frederick Douglass Film Company out of his Pacific Avenue home (below), producing four feature films that positively depicted blacks as distinguished, professional, successful citizens. Dr. Cannon's cinematic efforts helped establish early African American cinema and paved the way for future black filmmakers. (Courtesy of the Afro-American Historical Society Museum.)

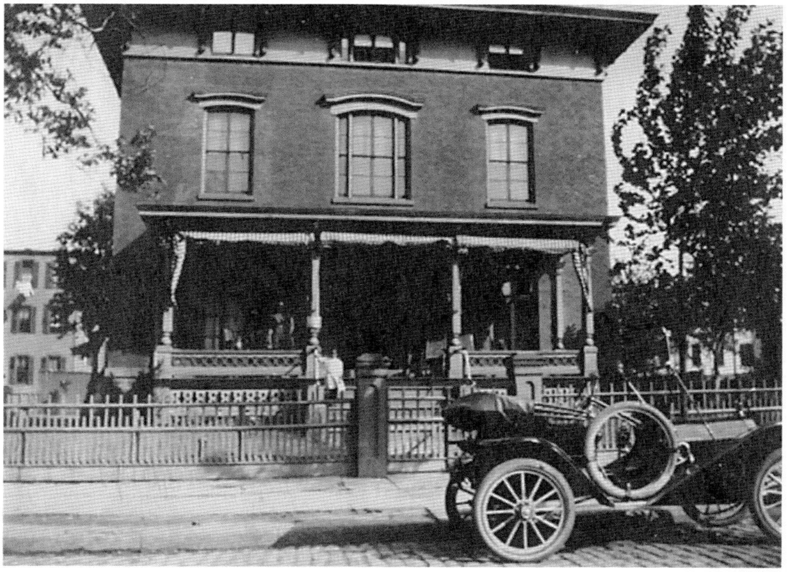

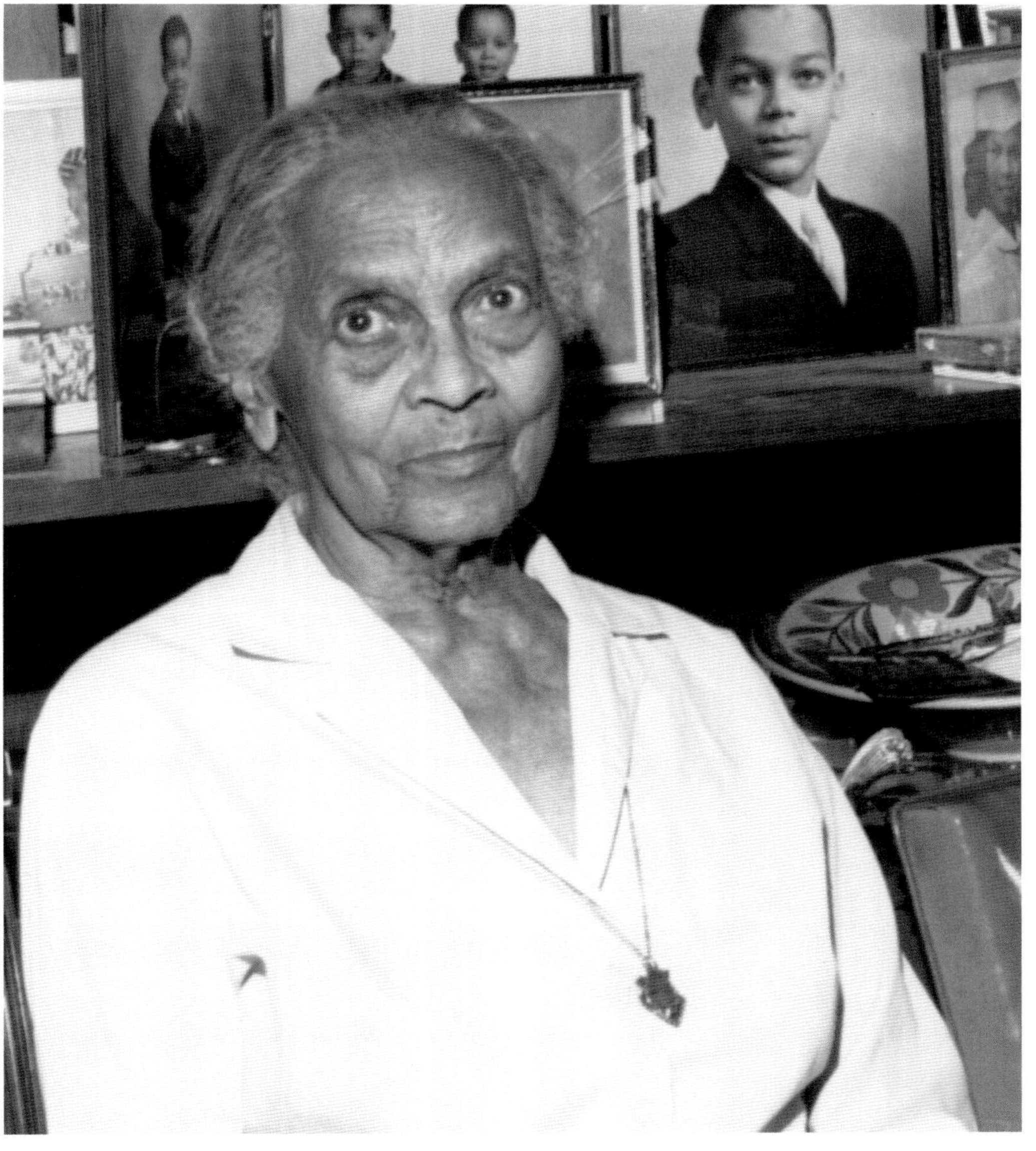

Dr. Lena Edwards
With the unexpected death in 1925 of Dr. Cannon—he died of an apparent accidental fall—Dr. Lena Edwards (1900–1986) arrived from Howard University to fill his void, though ultimately in her own distinct way. While raising her own family in Lafayette, she opened a prenatal practice on Pacific Avenue that focused on serving immigrant factory workers. When the world-class Margaret Hague Maternity Hospital opened in 1931, Dr. Edwards started what would become a legendary career there—she would deliver over 5,000 babies—though she was denied a residency until 1945. Compelled by faith, she eventually took a vow of poverty while a member of the Third Order of Franciscans. Dr. Edwards's calling surpassed the boundaries of Jersey City, and in 1954 she returned to Howard to teach obstetrics and, in 1960, established a maternity hospital for migrant mothers in Texas. This act of humanity won her the Presidential Medal of Freedom from Pres. Lyndon B. Johnson in 1964. (Courtesy of the Afro-American Historical Society Museum.)

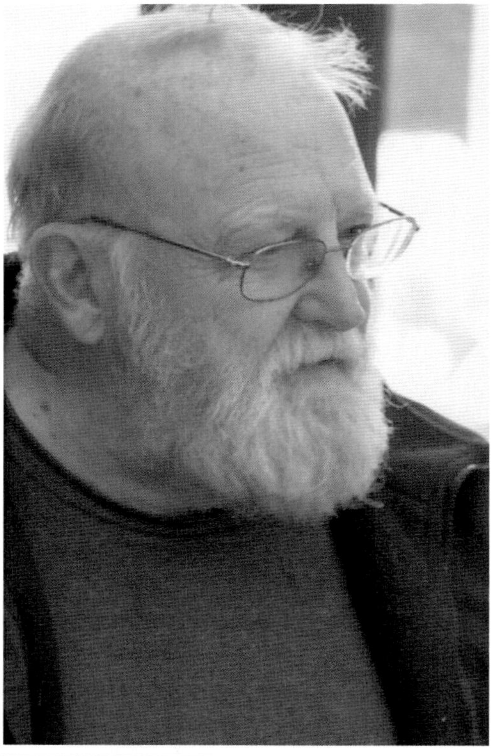

The Rev. Robert W. Castle

Throughout the 1960s, Jersey City was at the forefront of the civil rights conflict, and leading it was the Rev. Robert W. Castle (1929–2012), the rector of the now abandoned and crumbling St. John's Episcopal Church. "Bobby" was determined to lift local African American and Latino residents out of substandard living conditions and alter the apathy inside city government. From the pulpit and the porch, he waged war with Mayor Thomas Whelan and was even arrested on the steps of city hall for dumping debris pulled out of torched tenements. In 1968, the Reverend Castle was fired by the Episcopal Diocese of Newark for his close involvement with the Black Panthers. Over the next several decades, he practiced ministry in Vermont and Manhattan before beginning an acting career under the direction of his Hollywood-based cousin Jonathan Demme. In the late 2000s, at the invitation of the Jersey City Landmarks Conservancy, Bobby returned to Jersey City where he was publicly lauded and celebrated for his civil rights legacy. (Archival image collection of Dennis Doran.)

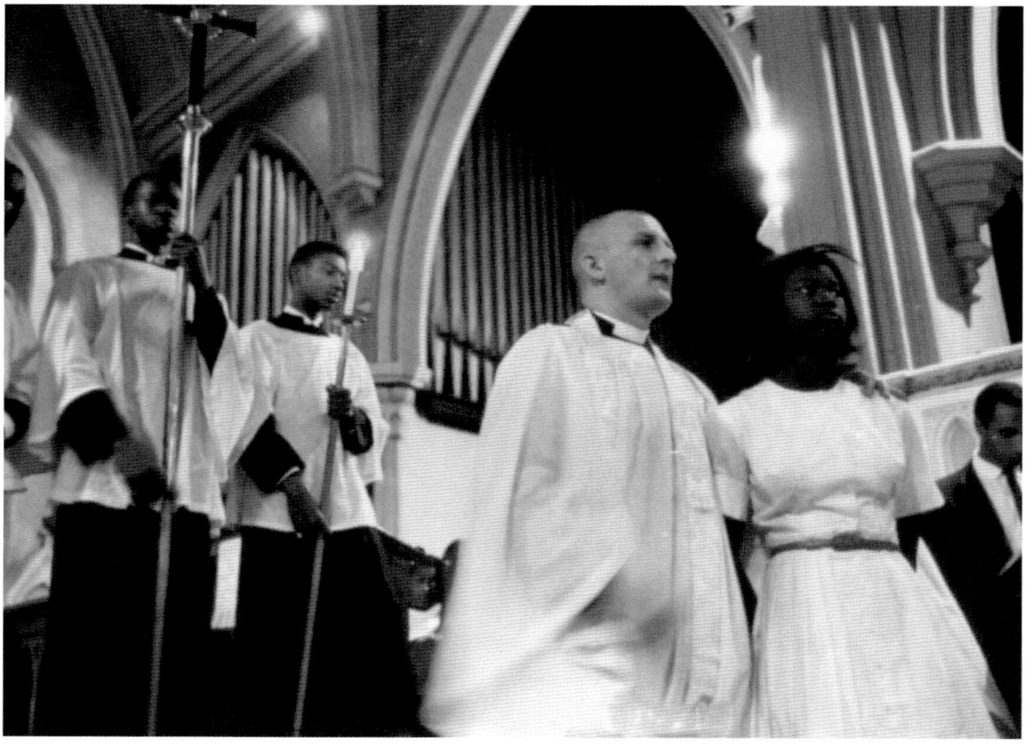

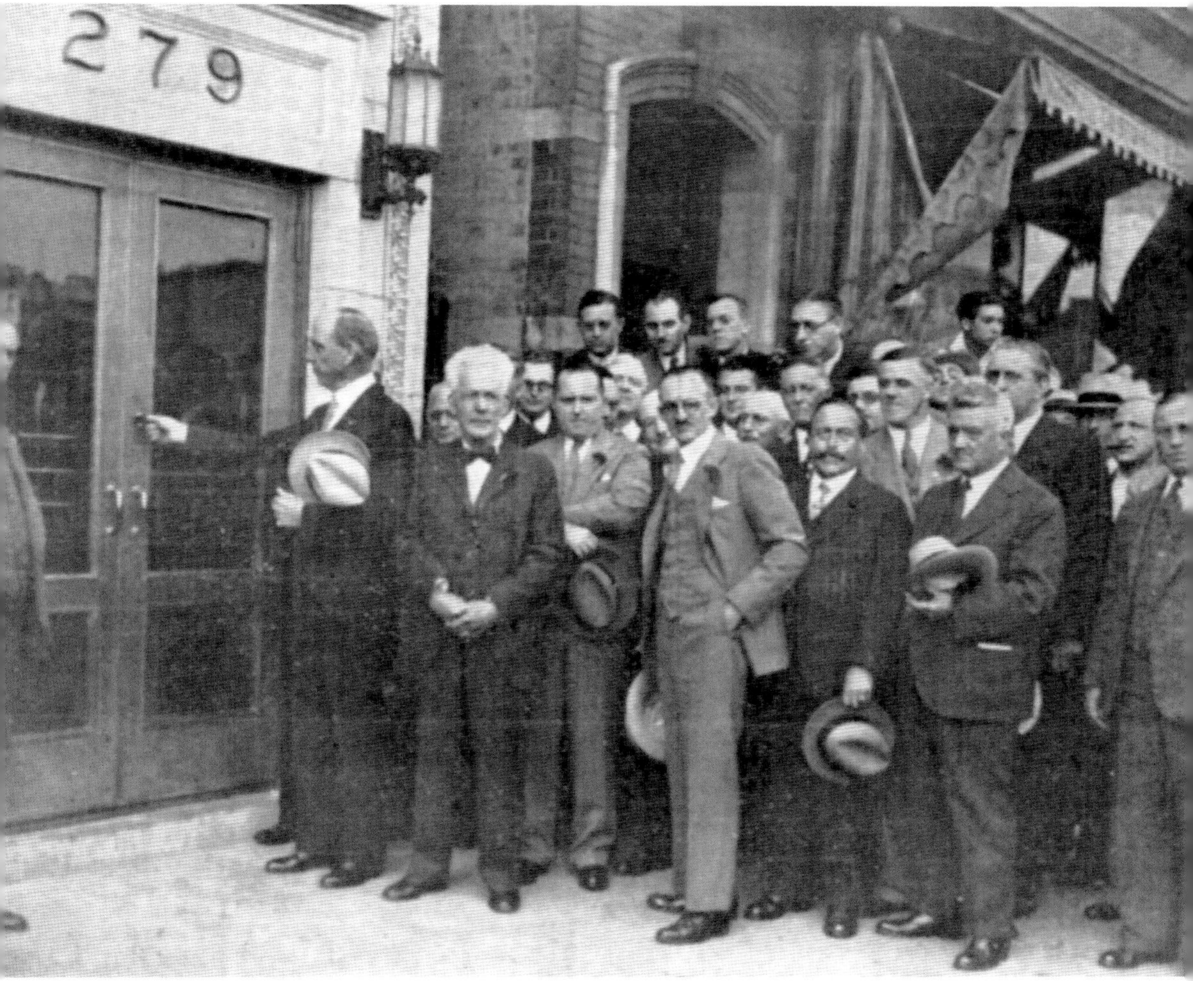

Frank Hague

While historians have highlighted the often unjust governing style and tactics of Mayor Frank Hague (1876–1956), locals still hold him in high esteem. Under Hague's regime, every resident had free access to the most modern medicine at his beloved Jersey City Medical Center complex, erected with Works Progress Administration (WPA) funds during the worst years of the depression; streets were spotless; and parks were plentiful. It did not matter that city employees' salaries were surreptitiously siphoned every pay period—so goes the great municipal myth—or that the likes of Leon Trotsky were jailed and tossed out of Jersey City during "Red" rallies. Hague turned the ceremonial keys of new banks, businesses, basilicas, and ballparks; schoolhouses soared with the growing population; and veterans were venerated with new housing projects. Amazingly, the ideals of Hague's urban utopia, though harshly criticized and lambasted during its heyday, have lived on, leaving behind a legacy wrought by one leader. (Courtesy of the Jersey City Free Public Library.)

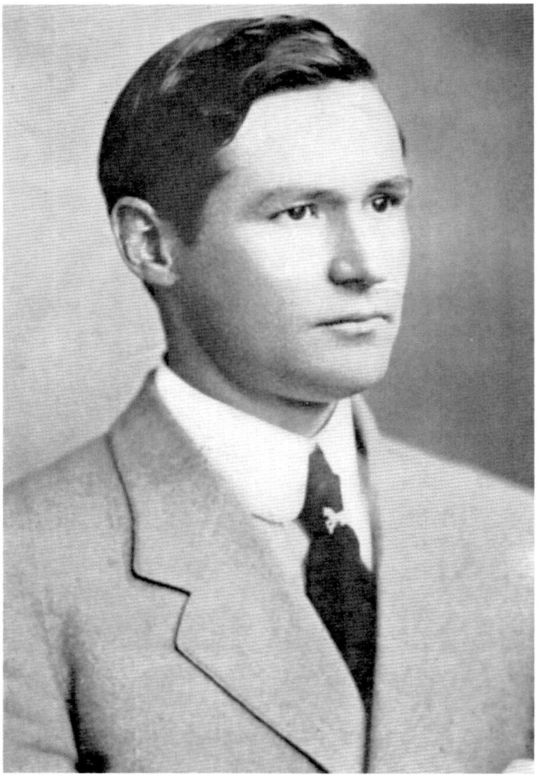

A. Harry Moore

A. Harry Moore (1879–1952), the three-time governor of New Jersey (1926–1929, 1932–1935, and 1938–1941) and US senator (1935–1938), was born and raised on Pine Street in the ancient Lafayette section of the city. A congregant of the historic Lafayette Dutch Reformed Church on Communipaw Avenue, Moore attended Cooper Union and the New Jersey Law School at Newark and was admitted to the bar in 1922. He started his long political career in Jersey City as city collector (1911–1913), a position he inherited after the death of "Boss" Robert Davis, and Jersey City commissioner (1913–1925). When his colleague Frank Hague became mayor in 1917, Moore was encouraged to run for governor. During his three nonconsecutive terms, Moore was seen as a children's advocate, establishing the A. Harry Moore Home for Crippled Children, one of the first of its kind in the country. (Courtesy of the Jersey City Free Public Library.)

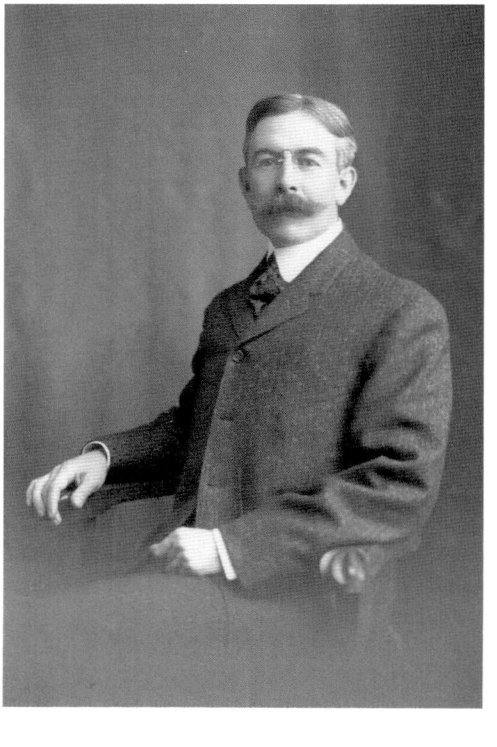

Mark Fagan

An undertaker by trade and profession, Mark Fagan suddenly splashed onto the political scene in 1902 when he was elected Republican mayor, shattering the domineering Democratic machine. Fagan, a disciple of the New Idea movement, set out to transform Jersey City into a cosmopolitan capital. During his multiple tenures (1902–1907 and 1913–1917), he built the Neoclassical-style Dickinson High School on the elevated picturesque site of an ancient barracks, erected the new City Hospital on Baldwin Avenue, and laid out city parks and plazas following the nationally adopted City Beautiful movement. (Courtesy of the Jersey City Free Public Library.)

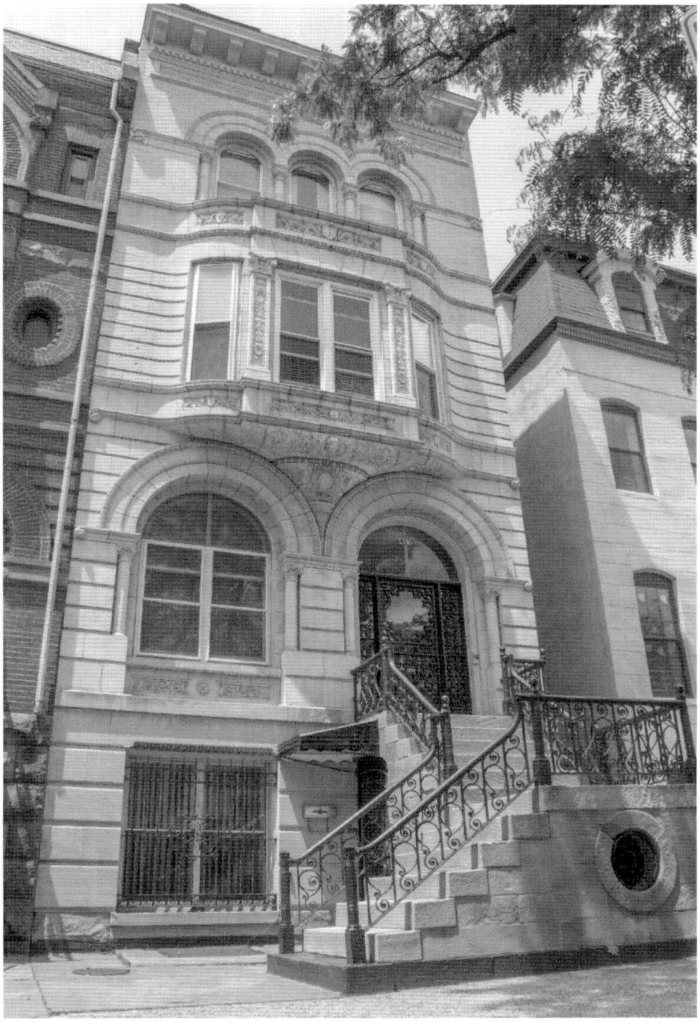

Cornelius R. Parker Jr.

Now in his late 90s and living outside Jersey City, Cornelius R. Parker Jr. is still a prominent citizen of the city. His legacy—as the generational owner of a funeral parlor business, a prominent NAACP and board of education member during the 1960s, a lifelong congregant of the historic Metropolitan AME Church, and a caring Ward F councilman during the administration of Thomas F.X. Smith—has never faded. A pocket park named for him on Madison Avenue in the brownstone-decked Bergen-Lafayette section is just one reminder of the legend who can trace his roots in the city to exactly 1895 when his father, Cornelius, opened Hudson County's first African American–owned funeral parlor. The young Cornelius took over the business starting in 1937 after graduating from the New York School of Embalming and Restorative Art and receiving the highest score on the prerequisite state board examinations. He was, the local newspapers reported, the youngest mortician in New Jersey. In 1968, he was instrumental in having the Rev. Dr. Martin Luther King Jr. visit Jersey City; the next year, after King's death, he successfully lobbied to have the new P.S. No. 11 School renamed in Dr. King's memory and connection to Jersey City. As councilman, he brought prodigious changes to Ward F, including the building of affordable housing, the installation of underground utilities and trees, and the preservation of the district's historic fabric.

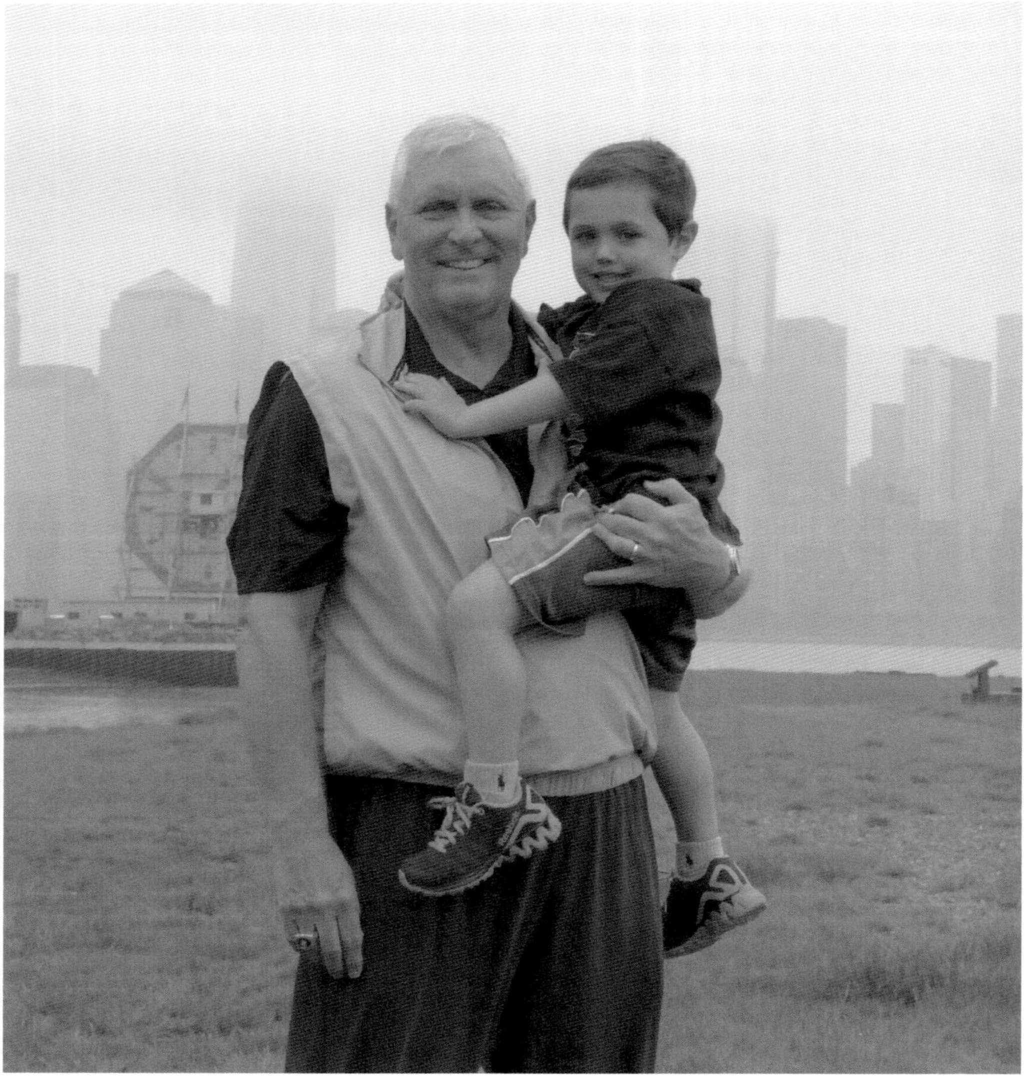

Bob Hurley

No one loves Jersey City more than Bob Hurley. The proof is in the Friars, his legendary high school basketball team at St. Anthony High School, where he has not only led the team to local, state, and national championships but has also shaped future hoop stars and model citizens; in his almost 30-year-career as a probation officer, trying his best to set troubled adults on the right course; and in his decision to continue to live in the city of his youth and Irish ancestors, pointing out that "for all the imperfections of this town, I will not leave. It's the one you're committed to." Hurley, who was inducted into the Naismith Basketball Hall of Fame in 2010, has been coaching since the late 1960s and will not retire until St. Anthony's shuts down, which is a real possibility in this age of parochial school closures. Whatever happens, Hurley has made his mark on the court as well as in major documentary works like author Adrian Wojnarowski's *The Miracle of St. Anthony: A Season with Coach Bob Hurley and Basketball's Most Improbable Dynasty* (2006); *The Street Stops Here* (2010), a feature film by Kevin Shaw; and *Chasing Perfect: The Will to Win in Basketball and Life* (2013), written by Bob Hurley and Daniel Paisner—with all proceeds going directly to St. Anthony's.

CHAPTER TWO

The Storefront Legacy

The storefront business—long the historical core, communal bond, and economic generator of all cities—can be found in every neighborhood in Jersey City. Most times, the business is a physical store with a sign, windows, counter, and cashier; a classified center, a place, where the space may be modest in size, sometimes narrow and tight, but the ambitions are monumental. Other times the business is Internet-based, without walls, a start-up steadfastly devoted to the city where it begins on a laptop and manifests with time. Whatever the type, the city business carries a shared storefront legacy; blood, sweat, and tears keep it standing; and personal sacrifice is evinced in the continuum of commercial days.

Lift up any library-archived city directory from the 1850s onward and observe a world of entrepreneurship that not very long ago existed, thrived, and gave substantial semblance to a growing Jersey City. Imagine these mom-and-pop owners opening the small store every day, year after year—uncranking striped cloth canopies, wiping down wide float-glass windows, staging deep showrooms, and stocking high wooden shelves and glass showcases with dry goods, candies, and household products. Within these very spaces, some of which are amazingly still here, though unrecognizable due to repeated renovations and reconfigurations, dramas were played out. Customers came not only to buy, but to participate in a culture; not only to fill up their cupboards and ice boxes, but to bring back an essence of the city. Such was 19th-century Jersey City storefront business life along a horse-truck gridlocked Newark Avenue in the downtown area; on Central, Palisade, and Summit Avenues in Hudson City or the Heights; on Monticello and Jackson Avenues in the Bergen Hill and Claremont districts; on Bergen Avenue as it stretched through the South Bergen and Greenville wards; on West Side Avenue in the Marion and West Bergen neighborhoods; and the side-street storefronts too numerous for history to grasp. Cobbled city lanes and avenues were lined up and down with tobacco emporiums, furniture showrooms, and chain stores with mom-and-pop atmospheres, including the Great Atlantic & Pacific Tea Company and F.W. Woolworth.

As decades pass and cities dramatically change, the storefront entity remains intact. It never ceases; it takes on new guises. Boulevard Drinks, Bag the Habit, Stan's Square Records, Second Street Bakery, Garden State News, Lee Sims Chocolates, Madame Claude Cafe, Laico's Restaurant, Andrea Salumeria, Light Horse Tavern, Goehrig's Bakery, and so on—though distinct and delineated by their own personal histories and goals—all come from the same municipal mold where dedication is the definition of longevity and commitment is their secret. Businesses like the 1939 World's Fair–produced White Mana do not exist as landmarks for nothing; owner Mario Costa had to buy the futuristic diner back from its new owner after he learned of plans to level it. General Pencil Company has been owned by the Weissenborn family since 1889 and still operates in the same brick building. Burns Brothers has been customizing stone memorials, monuments, and markers out of its Tonnelle Avenue shop for decades. The Rambusch Decorating Company, founded in 1898, with studios, offices, and warehouses on Cornelison Avenue, remains one of the greatest allied arts businesses in the world.

In Jersey City, local businesses—closed for decades or open at this moment—are timeless. Clocks never stop; centuries that separate one storefront from the next are passable. The proprietor across the ages and across neighborhoods is a pursuer of American dreams, always giving back to employees, customers, communities. They are part of a preserved commercial calling—a storefront legacy that can never fold.

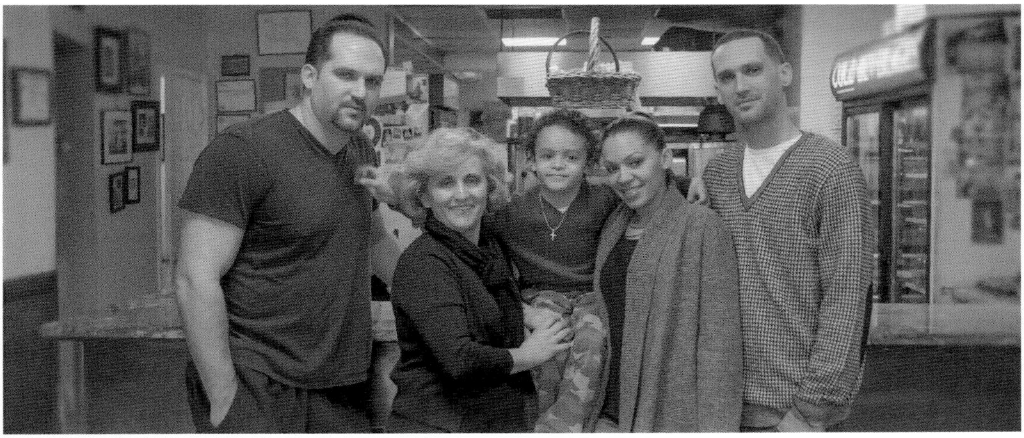

The Papageorgiou Family

The black-and-white photographs hanging on the walls inside Larry & Joe's Pizza tell the storefront tale that was started 35 years ago and belonged to the late Theodoros Papageorgiou. Today, his dedicated wife, Christina, and two sons, Demetrios and Spyros, are humbled whenever customers point at the images of "Teddy" and Christina in Greece—young, newly wedded, and on the verge of journeying to America to seek out their dream of business ownership. Settling on Newark Avenue in 1978, the couple initially opened a combination liquor store, deli, and restaurant. But then, in 1996, they seized the opportunity to purchase an established pizzeria and make it something extra special for the neighborhood, with fresh, affordable pizza and hot foods for nearby courthouse workers and visitors, as well as local high school students and teachers. Over time, Christina has also added her own character and bits of business wisdom to the place; never shy, she shares secrets like "Be friendly, be here!" and "Give customers the best." It has been a few years since Teddy died suddenly of cancer, but his presence is powerfully felt inside the store and on the streets, where everyone knew and loved him intimately. Looking at the photographs, Christina comments, "These are priceless pictures for me—now, more."

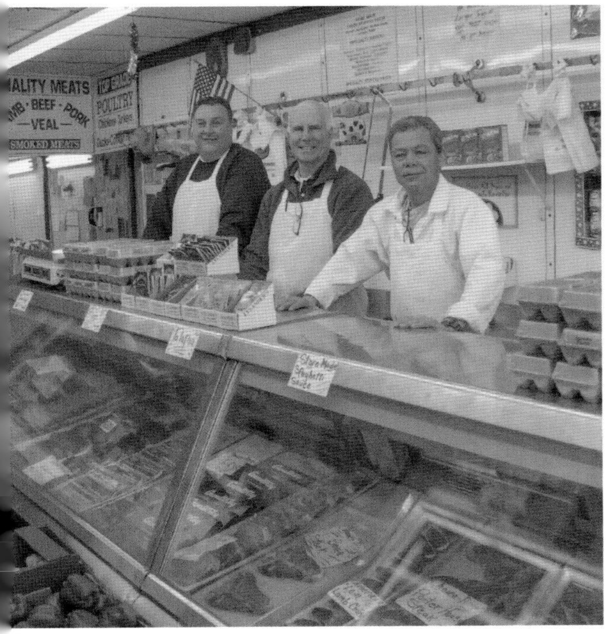

Moloney's Market

Tom Moloney (center) has been at it since 1967 at Moloney's Market on Newark Avenue in the historic Five Corners commercial district. Forty-six years is nothing considering that the first Moloney started out in 1875 in nearby Bayonne. A fourth-generation butcher, Tom is a sort of business showman who converses constantly with his customers and knows more about the history of the area than most historians. Tom's staff has been with him virtually as long as he has run the business. Almost in unison, they all brag about Moloney's famous hot lunches, crafted soups, prime meat cuts, and packaged Irish holiday foods. For St. Patrick's Day, they sell barrels of corned beef made the old-fashioned way, sitting and basting in brine. Perhaps the most visible signature inside the store is the saw dust on the floor, which Tom has to drive 100 miles, twice a year, to purchase.

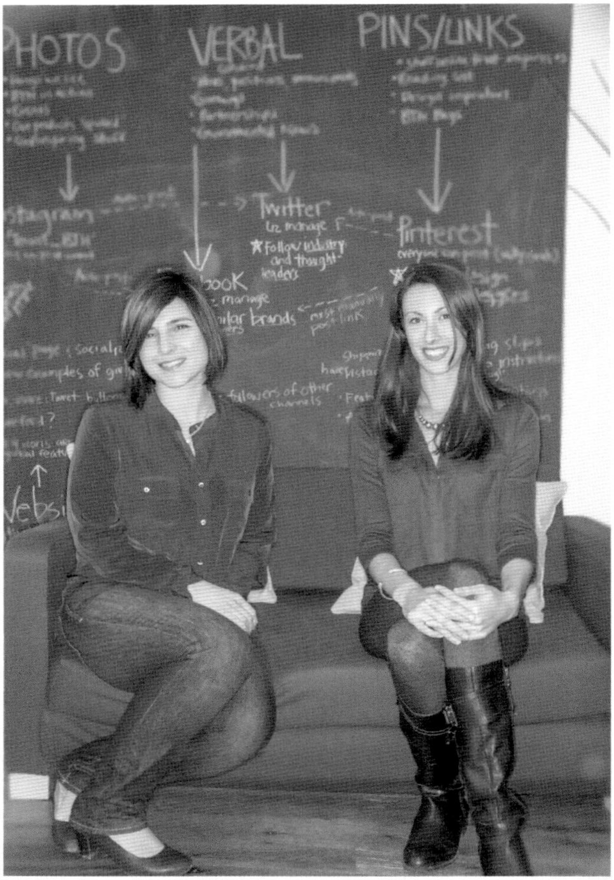

Holly Tienken and Liz Long

One day in 2007, without intention, Holly Tienken and Liz Long (left to right) started their environmentally sustainable Jersey City–based online business, Bag the Habit, over a cup of chai tea. In the tradition of the ancient tenement storefront business, the two close friends started with a vision and, with sheer determination and mindful planning, manifested it into a real venture that found commercial success and continues to grow till this day. The spark that Liz had seized upon was seeing someone double-bag a small tube of toothpaste—to her not only a complete waste, but also utter disrespect for the environment. Liz and Holly, with degrees between them in design, communications, and media, decided to challenge and counter that image with a fashionable line of recycled plastic-derived fabric that could be turned into reusable bags and totes. "The idea," says Holly, who designed the company logo of a leaf transitioning into a city skyline, "was that consumers can be in harmony with nature by showing their respect for it." The synthesis of their separate roots became the underlying secret to their eventual success. Liz had grown up in rural Pennsylvania, spending her youth amidst farms and fields and watching her grandmother fight to preserve open space and historic resources from over-development. Holly came from a background of mom-and-pop businesses, including her great-grandfather and grandfather's Little Italy–based bakery and cafe. With these meaningful foundations, they launched the company's dynamically designed website and established physical company offices on Grove Street. The duo have been recognized for their products, appearing in *USA Today*, the *Huffington Post*, *People*, *Planet Green*, and an episode of the Sundance Channel's *Iconoclasts*. Liz and Holly recognize the value of the local business enterprise to Jersey City. "People comment on the strength of the community here," says Liz, "and the business owners play a central role in that."

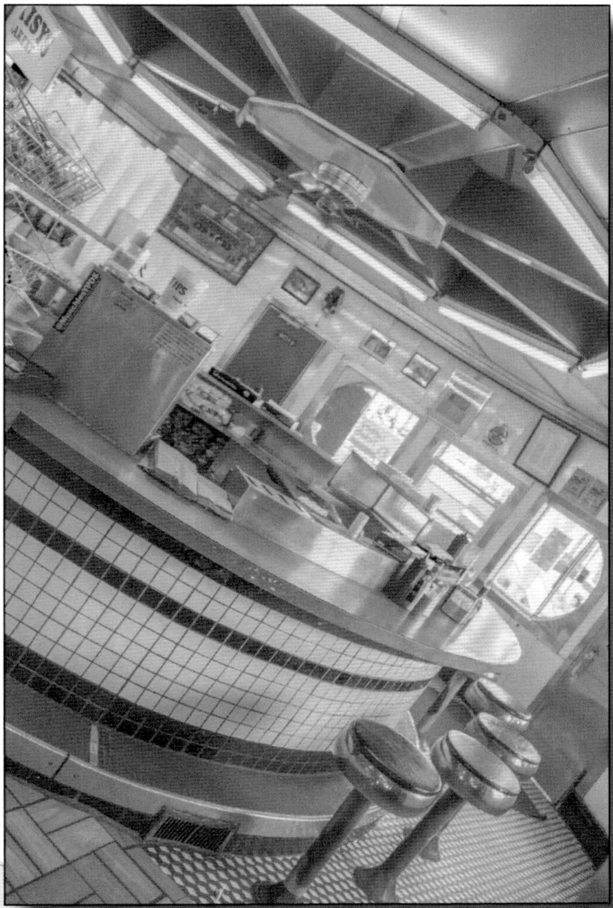

White Mana

Mario Costa is not just the proud proprietor of a famous local eatery in Jersey City, he is also a hero of landmarks. When he sold the White Mana diner in 1981 to a developer, he was stunned to learn of plans to demolish the Depression-era "diner of tomorrow" to make way for a donut franchise shop. So, in a leap of financial faith, he bought the cylindrical dining capsule back and has been its steadfast protector and vocal promoter ever since, leading the site toward official local landmark designation and true cultural destination status. Designed and patented in 1937–1938 by Arthur E. Sieber, exhibited in 1939 at the World's Fair, and fabricated in a limited edition of five by the Paramount Diner Company, the White Mana made its way to Jersey City in 1946 at the corner of Manhattan Avenue and Route 1/9. The pioneering pod-like fast-food structure still features Formica laminates, geometric floor tiles, porthole window banding, and chrome bar stools encircling a stainless steel drum counter.

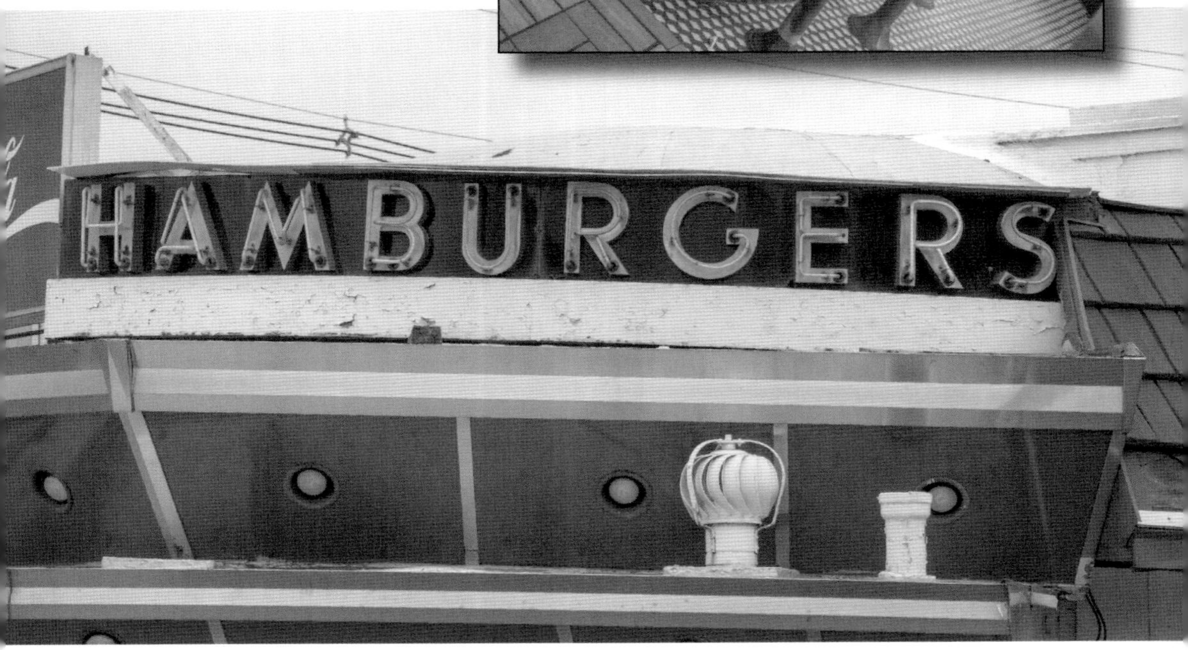

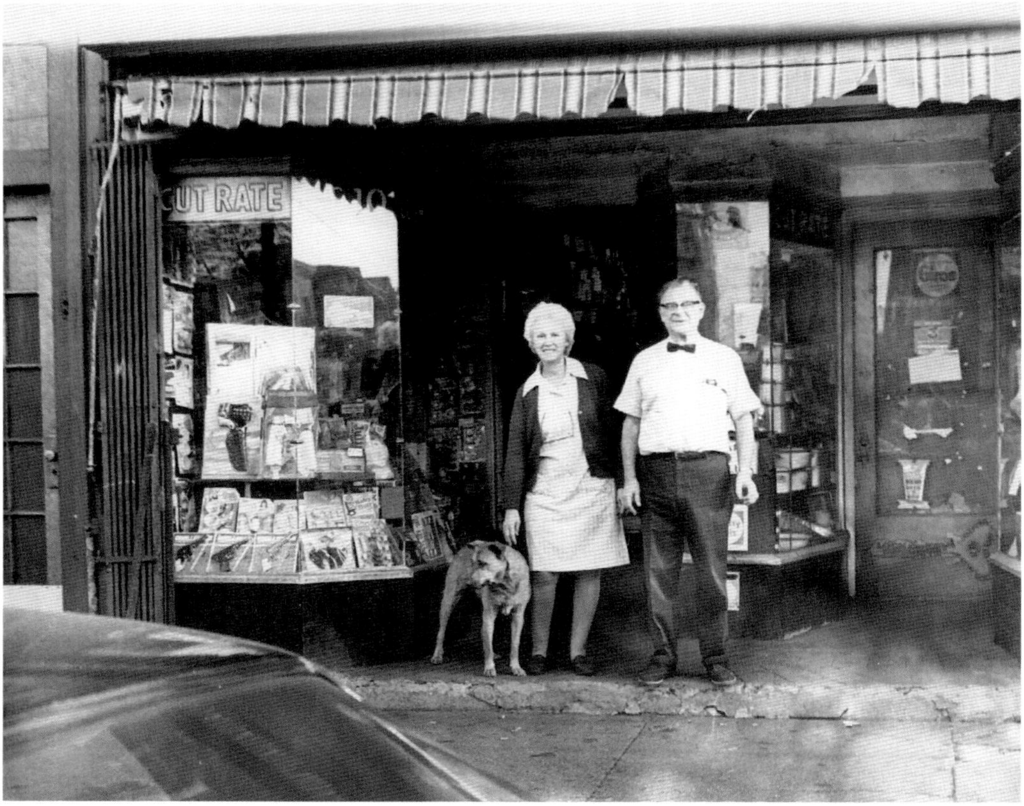

Pacific 5&10

Although his parents' F.W. Woolworth–like variety store, Pacific 5&10, closed in 1979 after 42 years of serving the community, Jeff Kaplowitz often shares two intrinsic treasures—animated anecdotes about the times he and his sister Phyllis spent, and the life lessons they learned, behind the counter interacting daily with the diverse Lafayette neighborhood residents, who became close to the entire Kaplowitz family; and, most profoundly, a series of stunning 35mm black-and-white photographs that Jeff took, at the urging of a Rutgers professor, to document the store in a single day—that, together, keep the storefront very alive. In his poetic images from 1974, Jeff, a former city planning commission chairman and now a highly respected real estate broker, captured a Pacific Avenue business neither failing nor fading, but pulsing with history and familial spirit; split-second shots of his mother, Sadie, and father, Herman, in action with customers or alone in contemplation; commercial products no longer the norm, like 45s and tube televisions; and other Pacific Avenue businesses now, like his parents' emporium, replaced on the streetscape. Jeff remembers the best-selling stock items very well, including comic books, cosmetics, clothing, candy, greeting cards, hardware, and dry goods—"If there were space for it we sold it," he says. To Jeff's pleasure, their type of business model—a small space managed by a father and a mother who work long hours, with their young children spending time there after school and on weekends learning the trade with the hopes of taking it over—can still be seen today in the form of the Dominican bodegas and restaurants along Communipaw Avenue or the many Asian- and Arabic-owned businesses in the Journal Square and Jersey City Heights districts. To Jeff, the community store is the true lifeline of the city. "Today you have the convenience of the mall," he says, "but you don't have the connection to the people." (Courtesy of Jeff Kaplowitz.)

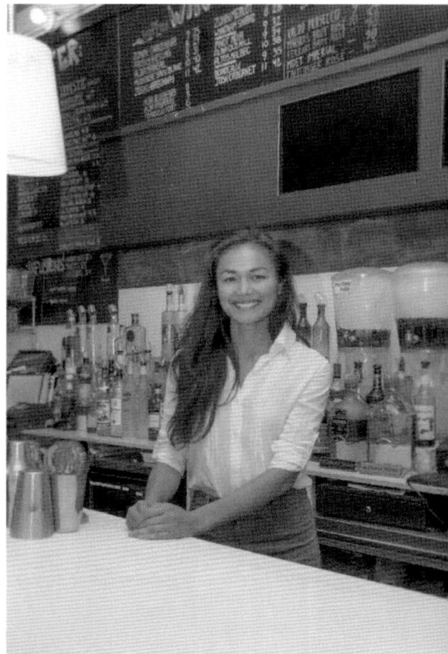

Jelynne Jardiniano

LITM (Love Is The Message), Jelynne Jardiniano's immensely popular "hip bar/restaurant and gallery" business on Newark Avenue, has in exactly 10 years taken the concept of the storefront to original limits, shaping and supporting the city's social and cultural scene. Local beer enthusiasts frequent the place; artists seek out its curators for exposure and opportunity; those who appreciate crafted burgers and creative salads fill its stools and tables. LITM emits a strong sense of tradition, of a dream having been fulfilled. A graduate of the local public school district's prestigious Acceleration and Enrichment Program (AEP) and McNair Academic High School, Jelynne, who immigrated to Jersey City from the Philippines with her family when she was only five years old, has fond memories of working after school at the legendary Lee Sims Chocolates on Bergen Avenue, an experience that prepared her for the Cornell University School of Hotel Administration where she earned her bachelor's in food and beverage operations. Jelynne's ambitions have reached outside LITM; in 2010, she published *Restaurant from Scratch: How to Trust Your Heart, Listen to the Market and Beat the Odds*, a motivational business book.

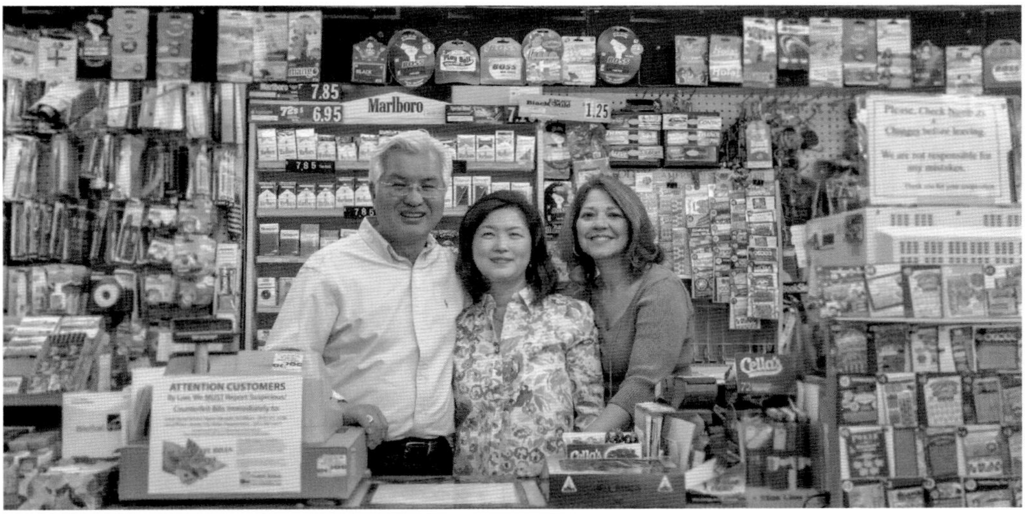

Garden State News

Since opening Garden State News in 1981, Michael Yun's newspaper shop has been the unofficial community center of the densely populated Jersey City Heights section. Michael and wife, Jenny, are not only dedicated business owners—they open the store at 7:00 a.m. and close it at 7:00 p.m., seven days a week—they are also tireless activists in the neighborhood they have adopted as their permanent home. From fighting for adequate bus service up and down the Central Avenue shopping district corridor to joining the fight to preserve historic Reservoir No. 3, the Yuns keep plugging away and assisting customers beyond the store counter. Michael is proud that many of the store's student employees have gone on to achieve success, due in large part, Michael brags, to his and Jenny's demand for commitment, honesty, and the acceptance that life is not just about money, that caring for the community is key, and, like Michael's father instructed him years before, that staying busy doing good things will not allow any time for doing bad things. In 2013, Michael was elected councilman of the ward where Garden State News thrives.

Andrea Salumeria

Once a week, for the process is time consuming, Pete Soriano, the owner of Andrea Salumeria on Central Avenue in the Jersey City Heights section, handcrafts glistening, fennel-filled Italian sausage links, and will only wait for the best possible product to be delivered before beginning the secret ingredient recipe mixtures and meat grinding methods handed down to him by his now-retired uncle and business namesake, Andrea. The making of mozzarella, too, is a gifted affair, though far less complex, allowing Pete and his long-employed chef and server staff to bring out watery trays of the white lumpy delicacy five times a day, sometimes more. It is this type of devotion to high-quality food that makes the business, started in 1975 by Uncle Andrea, legendary. Pete's gourmet sandwich shop and imported Italian foods emporium is arguably the finest in the municipality; the long lines inside the tiny shelf–stocked and coldcut case–lined space are definitive proof. Pete believes, however, that people tolerate the wait not just for the superb food, but also the conversation, the closeness that he and dedicated workers like Ben Fossetta provide. Regular residents enter the store daily, but so do prominent politicians, police officers, firemen, and educators, all rubbing shoulders, sharing gossip, growing older amid the hanging salamis, canned imported peaches, and boxed babka cakes stacked high on counters. To Pete, who works 10 to 12 hours, six days a week, his customers are not only unwavering, but also are everywhere, even outside the city limits, be it in the apple picking fields or on a cruise ship, stopping in excitement to greet and talk to him, as if they are in the store. "That's what keeps me going," Pete says. "The personal touch, the relationships; you don't get that in chains." And to top it all off, Pete donates generously to local little leagues and children's leukemia causes. "I do my share. As a business owner, it can't be one way."

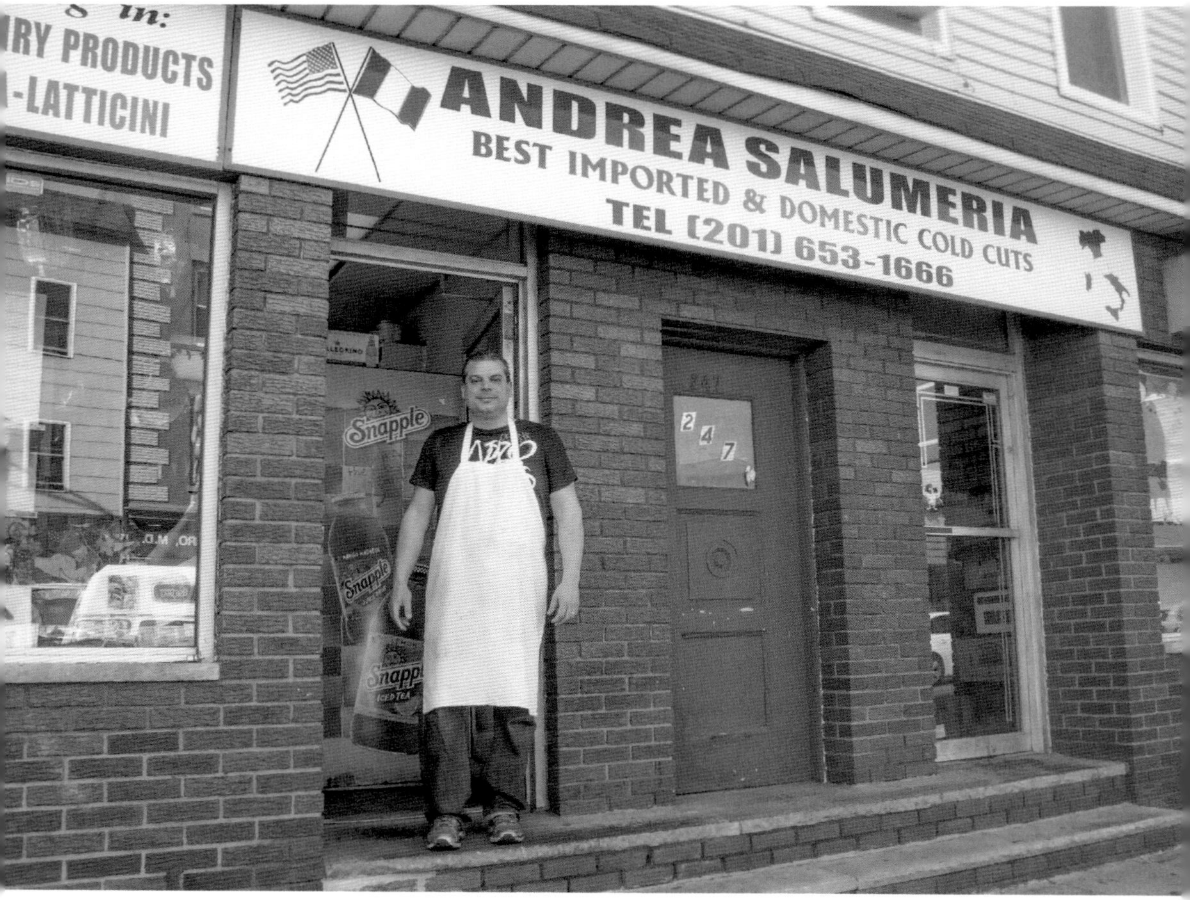

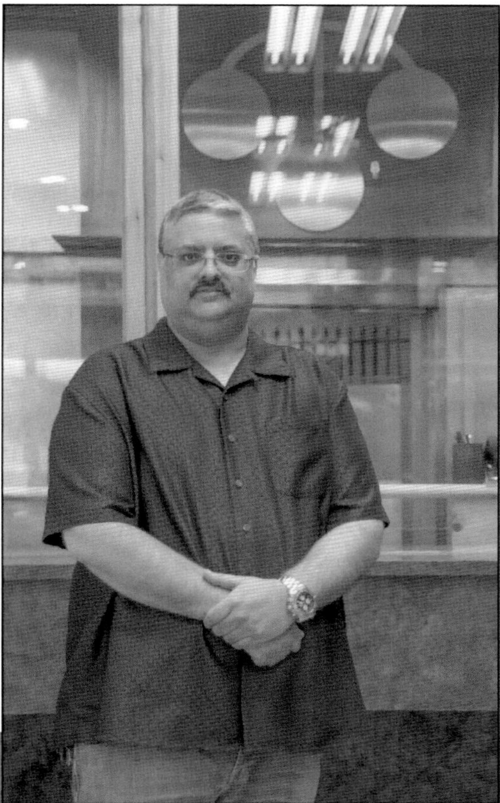

H. Schoenberg Pawnbrokers & Jewelers

Manuel E. Vidal, the owner of H. Schoenberg Pawnbrokers & Jewelers on Bergen Avenue (pictured below, far right), first became aware of the historic business when he got a job in a toy shop right next door. Manny was a hard worker and drew the attention of Paul Schoenberg, who, with brother Kenneth, proudly continued the family business that was founded in 1895. In 1988, Manny was hired by the Schoenbergs and began a proud affiliation that culminated in 2003, when he bought the business and renovated the interior but kept the historical name. (Archival photograph courtesy of the Jersey City Free Public Library.)

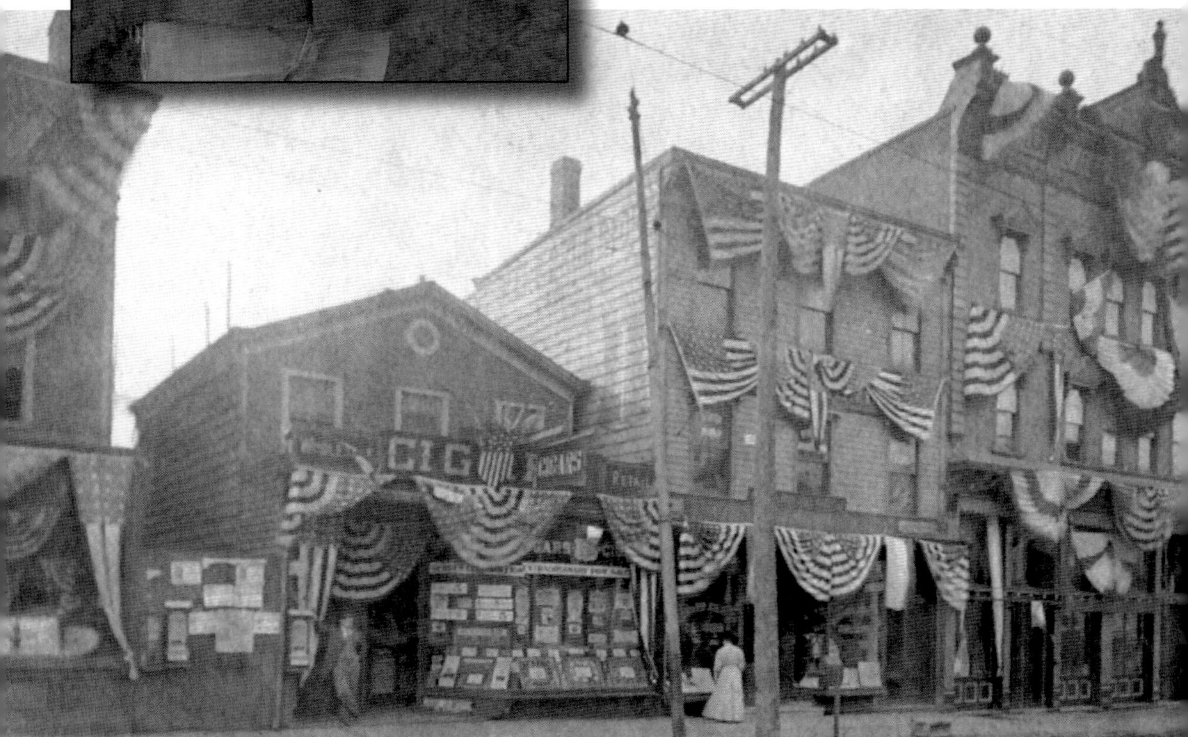

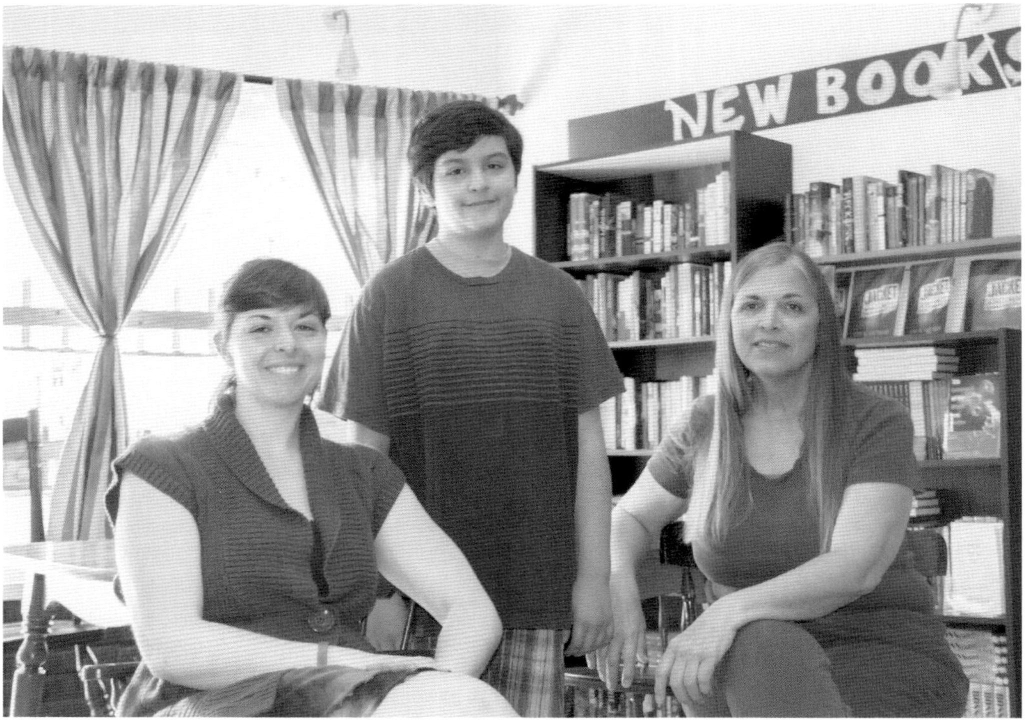

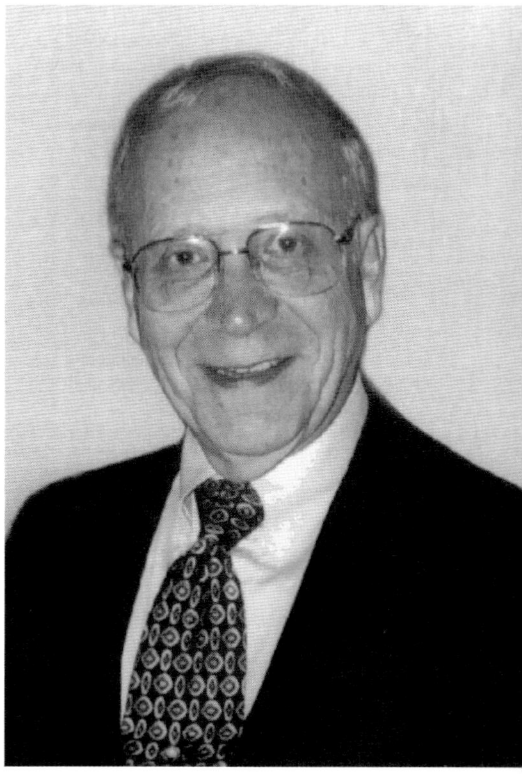

Bardack Realty

As Allan Roy Bardack has often told, Bardack Realty, Jersey City's oldest family-run storefront brokerage business, was founded by the luck of the silent moving picture industry. His father, Herman Bardack, working for Universal, used to go around soliciting local businesses to advertise in neighborhood nickelettes between reels. One day, according to Bardack business lore, Herman inquired with a one-man brokerage firm, and instead of walking out with a sale, he walked out with an offer of partnership. By 1920, Herman had broken out on his own, a bold move that resonates over 90 years later. Allan, whose father was his mentor—he taught him about all housing types and instilled in him a love of architecture, neighborhoods, and, most of all, people—later followed suit and obtained his brokerage licensure in 1951. From the 1970s through the 1990s, Allan teamed up with local preservation giants Thomas Stanton Jr., Theodore Conrad, and Morris Pesin to rehabilitate abandoned brownstone districts and to fight to protect individual monuments like the c. 1690 Newkirk House, the 1929 Loew's Jersey Theatre, and Liberty State Park. (Courtesy of Allan and Ruby Bardack.)

Tachair Bookshoppe (OPPOSITE PAGE)
Three years ago, at the age of eight, Paul Valleau, the inspiration behind his family store, Tachair Bookshoppe, climbed a stool to reach the podium microphone stationed right in front of the city council dais. Holding up a poster he created with the help of his mother, Aleta, and grandmother, Carol, which said, "Make A Splash, and Please Budget the Cash," Paul implored the governing body to save local libraries by keeping branches open, preventing layoffs, and not cutting back on materials so essential to the public. The large crowd in attendance gave a standing ovation, and suddenly, Paul was being featured in the local newspapers. But the young visionary had already been gaining attention in public as a smart seller of used books on sidewalk tables and at neighborhood fairs and markets, calling his campaign the "Opus Jr. Library Champion," with all proceeds being donated to the Jersey City Free Public Library. Eventually, seeing a need for a local bookstore, Paul, Aleta, and Carol decided to open Tachair Bookshoppe on Newark Avenue, which has quickly become a popular cultural destination in the city with a full schedule of author readings and signings, meet-and-greets, children's activities, and art exhibitions.

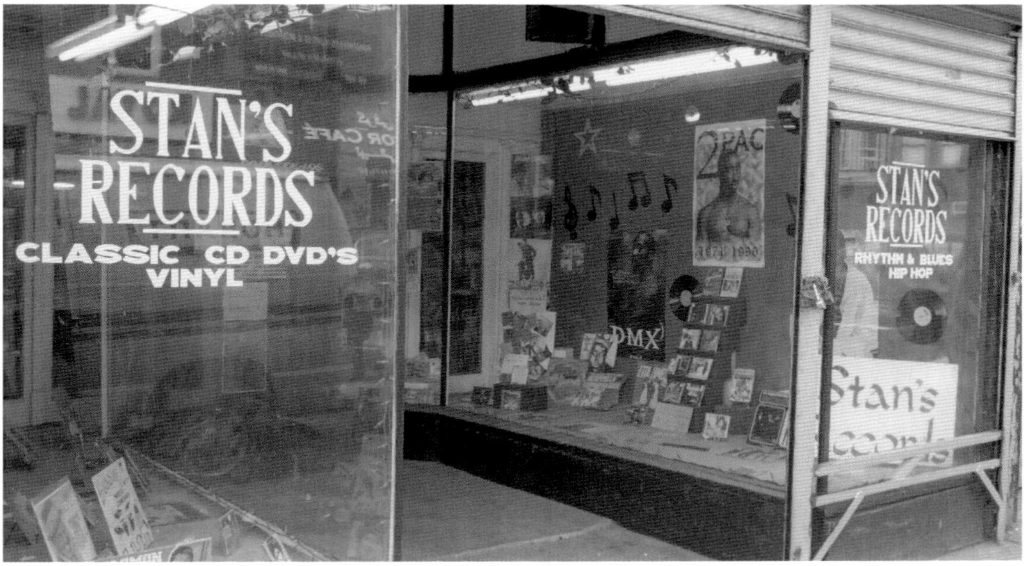

Stan's Square Records
Stan Krause, the founder and owner since 1965 of Stan's Square Records, is a living institution. Framed photographs signed by local musical legends plaster the walls of his time-capsuled store as proud proof of his influence. Vinyl records and albums, categorized by artist, era, and genre, are the store's main sale items and add to the interior aura and magic. A vintage jukebox is stationed in the back as a symbol of Stan's faith in the lost form and art of pressed records, whose sounds, he says, are deeper than digital and truer than online streams. For all its displayed nostalgia, Stan's Square Records, which started out in Journal Square but made its way to McGinley Square on Bergen Avenue in 1973, is always current, selling the latest musical movements in hip-hop, alternative, rock, and rhythm and blues, all categorized inside counter-top binders. Stan, whose father pressed independent records in a Little Ferry warehouse and who played Big Band music in the house, insists that he runs a business, not a museum, though the historical arc of Jersey City's modern musical heritage can be traced to his double-platform showcase window store. Starting out, Stan wanted to be close to the streets where real vocal harmony groups, like a capella, blues, and doo-wop, sang on corners and stoops, their songs soulful reflections and meditations on their lives and experiences in the city. He also wanted to discover, produce, and manage up-and-coming singers and bands, and in tandem with the store's opening, he launched Catamount Records, a company that still publishes talented singers on the rise. "Music is the binding of people," says Stan from behind the counter. "It can shape generations."

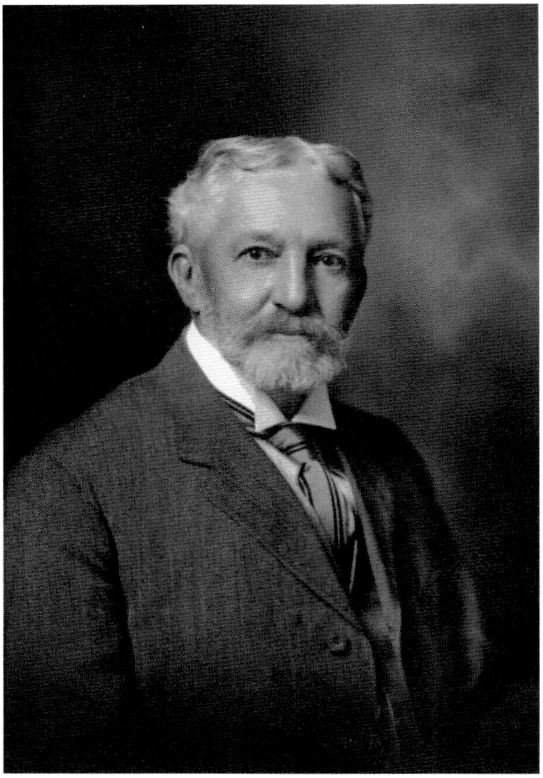

E.S. Wells

E.S. Wells (1841–1913) was the entrepreneur of his era; he was an experimental chemist and over-the-counter "doctor," who started off penniless but worked long hours to build up his modest Monticello Avenue storefront into an internationally renowned drug manufacturing company. His first inventions were potions that purported to cure baldness, hives, and warts; even unnamed horse ailments. But Wells was destined to transcend his own hopes and dreams. In the early 1880s, his Rough on Rats was born, becoming a national and global commercial blockbuster. The folk druggist invented over 100 Rough on products, including a "life renewer" potion. No matter the outrageousness of his products' claims, Wells was the epitome of the local success story, and today, archivists and collectors alike seek out his original ads. (Left, courtesy of the Jersey City Free Public Library.)

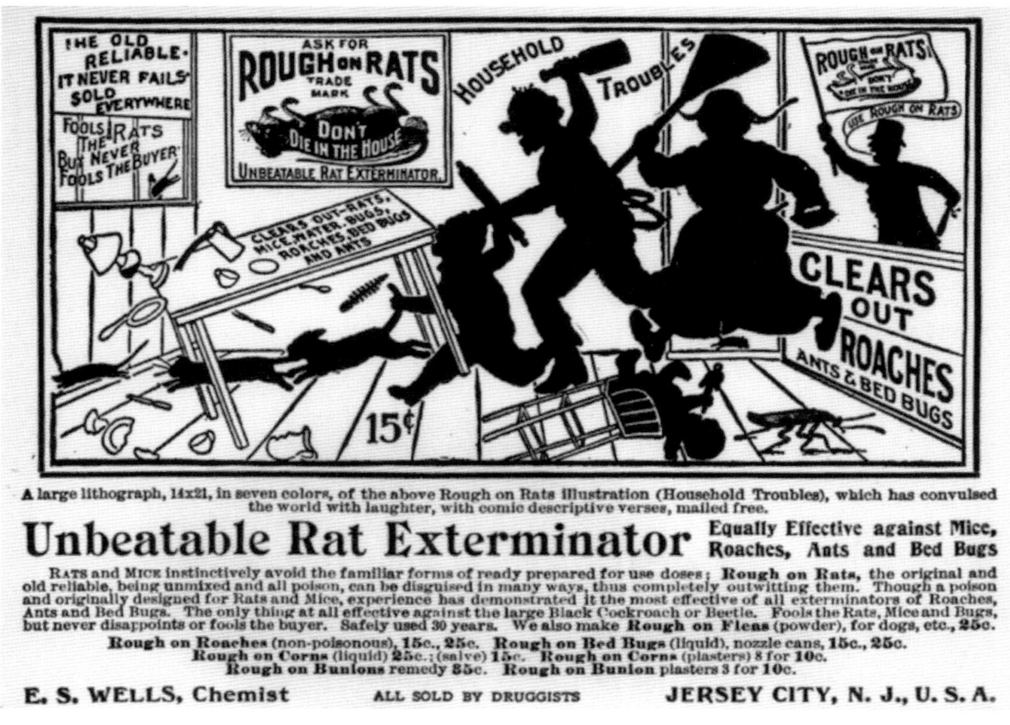

CHAPTER THREE

City of Creativity

If Jersey City were a lone municipal edifice and if all of its architecture-rich neighborhoods could be consolidated into a single tripartite monument, creativity would be its illuminated tower, with clocks on all four sides, with carillons constant in their soundings. Artistry and imagination would be its great, soldiered columns, colossal in their tiers and tridents, endless in the invigorating light they emit.

For the last 150 years, this vertical image has been present in the local skyline. It is inexplicably sensed every October when local artists across the city reveal and share their work with the public during the Artist Studio Tour, brilliantly organized by Pro Arts and city agencies; when every first Friday of the month JC Fridays features exhibitions and other exciting cultural events sponsored by the progressive Art House Productions; and when the doors to the Hudson County Justice William J. Brennan Courthouse are left open so that visitors may view American Renaissance-era murals executed by nationally renowned painters, including Charles Yardley Turner, Kenyon Cox, Edwin Howland Blashfield, and the Titanic-fated Francis David Millet.

Decade after decade, artists of all genres have been energized and impacted by Jersey City's dynamic neighborhoods and the everyday citizens who have populated and dramatized them. In the mid- to late 19th century, August Will, the city's preeminent landscape portraitist, carried his canvases through immigrant wards filled with Gothic tenements and debris-clogged canals, capturing a fading yet archetypical face of the city. His contemporary, Theodore Gubelman, a groundbreaking studio portrait and architectural landscape photographer, heaved his heavy tripods and large-format cameras through districts to document newly minted landmarks, some still standing. On Sherman Place, an unexpectedly quaint Jersey City Heights lane lined with owner-restored vernacular Victorian manses and matching carriage houses and deep rear gardens, a forgotten artists' community is still seen in the former homes and studios of muralist Vincent Aderente, Tiffany Glass Company–trained artisan F.E. Freund, sculptor and painter Pauline Ward Mount, and abstract expressionist Charles Seliger.

Artistry comes alive everywhere in Jersey City—at local Provident Savings Bank buildings, where the framed historical murals of Ruth Wilcox depict scenes from Jersey City's cascading timeline; in the postmodern commercial towers along its transformed waterfront, whose lobbies have been commissioned with history-filled paintings; at Hudson-Bergen Light Rail stations, which feature 3-D moving sculptures, wrought-iron benches, canopy mobiles, etched glass-block walls, and metal platform maps; and at the municipality's public housing projects, where sculptural works like Melvin Edwards's *Holder of the Light* (1985) glisten in the sun.

Classical and modern dance companies, like the Kennedy Dancers and Nimbus Dance Works, keep the genres going and turn out professional dancers. Master glazier Barbara Meise refuses to allow a medieval tradition die; her restoration work inside local houses of worship are a testament to her passion. Local photographers Edward Fausty, Andrzej Jerzy Lech, E. Jan Kounitz, and Leon Yost have utilized ancient and current photographic technologies to not only capture and document the city that has been their home and their personal diorama, but to also preserve its ever-fragile and ever-fading architectural grid. Laryssa Wirstiuk will think back to her Ukrainian grandmother's Jersey City home for inspiration for her beautifully rendered short stories; Charles Kessler will launch and fight for an arts community in the midst of overwhelming commercial development; Nick Taylor will write and shoot his independent feature films in the city he grew up and works in, continuing the work of the Pathe and Fox film studios of a century before; Grigory Gurevich and his son Alex will perform the mystical and ancient art of pantomime, mesmerizing their audiences in their small brownstone apartment space.

Jersey City is a city of creative geniuses throughout time; a city of intrinsic offerings; a city of impetus and inspiration—an aesthetic force formed and forged from legacy, rising up to that illuminated tower.

Archimedes Giacomantonio

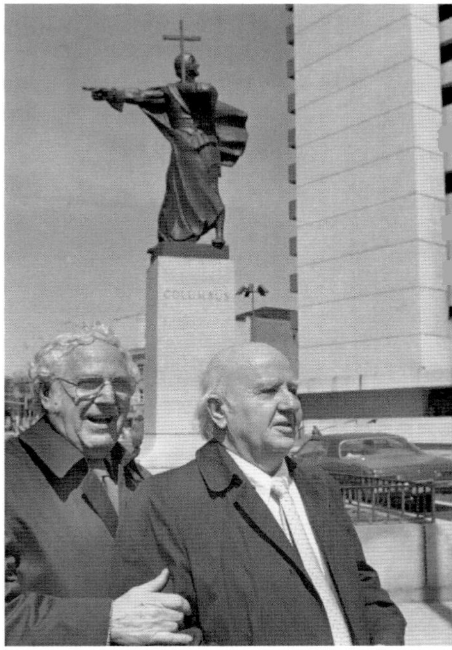

The name Archimedes Giacomantonio (1905–1988, pictured at right) rings with the sound of art. He is Jersey City's only sculptor of national renown, and his colossal bronzes are admired in public and private spaces around the city, Hudson County, and throughout the country. Born in Jersey City to Italian immigrant parents, Giacomantonio's genius was locally lauded after he cast an interpretive effigy of a young Abe Lincoln (*The Rail Splitter*, 1925) for Lincoln High School. In 1926, with the *Jersey Journal* rhapsodizing the wunderkind in a feature article, Giacomantonio sailed to Italy to apprentice with world-famous Neapolitan sculptor Vincenzo Gemito. A few years later, Giacomantonio returned a true master. Over the next 50 years, he designed major works, including *Police Monument* (Jersey City, 1935), *Mohammad Reza Pahlavi, Shah of Iran* (New York/Washington, D.C./Iran, 1945), *The Wounded Soldier* (Jersey City, 1947), *Gen. Dwight D. Eisenhower* (Washington, D.C., 1948), and, perhaps most famously, *Christopher Columbus* (Jersey City, 1950). (Courtesy of Sam Pesin.)

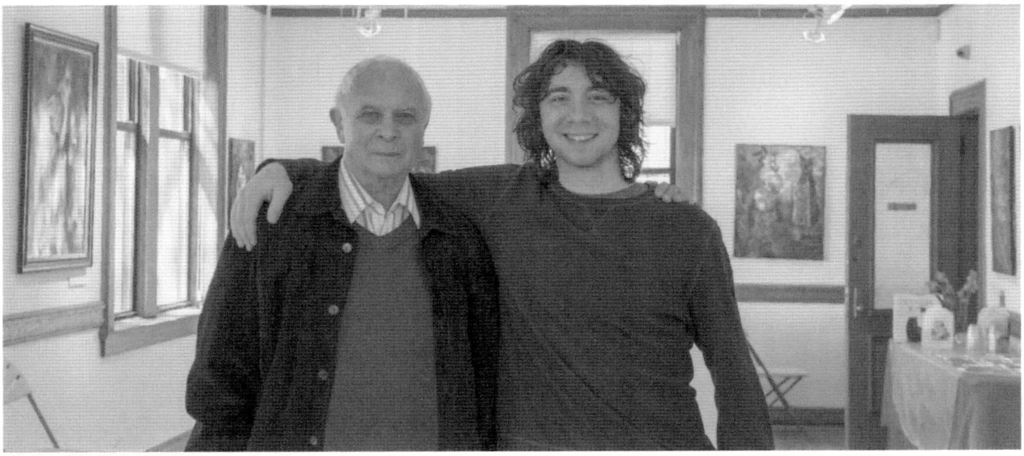

Grigory Gurevich

Grigory Gurevich recalls the moment in 1961 when he watched the great pantomime Marcel Marceau (1923–2007) perform on a Leningrad stage; it was spellbinding, poetic, and earth shattering. His meeting with the master, who befriended and encouraged him to take up the ancient "art of silence," was so profound that Grigory gave up his career as a promising architect for the largely poverty-stricken life of a pantomime artist. Miming had completely seized his soul, sending him traveling with his own troupe throughout Europe and Asia. In 1976, after hitchhiking through Vienna and Italy, Grigory boarded a plane for New York with $90 in his pocket. For two years, he lived in Brooklyn's famous Hotel St. George and then made his way to Jersey City to live in a Russian colony of brownstones on Barrow Street, where he has been ever since. In 1992, his son Alexander, today a gifted carpenter, prop artist, stage manager, and animated musical theater composer, was born, giving Grigory a permanent pantomime partner, traveling companion, and friend. In 1998, Grigory established Arts on the Hudson, a nonprofit organization offering various art classes to local residents and students, including scholarships for low-income families.

Laryssa Wirstiuk

Laryssa Wirstiuk knew she wanted to be a writer after she met the author John Rowell at Loyola University, Maryland. As an emerging writer, she had been exploring poetry, but Rowell, she says, "kind of blew my mind with short stories, and that was the beginning of an entirely new love affair." Laryssa began the compositions that would become her first book of short stories, *The Prescribed Burn* (2012, Painted Egg Press). Centered on an emerging artist named Veda, the eight connected tales take place in a Jersey City populated by young people searching for meaning and purpose.

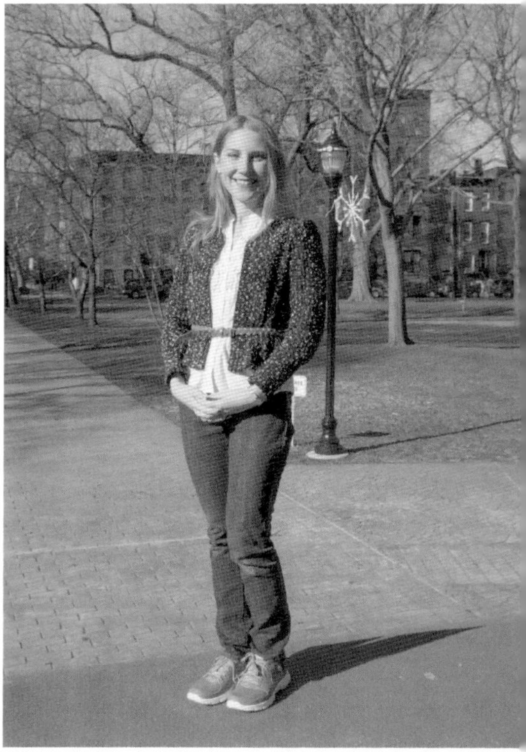

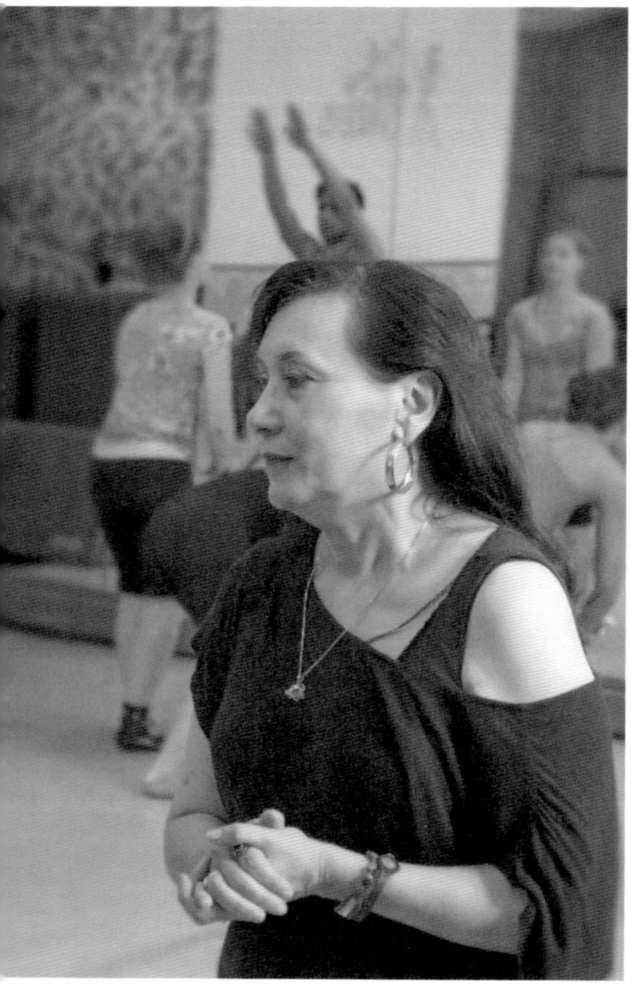

Diane Dragone

With the groundbreaking dance company, studio, and school she founded in 1976, Diane Dragone has become not only a legend of the art of dance but also a towering hero in the community. The Kennedy Dancers, where Diane is the executive and artistic director, is located in the heart of the Jersey City Heights but serves, as Diane will proudly point out, all neighborhoods. "Since its inception," she says, her company has "consistently expanded its programs to respond to the special needs of its constituency, including young children, at-risk and incarcerated teens, low-income families, persons with disabilities, and senior citizens."

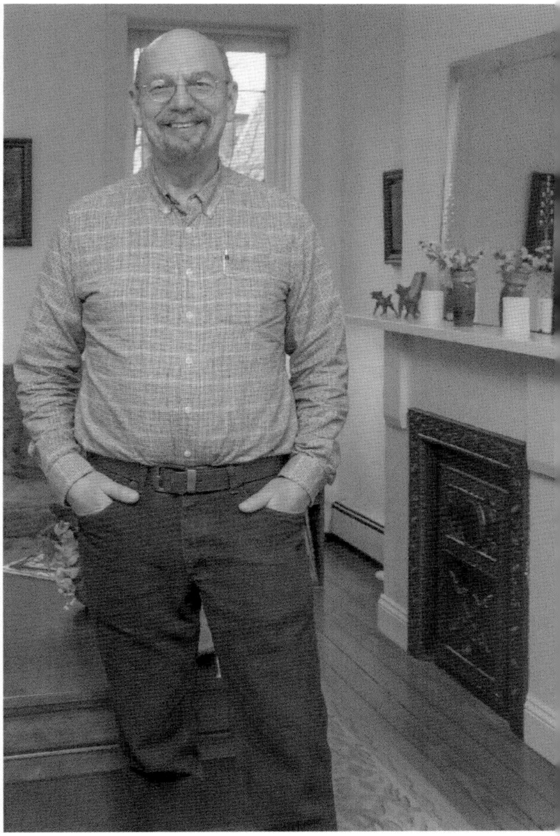

Charles Kessler

It is difficult to capture the complete legacy of Charles Kessler in the arts and historic preservation communities. He is the virtual inventor of the Jersey City arts scene, having initiated, decades ago, now-famous arts festivals, tours, and supportive nonprofit organizations. He helped establish the Jersey City Landmarks Conservancy in 1999 in the quest to save the then-threatened Hudson & Manhattan Railroad Powerhouse, and he is the moderator of Left Bank Art Blog, a highly regarded portal for art news, reviews, and criticism. If Charles's college education history is any indication, his trajectory as a pioneering artist and advocate was not supposed to happen. In 1961, he was a business major at the University of Massachusetts in Amherst. Curious, he took an art history class with the professor and soon-to-be museum director Carl Belz, best known to the general public as the author of the classic book *The Story of Rock*. Though impacted by the course, Charles found himself immersed in matrix algebra and early computer science at the Graduate School of Business at the University of California, Los Angeles (UCLA). But, following his instincts, he eventually switched his major to art history. There was nothing to regret, and by the late 1960s and early 1970s, Charles was at the center of the exciting California contemporary art scene, rubbing elbows with such legends as Andy Warhol and the Velvet Underground and rising art stars Bruce Nauman, John McLaughlin, Mike Todd, and Manny Farber. In New York, while a graduate student at UCLA co-curating a color-field painting exhibition for a seminar he was taking with the distinguished art gallery director Fred White, Charles met art world giants Clement Greenberg, Barnett Newman, and Frank Stella. As an emerging painter and art historian himself, Charles was influenced by Los Angeles artist Ron Davis. One day, Davis pointed out to him that he "wrote like an artist," and Charles recalls, "That what I was saying in my writing, I should be saying in my own paintings. This was a revelation to me, a bolt out of the blue." His destiny as a painter was cracked wide open. Later, in the early 1980s, he and wife, Annie Kessler, a former Los Angeles school teacher whom he met at UCLA and now an accomplished musical theater book writer and lyricist, moved to Jersey City to be close to Manhattan. Charles found himself drawn to the place, which revealed a colony of artists, with many of them being expatriates from Los Angeles. To change that—to make art more publicly accessible to the Jersey City public and to help provide the support and resources artists require to thrive as a community— Charles teamed up with other artists, newspaper editors, civic groups, and city departments to launch the art exhibitions, festivals, and tours that would define him. In 1990, with Pat Donnelly of *Gold Coast* magazine, he started the Jersey City Downtown Artists' Studio Tour, an annual event that today draws thousands of people. A few years later, in 1994, collaborating with artist Al Preciado, Charles founded Pro Arts, a professional artists' organization that also continues to thrive. Over the next decade, he was a founding board member of the Jersey City Landmarks Conservancy; he joined the fight to save 111 First Street, a complex of former Civil War–era tobacco warehouses that artists occupied and regarded as the core of the city's arts province; and he worked intensely with city planners and the Urban Land Institute to establish the Powerhouse Arts District (PAD), an initiative that has yet to fully materialize.

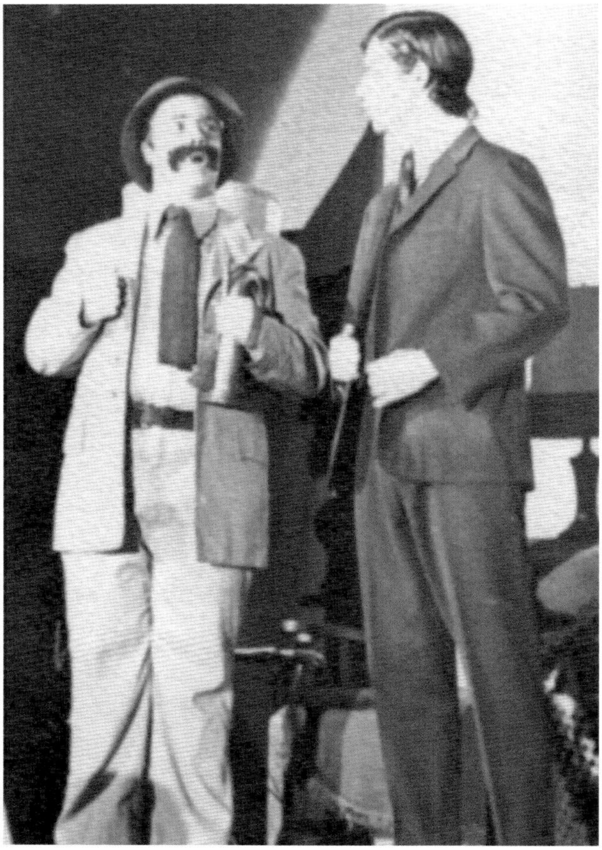

Nathan Lane

Born in Jersey City in 1956, Broadway legend and motion picture actor Nathan Lane attended St. Peter's Preparatory School in the early 1970s, where he acted in school stage productions (pictured at left). In 1992, Lane starred in the blockbuster Broadway musical *Guys and Dolls*, and breakthrough roles followed, including *The Birdcage* with Robin Williams and *A Funny Thing Happened on the Way to the Forum*, which earned him the Tony for Best Actor in a Musical. After a series of major film roles, Lane appeared with Matthew Broderick in *The Producers*, winning his second Tony. (Courtesy of the Jersey City Free Public Library.)

Richie Havens

The great folk-rock-blues musician and Woodstock legend Richie Havens (1941–2013), though born and raised in New York, decided to move to Jersey City over 30 years ago and call it his and his family's new home. While a fiercely private person, Havens never turned his back on his adopted city and surrounding neighborhoods, often performing at community concerts and small local gigs. Perhaps the greatest demonstration of Havens's commitment and connection to Jersey City occurred recently when he carried out a complete restoration of his c. 1875 home, a gesture that won him a preservation award from the Jersey City Landmarks Conservancy. (Courtesy of Landov Media/ Evening Journal Association.)

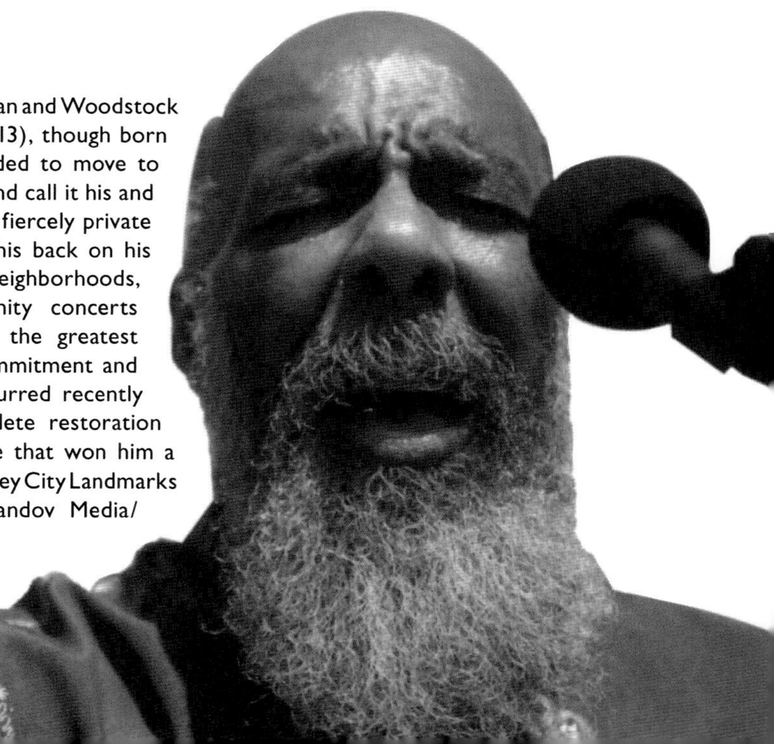

Christine Goodman

Over 10 years ago, Christine Goodman, the founder and executive director of Art House Productions, had a vision to establish an arts organization that would offer Jersey City residents quality theater, art exhibitions, and other cultural events. Since then, and without break, Art House has grown into a major nonprofit organization and offers dynamic cultural programs to the public, including original plays composed by local dramatists; JC Fridays, a seasonal festival of the arts; INKubator, a professional script development workshop; STAGES!, a youth theater company; and comedy shows, concerts, and film screenings.

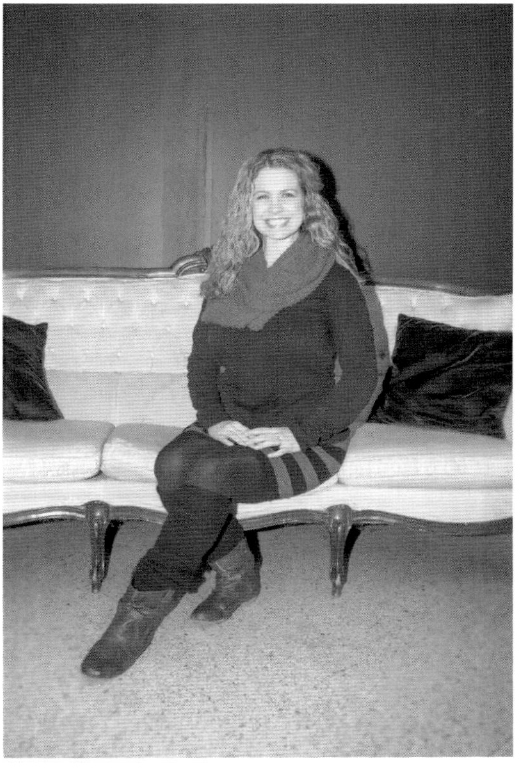

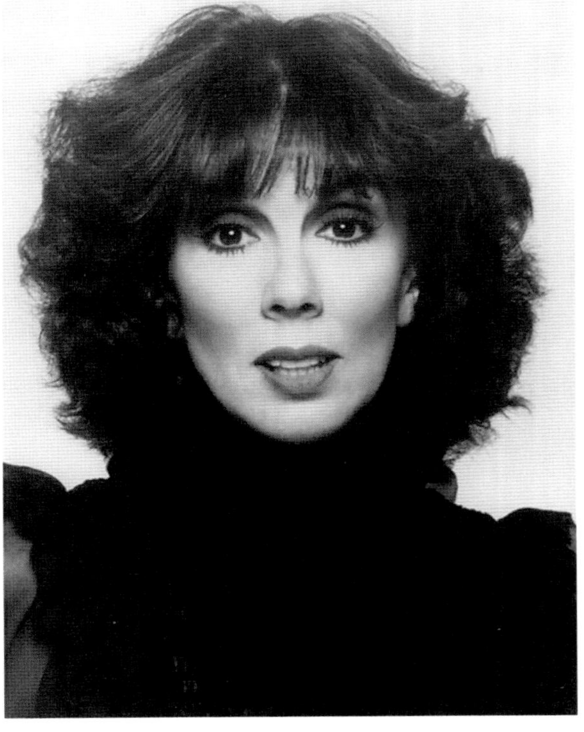

Phyllis Newman

Phyllis Newman, the Tony-winning actress and philanthropist, grew up in the Greenville section of Jersey City and started out at local vaudeville houses as "Baby Phyllis Baker." A graduate of Lincoln High School, Newman won a Tony for *Subways Are For Sleeping* and has appeared in cinematic classics like *Picnic* (1955) and *The Human Stain* (2003), starring Anthony Hopkins and Nicole Kidman. Newman is the proud founder of the Phyllis Newman Women's Health Initiative of the Actors Fund, which, she writes, "addresses the concerns women face when dealing with a serious medical condition." (Courtesy of Phyllis Newman.)

Vincent Aderente

Vincent Aderente (1880–1941) is the only American Renaissance painter to come out of Jersey City and achieve the level of fame reserved for the era's towering master muralists. A member of the vibrant Italian immigrant colony that populated the Jersey City Heights, Aderente assisted his mentor Edwin Howland Blashfield on four allegorical pendentive angels inside the 1910 Hudson County Courthouse (now the Justice William J. Brennan Jr. Hudson County Courthouse). Later, Aderente painted four mythical figure and landscape murals inside the main entrance and foyer of Dickinson High School, including *Knowledge* (1914) and *Wisdom* (1915). (Courtesy of Landov Media/Evening Journal Association.)

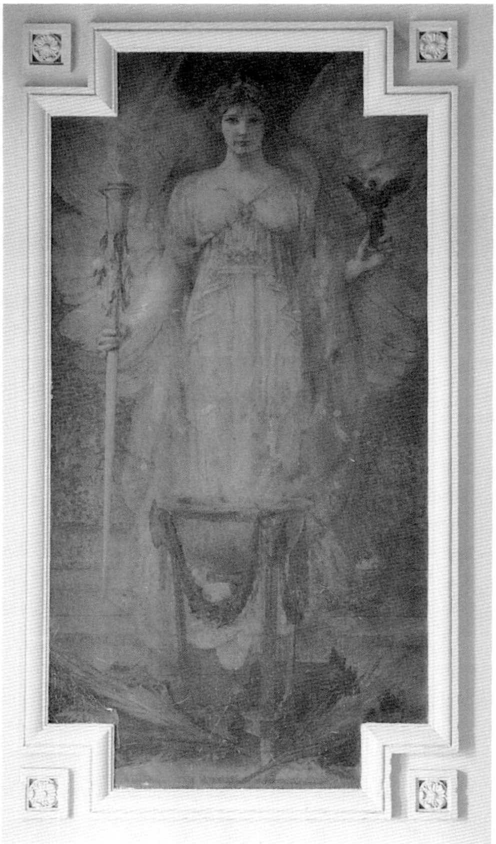

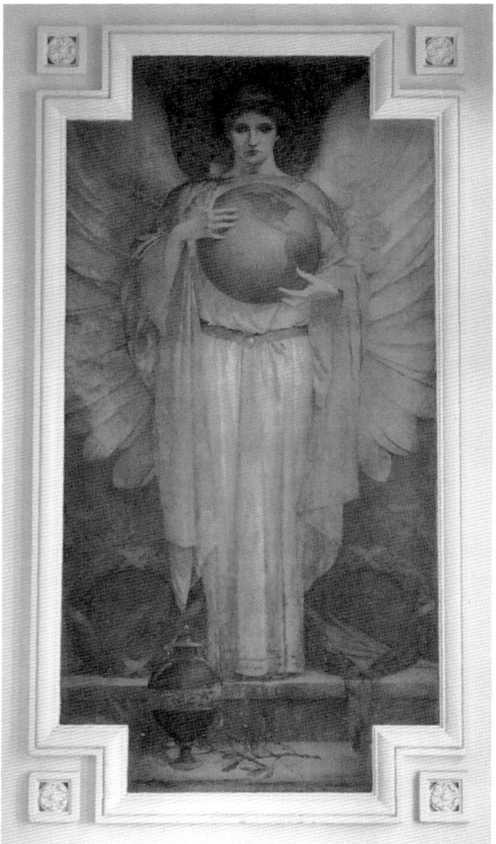

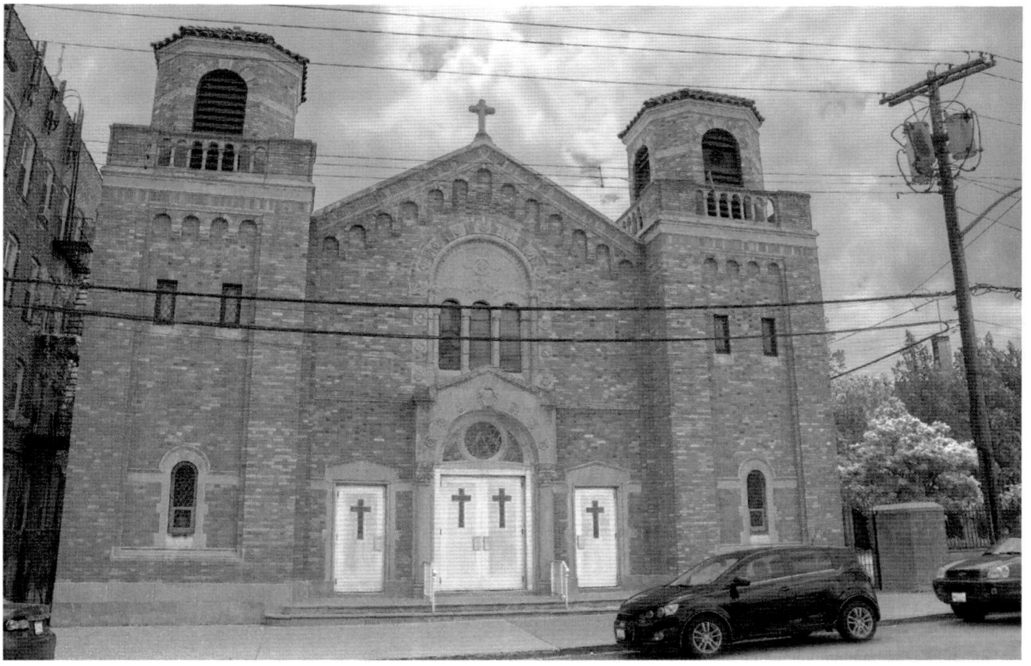

Frank Sinatra

Frank Sinatra's biographers tend to place the emphasis on his birthplace, Hoboken, but the legendary singer and actor also spent considerable time in Jersey City before his career took off in the early 1940s. The apartment building that he, wife, Nancy Barbato, and daughter Nancy lived in, at Audubon and Bergen Avenues, is still there, though unmarked; the Loew's Jersey Theatre in Journal Square where he sat, in 1933, mesmerized, watching Bing Crosby croon on stage, is preserved; the Margaret Hague Maternity Hospital, where son, Frank Jr., was born, still stands, though abandoned; and the doors to Our Lady of Sorrows where Frank and Nancy were married in 1939 remain open.

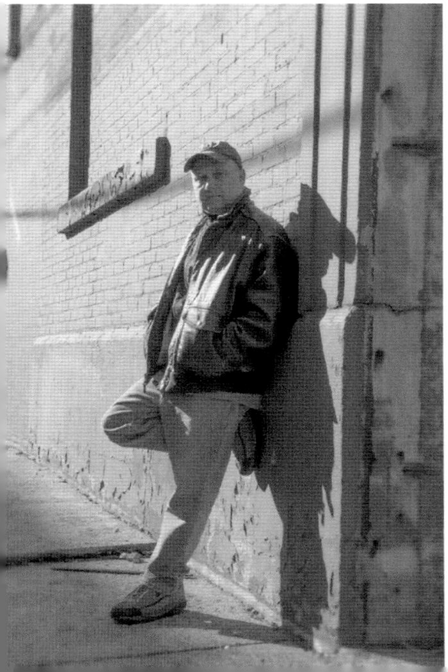

Nick Taylor

The independent feature films of Nick Taylor are enigmatic meditations on the municipality that has been part of his personality and psyche ever since growing up on North Street in the Western Slope ward of the city. In Nick's beautifully photographed and superbly acted films, Jersey City is not merely a backdrop—it is a profound presence. His features include the black-and-white 16mm cult classic *A Clown in Babylon* (1999) and the full-color *Paradise East* (2010), for which he won Best Director at the 2011 ITN New Media Festival, Best Dark Comedy at the 2011 New York International Film Festival, and Best American Feature at the 2011 International Film Festival Ireland. Nick's next independent feature, which starts production in 2014, will be shot on the streets of Jersey City, "a spectacular landscape for filmmakers," he says, and which he knows so well.

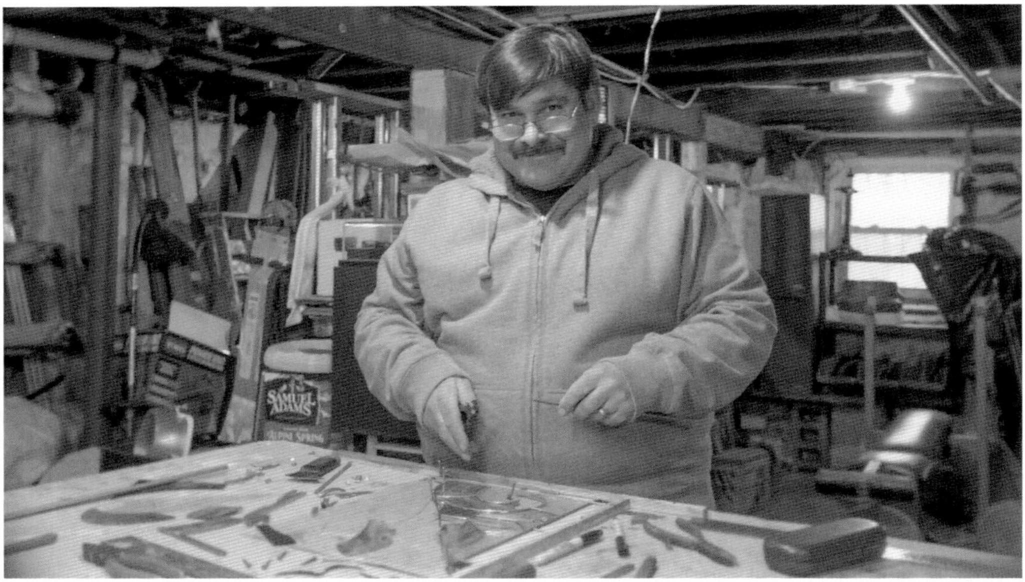

Chris Lynardakis

Chris Lynardakis is one of Jersey City's hidden stained-glass masters, honing the ancient craft quietly in his Kennedy Boulevard workshop basement, with his tools and instruments, including glass cutters, pliers, mallets, rulers, and leading tools, sprawled out on a wooden table in ordered chaos. A graduate of Pratt Institute, Chris has been creating and restoring art glass for commercial, residential, and ecclesiastical clients for over 25 years. Influenced by medieval and opalescent stained-glass collections at the Metropolitan Museum of Art, Chris is well versed in various special "decorative-glass processes," as he describes it, including intricate acid- and sandblasted-etched glass, as well as the copper foil method, which he taught for several years at the Newark Museum. "Stained glass is an unforgiving medium," he says. "Glass must be cut precisely to the patterns or the result will be less than perfect," a maxim that has stayed with Chris since the beginning.

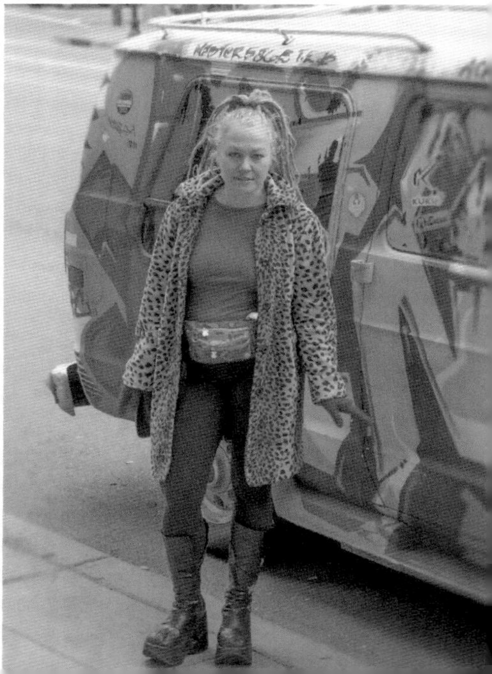

Uta Brauser

Uta Brauser, a local artist, sculptor, curator, gallery owner, public arts showcase organizer and promoter, and "experimental thinker," as she describes herself, can usually be spotted by the white van she proudly drives around Jersey City, tagged on every side with graffiti art. Her signature long, braided pink hair also identifies her. Parked every Friday inside the Grove Street PATH Plaza, she is always unloading supplies, furniture, and pop-up display tents for the weekly market, Creative Grove, which she is famous for. Founded by Uta and her colleague Laura Dejean, the wildly popular open-air, every-Friday festival is "a meeting place, market, art experiment and scene that involves the public, promotes art and culture, and builds community space as a forum for dialogue and exchange." For very low cost, Uta provides local vendors, including artists, designers, and collectors, tables and tents for displaying and selling their talents and goods.

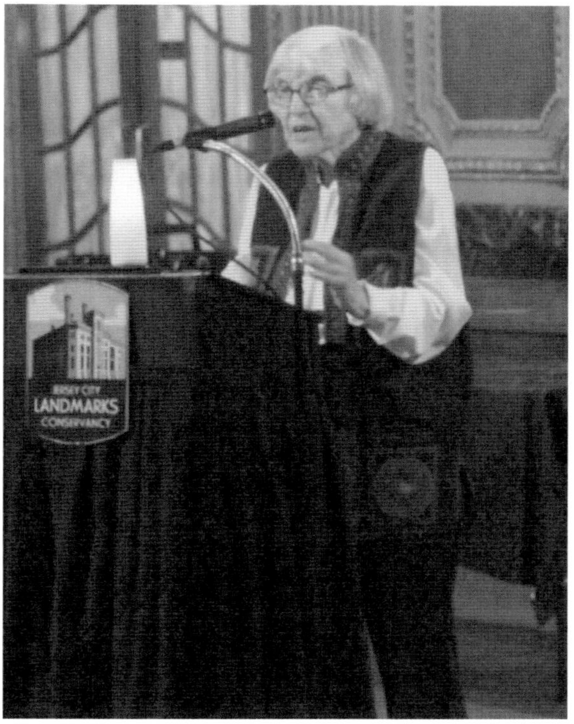

Lillian Morrison

Born in 1917, Lillian Morrison grew up in the Jersey City Heights, graduated from Dickinson High School, and worked in the New York Public Library system for over 50 years. In 2008, she won the J. Owen Grundy History Award from the Jersey City Landmarks Conservancy for *The Ghosts of Jersey City and Other Poems* (1967), which, in the words of the organization, "captures and conjures the historic sights and sounds of Jersey City." Other volumes include *The Sidewalk Racer and Other Poems of Sports and Motion* (1977) and *The Break Dance Kids* (1985). (Courtesy of Landov Media/Evening Journal Association.)

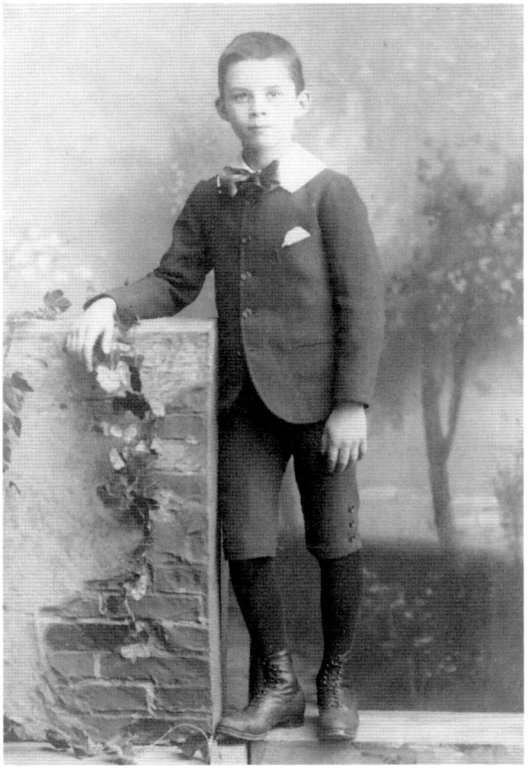

Theodore Gubelman

Theodore Gubelman (1841–1926) is to Jersey City what Alfred Steiglitz is to Hoboken: its first world-class photographer. A pioneer in instantaneous portrait photography—according to the *British Journal of Photography*, he invented it—Gubelman maintained studios in the downtown Jersey City area after serving in the Civil War as a field photographer for the Union army. The recipient of prestigious photography medals and citations at international conventions, including the 1876 Centennial Exhibition in Philadelphia, Gubelman captured hundreds of posed citizens and newly erected structures on glass plates. Sadly, most are now lost to time, but a few are in the collections of major museums. (Courtesy of the Jersey City Free Public Library.)

Pauline Ward Mount

Pauline Ward Mount (1898–1990) is a titan in Jersey City's 20th century art milieu, although today her legacy as painter, teacher, collector, and advocate is almost entirely eclipsed by new art motives, new art legends. Her majestic Victorian house on Sherman Place in the Jersey City Heights, with its setback carriage house, extending gardens, and great old-growth trees, is still occupied by the Mount family, which helps keep her pioneering patrimony in place. Born in Upstate New York and raised in Flushing, Queens, Ward moved to Jersey City in 1920 after marrying World War I lieutenant and medical officer Dr. Elmer Marshall Mount. In the 1930s, Ward (she used only her middle and last name in public due to the frequent sex discrimination she experienced) studied painting in the studio of Albert P. Lucas (1861–1945), a Jersey City native and nationally renowned painter. According to her son Dr. Marshall Mount, a Columbia University graduate, African art authority, professor, and author of the classic *African Art: The Years Since 1920*, Ward was enthusiastic about all forms of art, including Impressionism and Cubism, two trends strongly synthesized in her own canon. In the early 1940s, she became an instructor herself, offering courses at State Teachers College (now New Jersey City University) as well as private lessons at home. "My mother was the most generous of teachers," Dr. Mount says, "who shared everything she knew, combined praise with gentle criticism, and helped creativity along with a glass of champagne." Ward was serious about her profession, and the art world took notice. She founded the Painters and Sculptors Society of New Jersey and became famous for curating groundbreaking annual exhibitions at the Bergen (now Edmund W. Miller) Library on Bergen Avenue, including one show where one of her own paintings, *Freedom from Dogma*, which depicted three nuns dressed in black, was deemed inappropriate by library officials and pulled off the wall. Ward replaced the vacant spot with a worded poster objecting to the censorship, which was a radical act that drew attention in the newspapers. (Courtesy of Dr. Marshall Mount and Caroline Katz-Mount.)

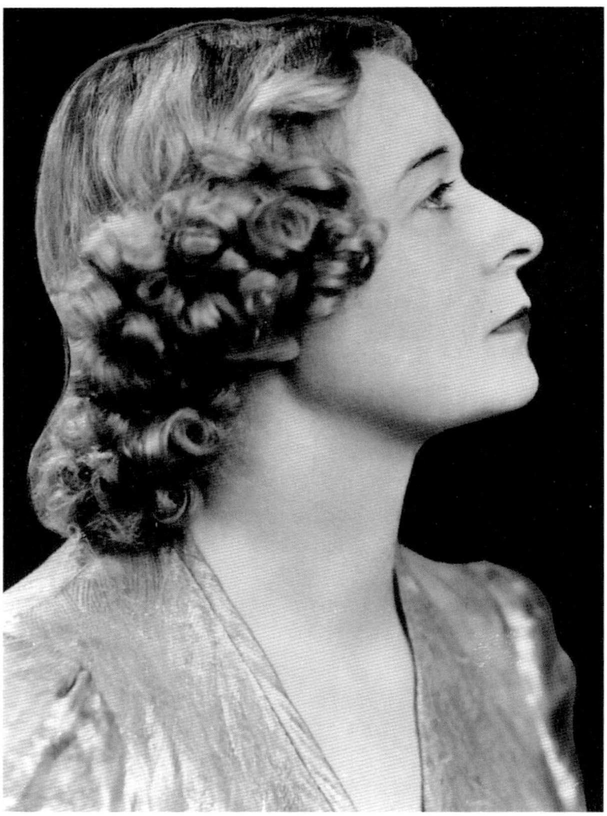

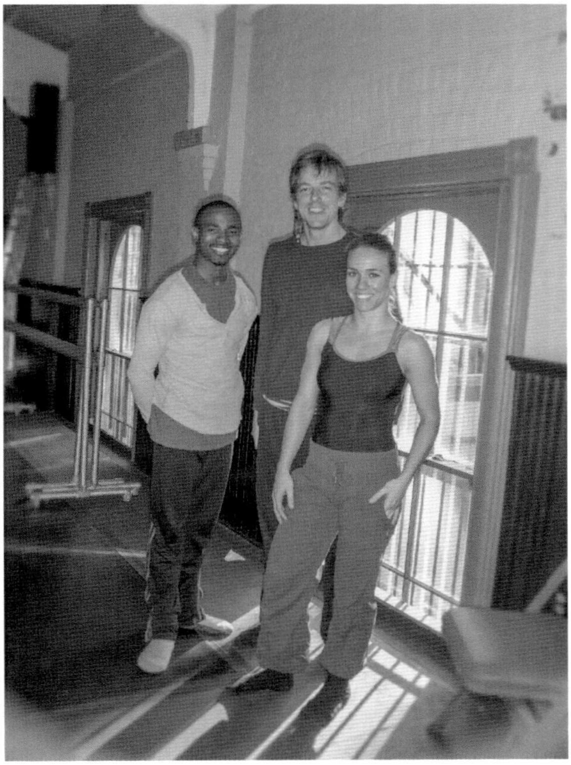

Samuel Pott

Samuel Pott (center), the artistic director of Nimbus Dance Works, the professional company he founded in 2005, recognizes the value of connecting communities with art. Growing up amidst the diversity of New York City and in a family that fostered creativity and conscientiousness, Sam launched Nimbus as a nonprofit organization of professional dancers, choreographers, writers, and musicians that offers ballet and modern dance classes, repertory featuring Sam's original compositions and choreography, and seasonal performances. Need-based scholarships allow students from around the city unique opportunities to experience, as the company's mission states, "programs of top-level artistry that inspire audience members while building close ties between individuals and communities."

Jerry Herman

In almost every interview he gives, legendary Broadway musical composer and lyricist Jerry Herman, though born in New York City, talks excitedly about growing up in Jersey City. A graduate of Snyder High School, he lived close to Journal Square's movie palaces, where major traveling Broadway productions were often staged. After studying at Parsons, Jerry attended the University of Miami before moving to Manhattan where he started writing and composing. In 1961, his first Broadway production, *Milk and Honey*, signaled a major new talent, and in 1964, *Hello, Dolly!* became his first theatrical monument. Two years later, in 1966, his second timeless work, *Mame*, appeared, and, in 1983, *La Cage aux Folles* became his third masterwork. In recognition of his canon, Jerry was inducted into the Songwriters Hall of Fame, received a star on the Hollywood Walk of Fame, was given a special lifetime achievement Tony Award, and, in 2010, was bestowed with a Kennedy Center Honor. In 2008, his connection to and nostalgic fondness for Jersey City was revealed in the PBS documentary *Words and Music by Jerry Herman*, where he led a film crew to his childhood home and haunts. (Courtesy of Jerry Herman.)

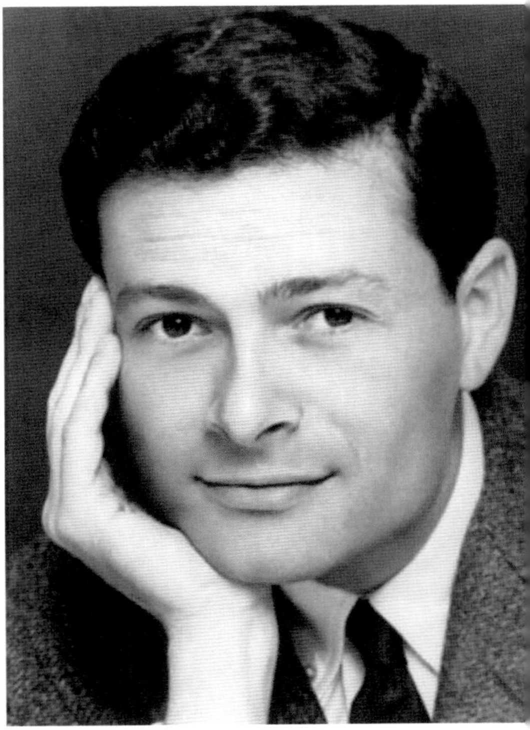

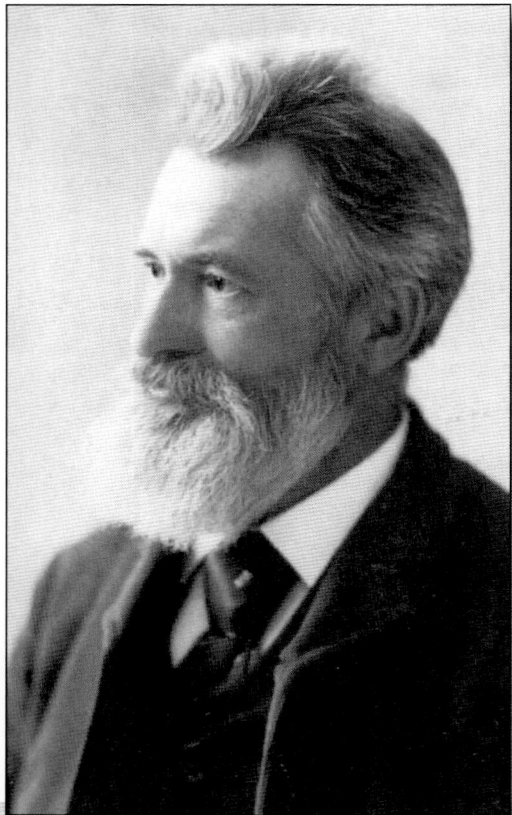

August Will

August Will (1834–1910) was and still is Jersey City's preeminent landscape portraitist, an old master who documented in watercolor, oil, and ink, municipal monuments and streetscapes virtually vanished from today's topography. His miniature and panoramic canvases, all part of the Jersey City Museum collection, are vernacular snapshots of bucolic, innocuous 19th-century scenes of great factory buildings with high smokestacks set back across rolling hills; canal footbridges intersecting with main stage and trolley turnpikes; and the spires and belfries of newly erected churches rising above rooftops. Will, born in Weimar, Germany, was recognized and celebrated in his lifetime and was often the subject of numerous news articles and retrospectives. A widely published magazine illustrator and professor of art in Manhattan, Will was a charter member of the Jersey City Art Club, which was formed in 1904 and situated in a studio on Communipaw Avenue to "bring together the many artists in this city," as the *Evening Journal* described it. With Will's influence, the club attracted prominent local painters, ceramic artisans, and photographers, among them Henry Harrison, Harriet Vreeland, Dr. Henry S. Drayton, Blanche Shafer, Charles H. Lefferts, Sarah Welsh, and Frederick Pansing. (Left, courtesy of the Jersey City Free Public Library; below, courtesy of the Jersey City Museum.)

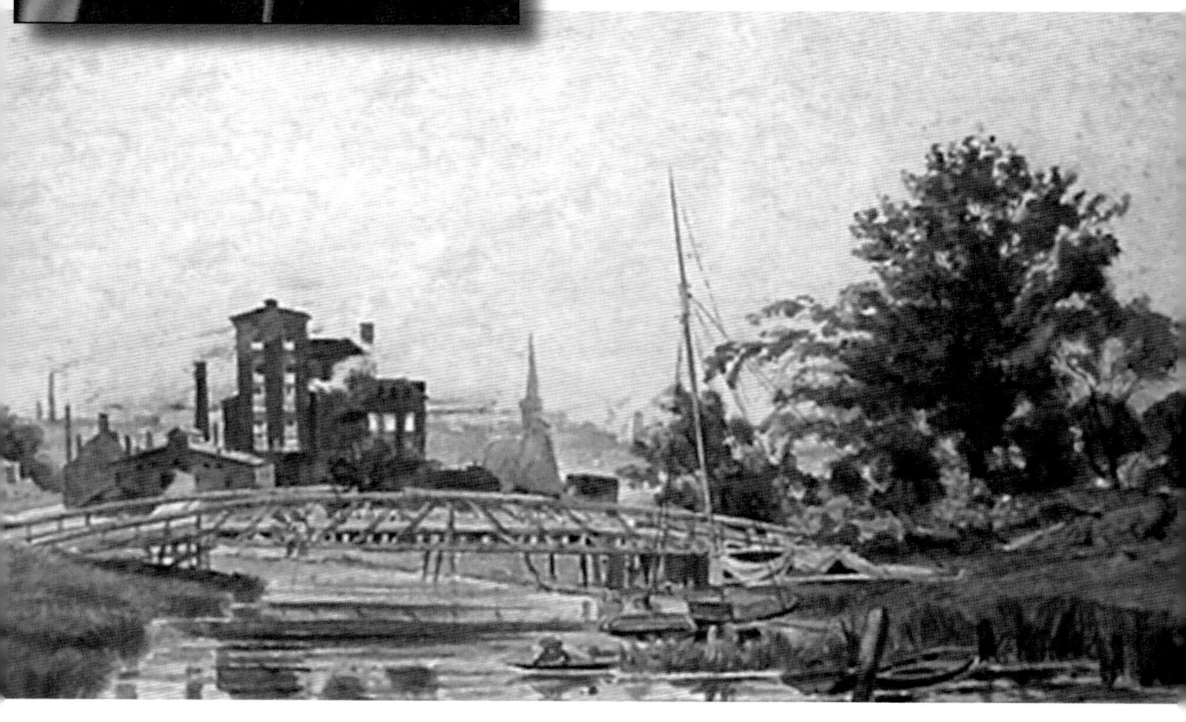

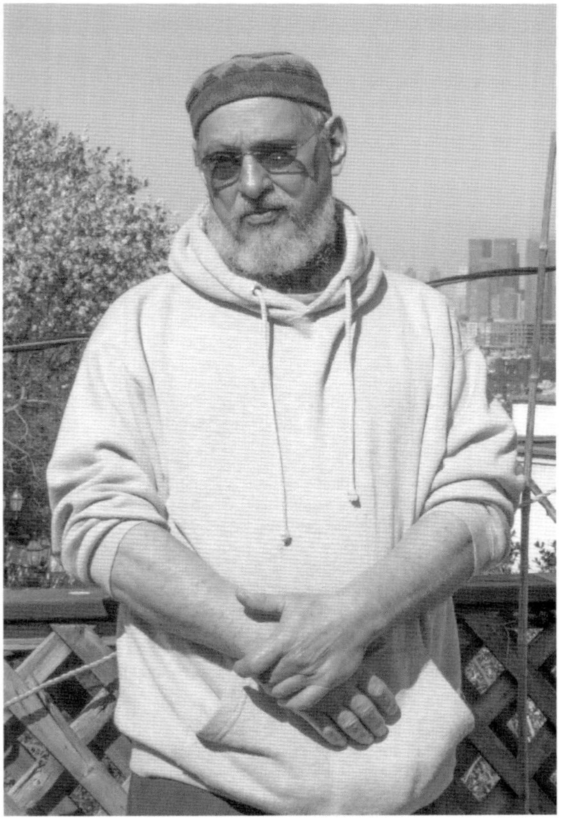

E. Jan Kounitz

When, on the last day of 1998, E. Jan Kounitz and his wife, Deborah Klein, attended a friend's New Year's Eve party on Ogden Avenue in the Jersey City Heights, far from their cavernous Tribeca loft where they were operating a progressive performing arts company, they set stunned eyes on their future home. By 1999, they were moving into their 19th-century property, and Jan, pulling out his well-worn cameras, started taking pictures of people in the surrounding neighborhoods. Over the last dozen years, he has been capturing local street scenes that seem staged but are actual and unmanipulated; everyday life in the city is being captured. His most visible photographic interactive projects include "Me-Hood" and "Dogs and Their People," which have brought him wide public recognition as a documentarian with an eye for municipal poetry and humor. (Below, courtesy of E. Jan Kounitz.)

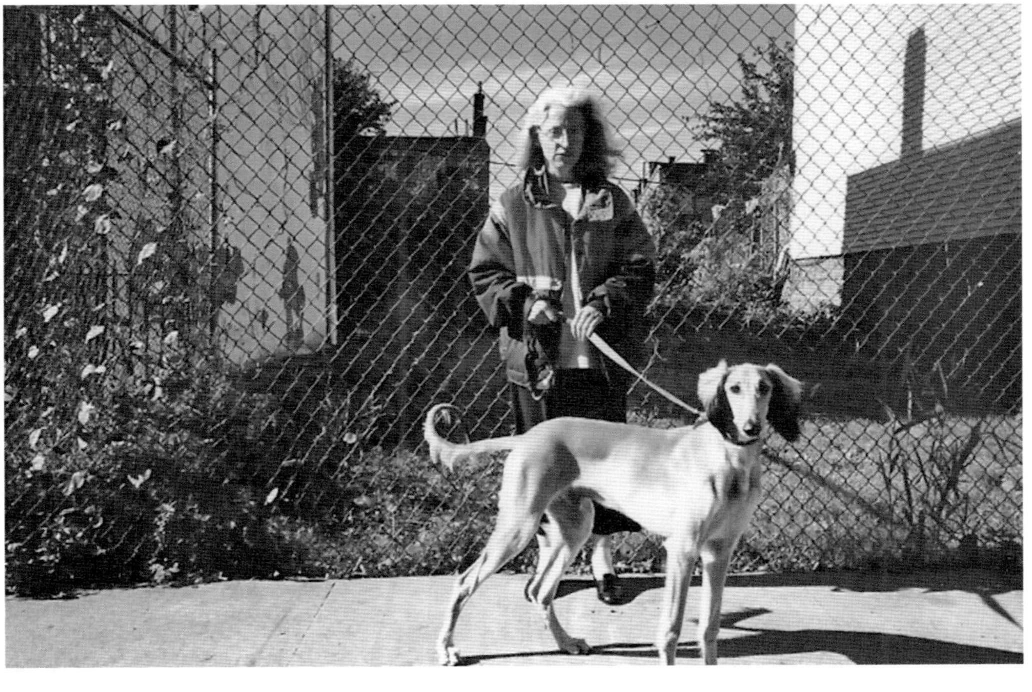

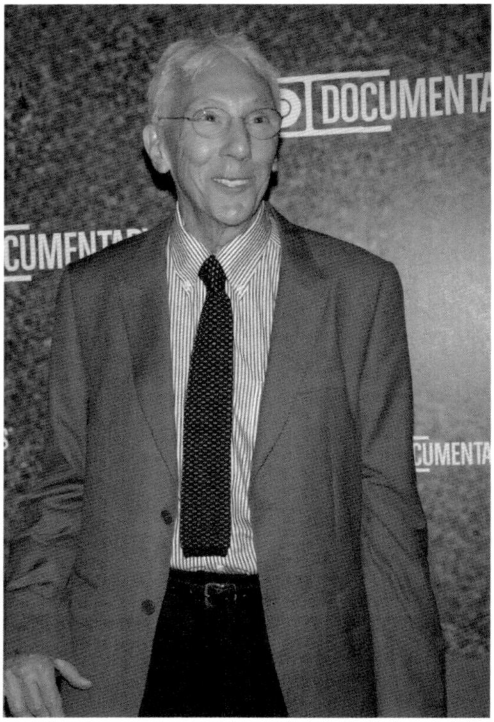

Leon Gast

In 1997, Leon Gast, who grew up on Stegman Parkway and attended Snyder High School in the Greenville section of Jersey City, received the Academy Award for Best Documentary Feature for *When We Were Kings*, his epic documentary about the legendary 1974 boxing match between Muhammad Ali and George Foreman. Gast has directed several other highly regarded documentaries, including *Our Latin Thing* (1971), *The Grateful Dead Movie* (1974), *Hells Angels Forever* (1983), and *Smash His Camera*, which won the Directing Award in the documentary category at the 2010 Sundance Film Festival. (Courtesy of Landov Media/Evening Journal Association.)

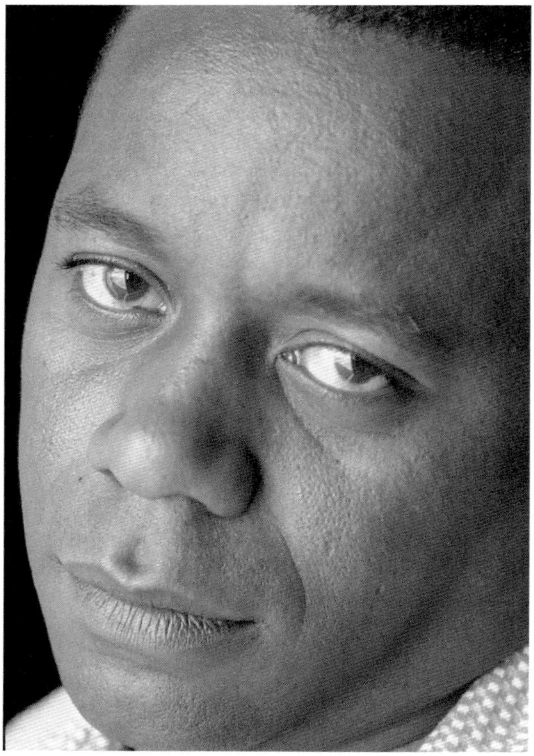

Flip Wilson

The pioneering African American comedian Flip Wilson (1933–1998) grew up in Jersey City in a large family. After a career in the US Air Force, Wilson was discovered in 1965 by Redd Fox and began regular appearances on *The Tonight Show*, *The Merv Griffin Show*, and *The Joey Bishop Show* (a fellow Jersey City native). *The Flip Wilson Show* became the first successful African American–hosted variety hour series, lasting four seasons (1970–1974). Wilson, who died in 1998 of liver cancer, was celebrated by his hometown in 1999 with the dedication of Flip Wilson Way. (Courtesy of Landov Media/Evening Journal Association.)

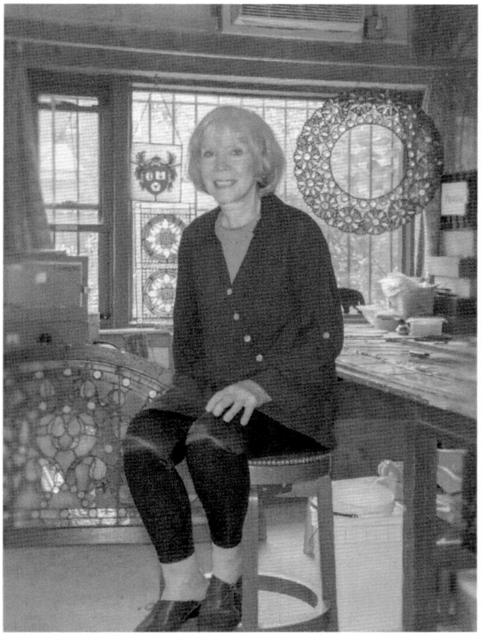

Barbara Meise

Despite the near ruination of her stained-glass studio during Hurricane Sandy, Barbara Meise continues to do what she has been doing—and what has brought her deserved renown and demand—over the last 40 years: firing architectural glass of supreme artistry from the kilns of Artbuilders, her Montgomery Street atelier. Born in Bavaria and educated at Cambridge, Barbara was apprenticed at the famed J. & R. Lamb Studio, the country's oldest ecclesiastical arts studio, where she learned the ancient crafts of stained glass, mosaics, and illumination. In 1989, after earning a master's of fine arts from Columbia University, she bought her tenement storefront property, launching her business and offering local houses of worship affordable stained-glass restoration services.

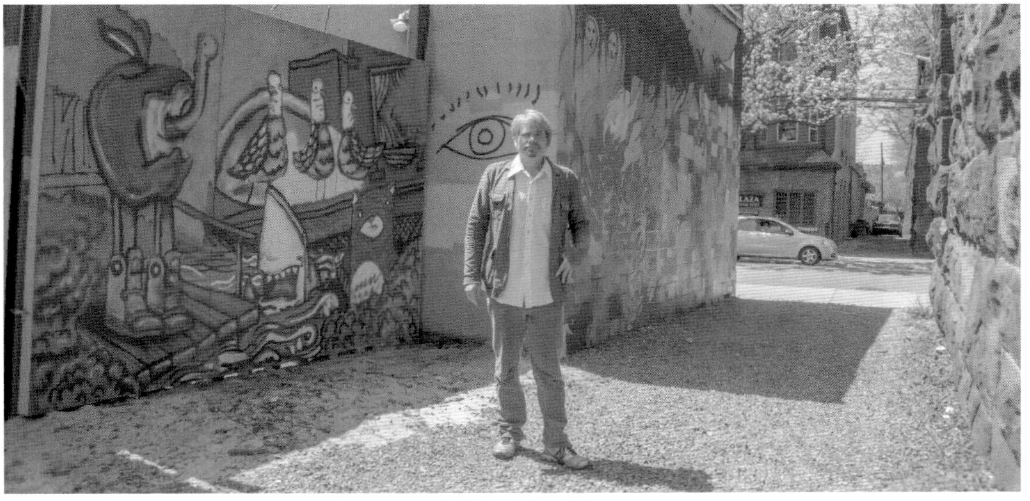

Thomas John Carlson

Thomas John Carlson is all over the place with his art. Easily found racing around Fifth Street and its brownstone environs, he is in the middle of expanding his Jersey City Art School, which has been a runaway success since its founding in 2009, to other sections of the city besides the downtown area. The school, in Thomas's words, focuses on the "growth of the individual artist—those involved can learn new skills, build a portfolio, or just hone their existing technique in an environment that fosters communication, even friendship, with others who have the same interest and talent," and it offers low-cost courses in painting, figure drawing, sculpture, digital photography, and animation. Filled with energy and vision, Thomas, a musician in the local band Papermaker, also collaborates with established arts organizations, like Pro Arts, Art House Productions, 4th Street Arts, and JC Comics, and is working with local architect Anne McTernan on Art Activates, an initiative for painting alleyway murals across the city accompanied by the creation of sustainable community art gardens.

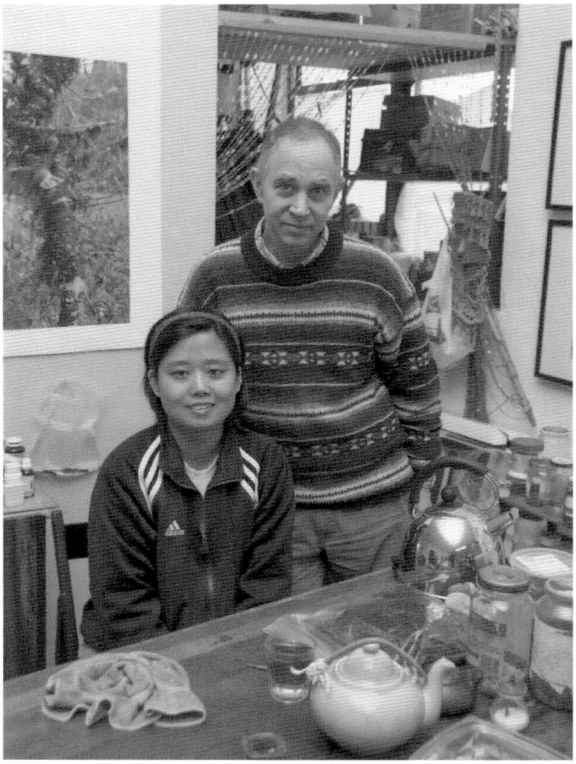

Edward Fausty

Edward Fausty (at left, with wife Feng Xiao) recalls his father's camera shop in Scarsdale, New York (below), very well; it was a magical place where it would not be uncommon for esteemed photographers like Barbara Morgan to walk in and where, at age five, he started using a roll-film camera around the neighborhood. By 11 years old, with his father's help, he had his own darkroom in a small bathroom in the basement. "The actual making of images with chemistry and paper was fun and magical for me," says Ed, who went on to receive his bachelor's of fine arts from Cooper Union, where he was strongly influenced by the great photographer Joel Meyerowitz, and his master's of fine arts from the Yale School of Art. Over the last two decades Ed has photographed the city's labyrinthine industrial rooflines and numerous artist studios, utilizing the intricate process of digital pigment printing that defines his canon and for which he has been lauded a master. (Below, courtesy of Edward Fausty.)

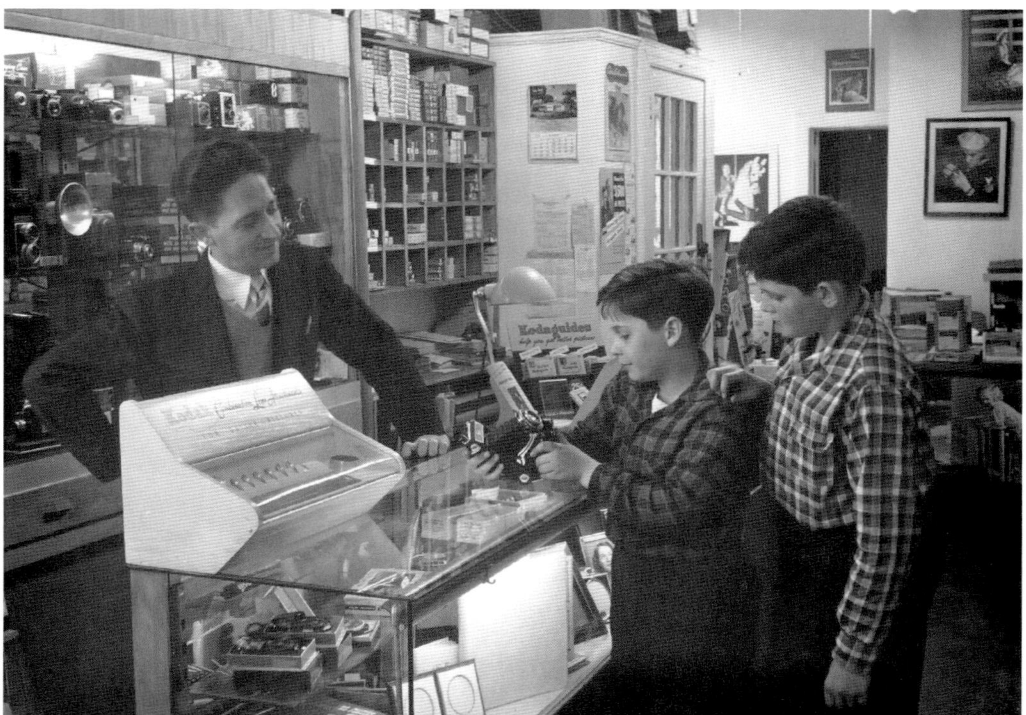

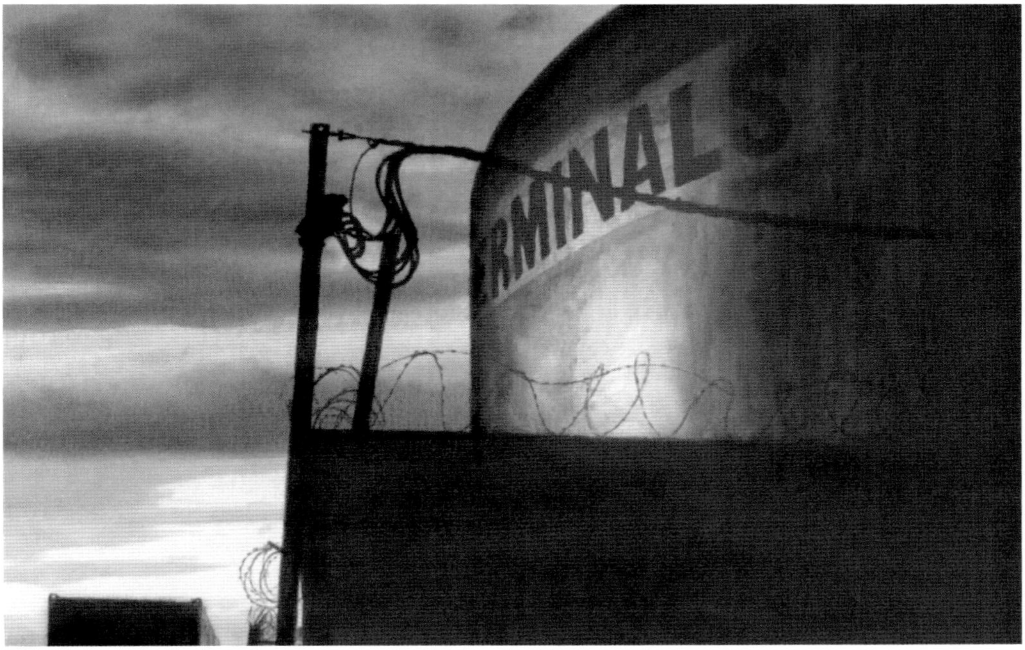

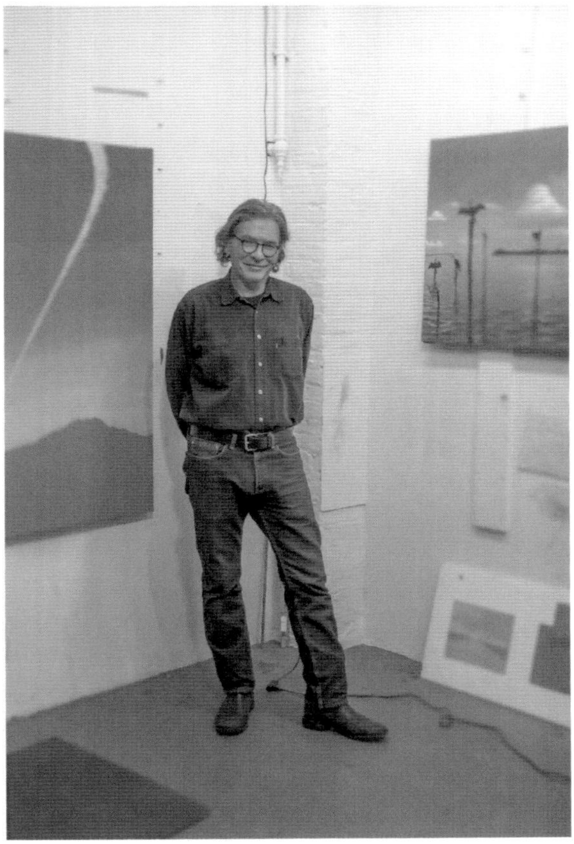

Tim Daly

In 1977, the Jersey City–born painter Tim Daly was living in a $100-a-month, five-room cold-water flat in Hoboken. The cheap rent enabled him to work as little as possible in order to have time to paint and mature as an artist. More importantly, Tim's day job at that time at a post office located in the Kearny marshes brought him close to a watery topography that would demarcate his future canvases and bring him legendary status. "I was in the meadows all the time," he says, "soaking up that unique New Jersey landscape," until a life-changing epiphany enveloped him while studying Renaissance paintings and drawing intently at night: he "came to realize that these places were a large and worthy subject. If I could manage to paint the roads, bridges and rivers I saw every day, I could learn to be an artist. It was an authentic subject matter for me." (Above, courtesy of Tim Daly.).

Tris McCall

When the great American author Cynthia Ozick read and offered glowing praise for *The Trespassers* (2012 Schrafft), Tris McCall's first novel, McCall knew he had entered a place not easily accessible to every emerging writer. He had earned it, having toiled hard on a book inspired, at its core, by the beautiful industrial wrecks of Jersey City, all since vanished to make way for development. With his self-printed book, Tris, an urban songwriter and musician and the music critic for the *Newark Star-Ledger*, has created a majestic factory-scaped world of young explorers who break into buildings not just for adventure but to be part of a community of wandering souls searching for answers. Tris describes the book's main character, Doran Satterfield, and his new group of photographer friends, as spending their days "taking pictures of the last few abandoned factories left on the Hudson waterfront: snipping bolts, shimmying up collapsed staircases, tiptoeing across crumbling catwalks, and marveling at the grandeur of the Garden State ruins." (Below, courtesy of Schrafft Books.)

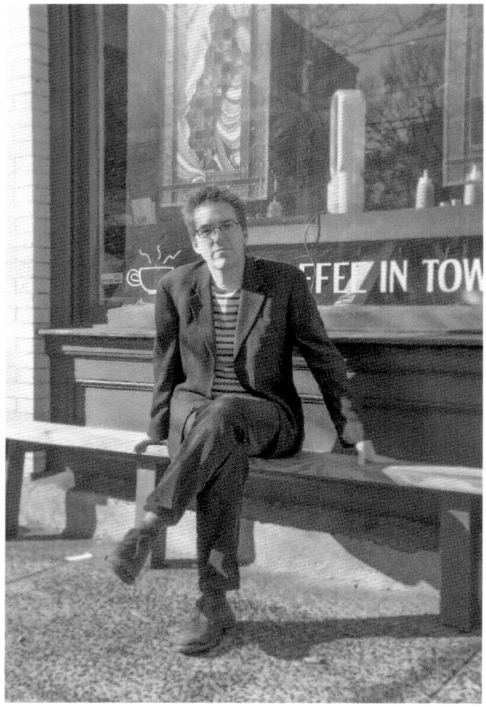

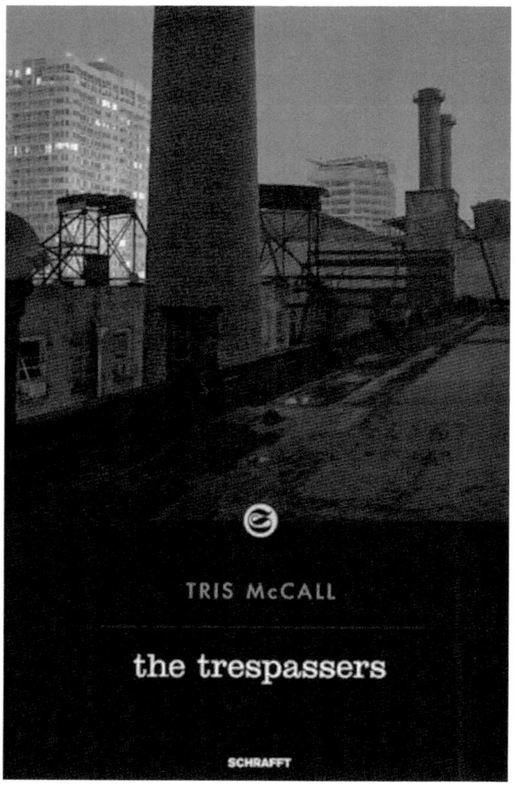

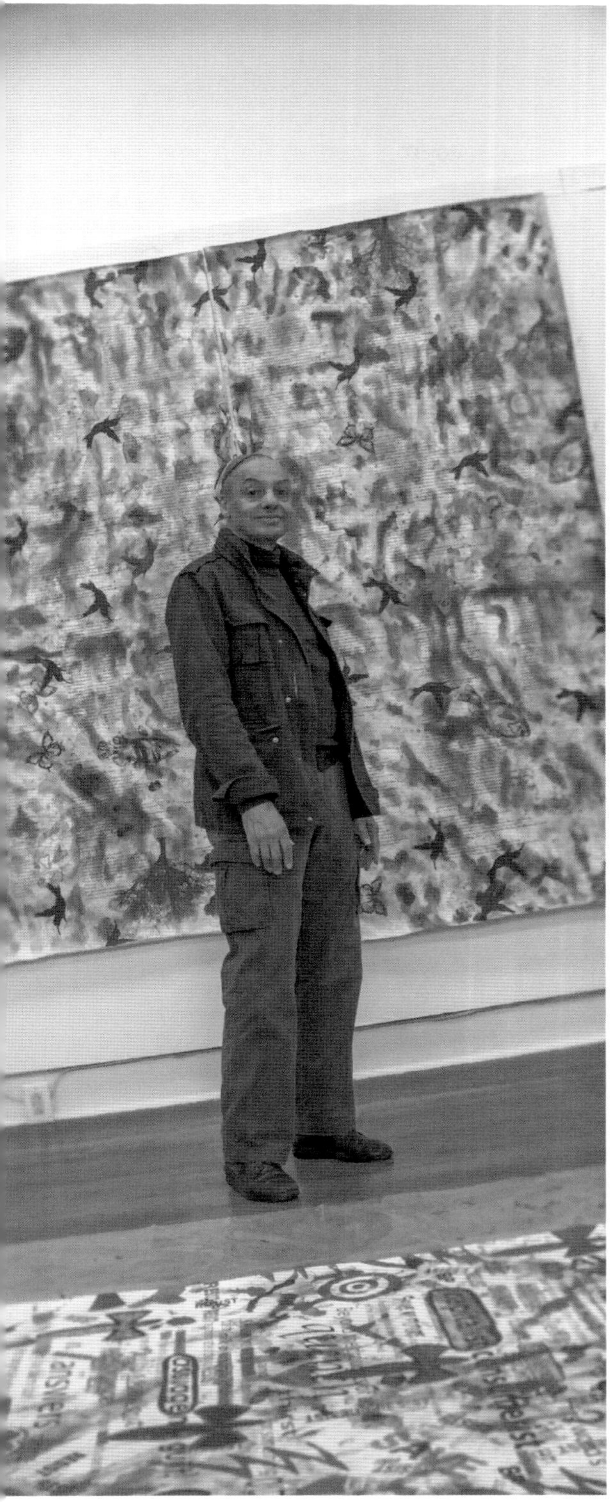

Ben Jones

When Ben Jones started teaching at Jersey City State College (now New Jersey City University) in 1967, he found a colony of art students who had hardly ever made excursions into nearby New York City or, worse, had never, despite being born and raised in Hudson County, crossed the Hudson River via ferry, car, or subway. To Ben, Manhattan was the greatest gallery in the world, and if his students wanted to become serious artists, they had to make the journey to its architectural canyons and temples of art. His job was not only to teach art, but also, he felt, to make it a part of each stroke of the fledgling brush. With that beginning, and all the way to 2010 when he retired as professor emeritus of art, came the conviction that cities and their "mythology of architecture," as he describes it, are essential art elements. Ben, who was born and raised in Paterson, New Jersey, has followed his own mantra and traveled the world over to study its modernist stone cities and beachfront hamlets and exhibit his own art. His resume unfolds across a dozen pages and acts as a life mask and map of his creative accomplishments and regard as a world-class artist. In Ben's work, African history and culture, which he has made part of his studies over the last four decades, are not just two means of inspiration—they are a collective connection to his muse and his municipality. Over the years, his diverse students have understood this credence and found their own historical voices. Ben, as he will explain, has not really retired; chapters calling for more travel and more explorations in art, including a new focus on environmental prescience, are turning.

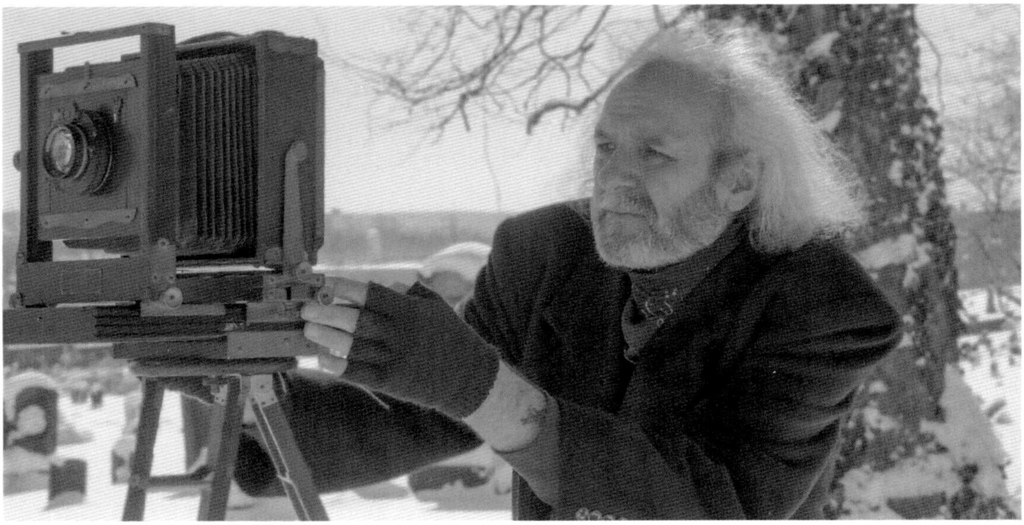

Andrzej Jerzy Lech

As Andrzej Jerzy Lech lugs his big wooden 19th-century view cameras and heavy tripods across Jersey City, which he has been doing for close to 25 years, he looks for local landmarks that are drawn to his antique glass lenses. To this great composer of visceral black-and-white, sepia-toned, and tea-dyed images, Jersey City is a municipal mirror of his ancestral Wroclaw, Poland, and keeps inspiring him to plunge deeper into its urban hamlets and wards. For his extraordinary work in documenting the city's poetic fabric, Andrzej was presented in 2005 with the Jersey City Landmarks Conservancy's coveted J. Owen Grundy History Award in recognition of his "photographic portfolio, which acts as a record of changing—and vanishing—landscapes." (Below, courtesy of Andrzej Jerzy Lech.)

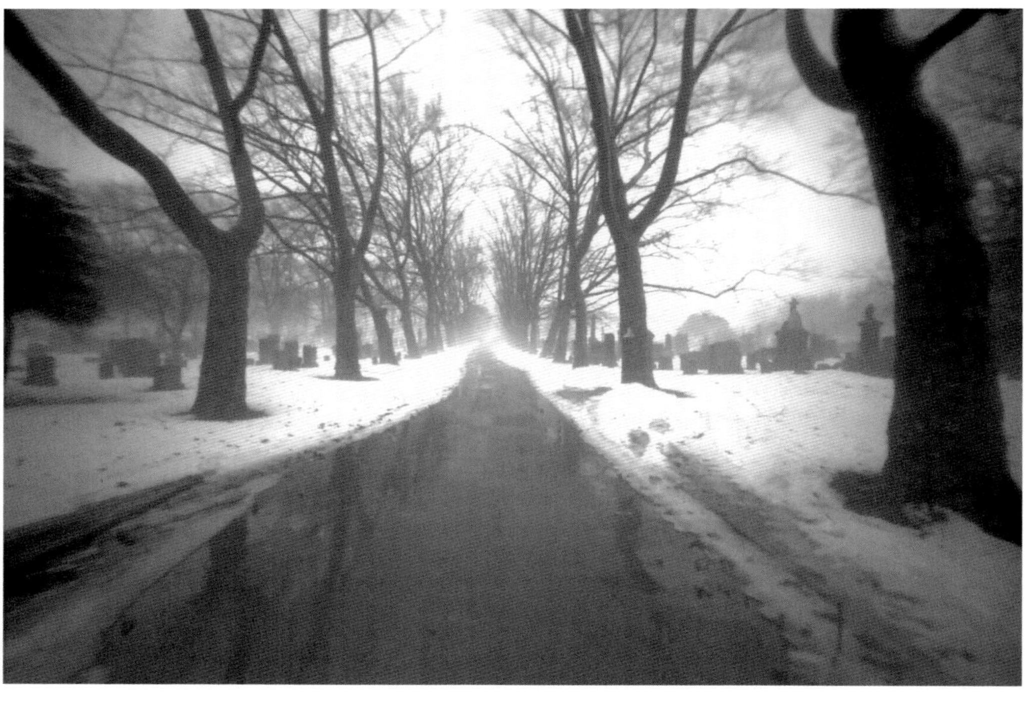

CHAPTER FOUR

The Historians

A city without historians is a city stripped of revelatory pages and erased from mysterious municipal time. Take away those scholars who hit the annals hard every day to make sense of events and epochs, and the public is left with tangled facets and facts, uncertainties, stories untold. Throw out the accounts and sketches of the chroniclers and compilers of the last two centuries, and the city is left with tremendous voids; the narrative becomes broken.

Historians are extraordinary public servants—heroes of humanity. Citizens require and rely on their fact pulling, their talent for transforming moments of mundanity into moments of meaning. None of it is easy. It may take years of research to create a single monument's monograph; looking for triggers and links between trends and periods may take on the aura of inefficacy; surveying illegible deeds and confusing conveyances could conclude, if all goes well, with finding that first owner; spinning microfilm rolls through outdated machines, day after day, in search of that one missing morsel of fact might end in discovery.

Over 200 years have been invested in keeping the city's history intact and accessible. In the early 1800s, Washington Irving must have been aware of the significance of his excursion from Manhattan to the foot of Communipaw Avenue to meet with John Van Horne and the Dutch-speaking citizens of the ancient hamlet of Communipaw. It was a research trip filled with rich myths and legends that found their way over the next two decades into such landmark literary works as the semifactual *A History of New York* and the magical collections of short stories in *The Sketch Book of Geoffrey Crayon* and *Wolfert's Roost*. A century later, William H. Richardson was running scholarly articles regularly in the *Evening Journal*, the city's first history columnist and historian for a new modern age. A young J. Owen Grundy dared to protest the Mayor Frank Hague–sponsored widening of Bergen Avenue in the 1920s—a devastating infrastructure project that wiped out many of the area's most intact and still lived-in 17th-century Dutch homesteads. From that one eye-opening experience, Grundy began his illustrious 50-year career as city historian.

The most accurate measure of the historian's talents lies with the city's young readers, listeners, viewers, and museum goers. Students get it; they respond excitedly to school visits from Bob Leach, Jersey City's only traditional storyteller and spinner of fantastic urban tales. When teachers take middle school students to the Afro-American Historical Society Museum on the top floor of the Greenville branch of the Jersey City Free Public Library, started in 1977 by Capt. Thomas Taylor and the late Theodore Brunson and curated today by his son Neal Brunson, they become immersed in African cultural traditions as well as the local African American experience. When high school students visit the

New Jersey Room on the third floor of the main branch of the library system, they find author Cynthia Harris, archivist John Beekman, and genealogist Danny Klein, three titans of local research. St. Peter's University professor Dr. Joseph McLaughlin will use the outside urban diorama as a classroom, allowing students in his sociology, architecture, and planning courses to experience a changing and yet preserved Jersey City up close.

Historians here are astoundingly dedicated. Some spend their entire lives and careers turning the heavy pages of precious maps and plat books; others orate the local history like trancing actors, letting facts and handed-down tales levitate or land where they may; and still others turn their efforts into bound books, e-books, articles, papers, and documentaries. Whatever genre each historian adopts, whatever form his or her Herculean tasks and endeavors take, a wedded culmination is apportioned across the entire city—as if one Jersey City book is being composed, one illuminated annal is under construction, with room for future chapters.

70

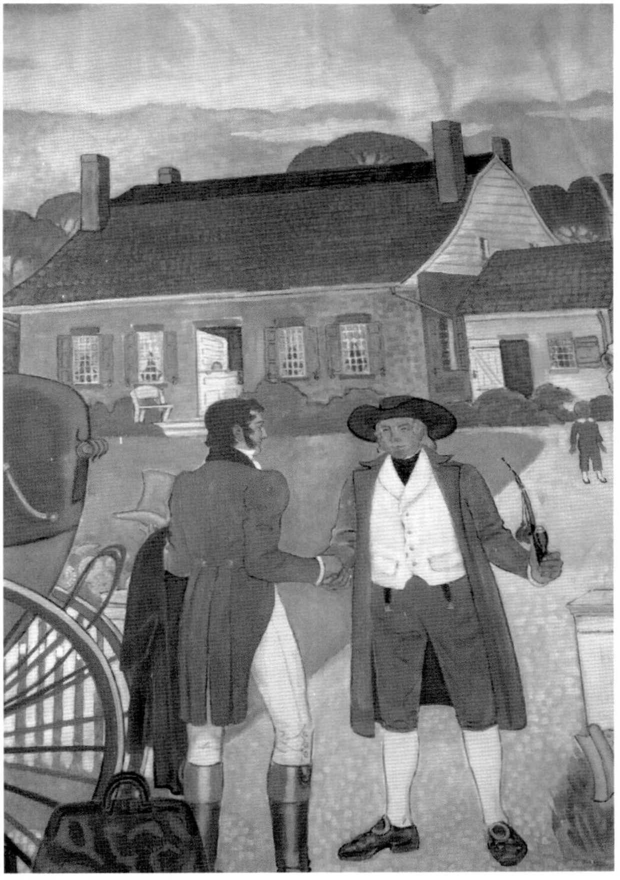

Washington Irving

Washington Irving (1783–1853), Jersey City's first historian, was also America's first internationally famous author. Nearly 200 years ago, the Dutch-speaking, red-stepped-roof hamlet of Communipaw, today's Lafayette residential district, captured and widened his imagination and led to literary works of great originality and world prominence. Irving, the author of the classics "Rip Van Winkle" and "The Legend of Sleepy Hollow," was a master of municipal hyperbole, a humorist-historian who in his early career turned well-researched facts into quasi-fiction, concocting in prodigious strides vanished coastal Dutch cities, mountainous glens, and, most famously, haunted hollows. With Irving, there was no line dividing reality and non-reality; ghosts and goblins walked the same realm as farmers and fishermen. In 1809, in his wildly popular *A History of New York*, Irving put Communipaw on the literary map, highlighting its "hereditary homesteads" and quirky inhabitants in biographical sketches and short stories. Communipaw, "the egg from whence was hatched the mighty city of New York," as Irving described it, was a forgotten city where gated gardens grew into colossal cabbage dens; where the upright Lenni Lenape inhabitants of off-road burial grounds were mysteriously topped with tied oyster sacks; and where the first Christmas occurred with a Santa Claus–semblance figure flying from gabled rooftop to gabled rooftop, delivering gifts. Later, with the 1855 publication of *Wolfert's Roost*, Irving revisited Communipaw in classic atmospheric stories like "Guests of Gibbet Island: A Legend of Communipaw." Though vanished, hints of Irving's Communipaw are etched in actual cemetery stones, land deeds, street signs, stained-glass windows, and, the only direct reminder of his presence, in a priceless Ruth Wilcox mural (pictured above) inside the Lafayette branch of the Provident Savings Bank showing him being greeted by John Van Horne at his mystical House of the Four Chimneys.

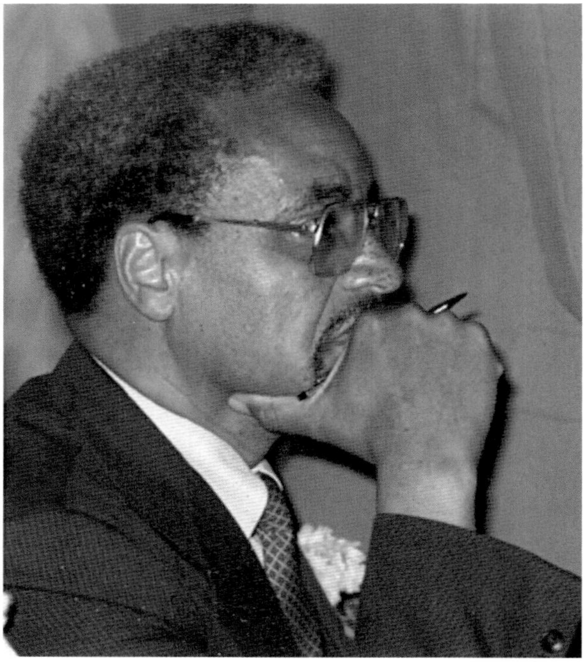

Theodore and Neal Brunson

Theodore Brunson (1925–2012) is a giant in the scholarship and advocacy of local African American history and culture. Because of his vision, Jersey City residents are able to enjoy the art, artifacts, and archival resources of the Afro-American Historical Society Museum, located in the Greenville branch of the Jersey City Free Public Library. Founded in 1977 as a special committee of the Jersey City branch of the NAACP, Ted worked closely with fire captain Thomas Taylor and other community stalwarts to establish an institution that would be a combined museum, archives, and meeting and performance space. Opened in 1984, with Ted as its first director, the museum features original African art and African American folk art exhibits, interactive period rooms, computer research stations, and local African American history timelines and interpretive wall text. Since 1998, Ted's son Neal (right), a practicing Newark lawyer, has been museum director, curator, historian, writer, lecturer, and proud keeper of his father's outstanding legacy. (Above, courtesy of the Afro-American Historical Society Museum.)

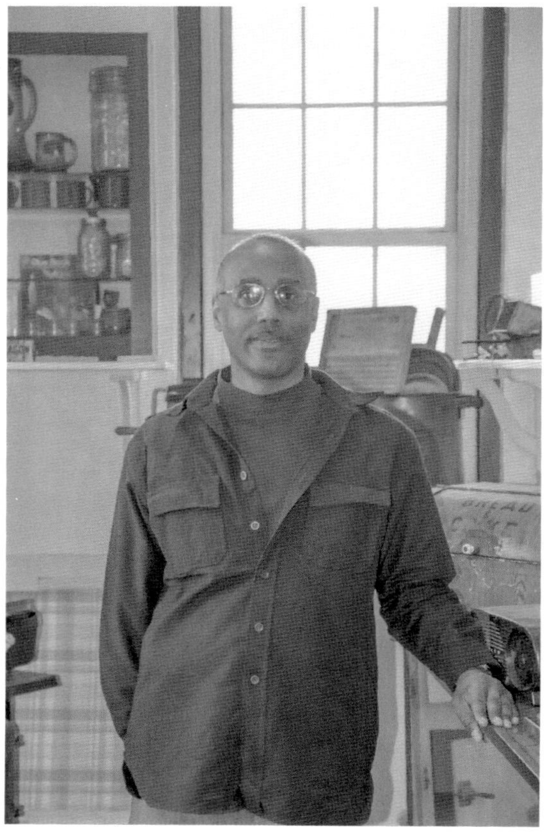

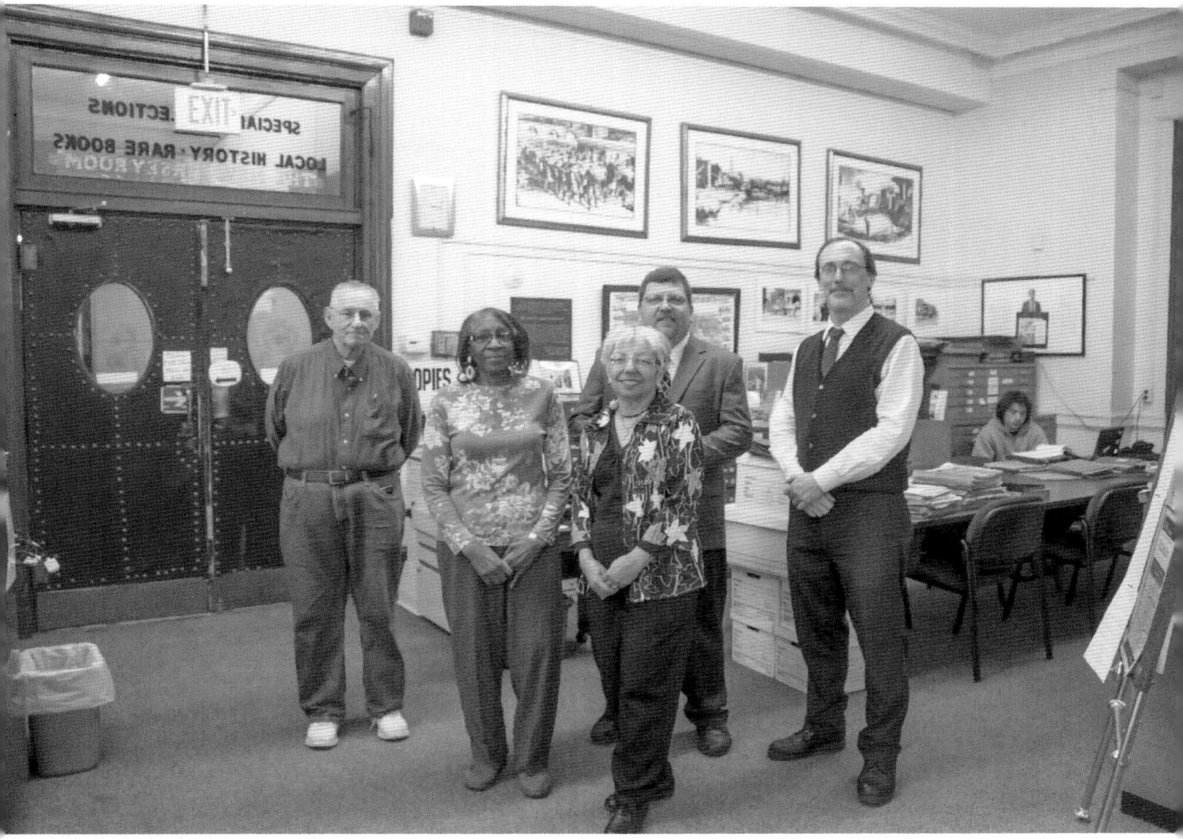

The New Jersey Room

Without the New Jersey Room in the central Jersey Avenue building of the Jersey City Free Public Library, locals would not be able to research, study, and touch the municipal records and archives so vital to historians, consultants, students, and other scholars in the writing of history books, articles, reports, websites, and sidewalk markers. Pictured from left to right, Bruce Brandt, Shirley Handy, Cynthia Harris, Danny Klein, and John Beekman are the room's visible vanguards; they are the people tasked six days a week to pull vertical files, rare texts, indexed microfilm reels, catalogued photographs, periodicals, maps, and special collections. For them, it is a labor of municipal love, a way of giving back to the community. Formerly managed by Joan Doherty-Lovero, author of the seminal *Hudson County: The Left Bank* (1986, Windsor Publications), and once frequented by the great local historian J. Owen Grundy (1912–1985), the space captivates patrons and librarians alike. "The highlight is the great satisfaction I get when I help someone find answers that they have been seeking, literally, for years," says Cynthia, the author with Leon Yost of *Changing Jersey City: A History in Photographs* (2009, Schiffer Books) and an authority on local school history. John, a graduate of Fordham, often finds himself helping patrons unearth the "story of a place," and Danny, a prominent local genealogist, monthly newspaper columnist, and founding trustee of the Hudson County Genealogical & Historical Society, pronounces, "Jersey City, and Hudson County, are subjects worth the attention of scholars because their history—our history—is the history of our nation."

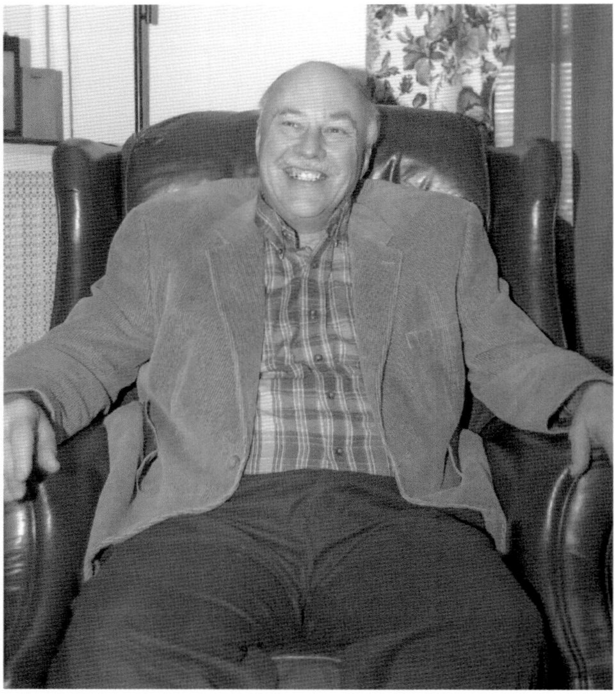

Bob Murgittroyd

Bob Murgittroyd specializes in the history of people, a vocation initiated by the birth of his first child. "The fact that I knew so little about my own family history," he says, "never having known any of my grandparents, I wanted to find a way to be able to tell my children something about their own heritage." That profound familial motive and a chance find at the National Archives in Bayonne, where an ancestor was unearthed in the 1790 census, culminated in 2007 with Bob joining up with other researchers in the area to form the Hudson County Genealogical & Historical Society. Bob, who has lived in the Jersey City Heights all his life, was the group's first president and still serves as a board member, researcher, and participant in special projects.

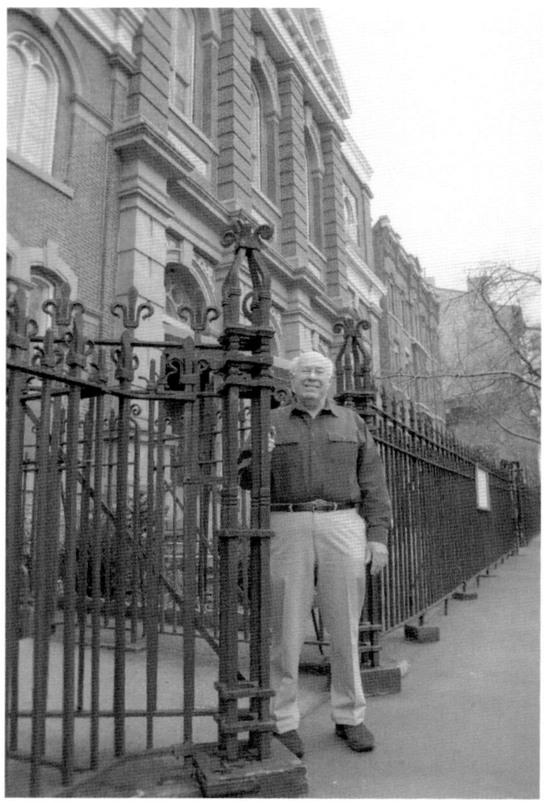

Randall Gabrielan

Randall Gabrielan has authored more full-length books on Jersey City and Hudson County than any other modern historian and has become an authority on the area's historic church buildings and their associated architects. Born in Jersey City, Randy's knowledge of architectural movements, styles, builders, and artisans is encyclopedic. His illustrated books, *Jersey City in Vintage Postcards* (1999, Arcadia Publishing) and *Jersey City: A Monumental History* (2007, Schiffer Books), are widely available and referenced by local historians and students. Through his involvement with the Keely Society, Randy has become an expert on the master Irish architect Patrick C. Keely (1816–1896), the "pioneer Catholic architect of America," as the *New York Herald* described him in an obituary, who built four colossal Catholic churches in Jersey City, including St. Peter (1864–1866), which is now demolished; St. Patrick (1870–1877); St. Michael (1873–1876); and St. Bridget (1886–1889).

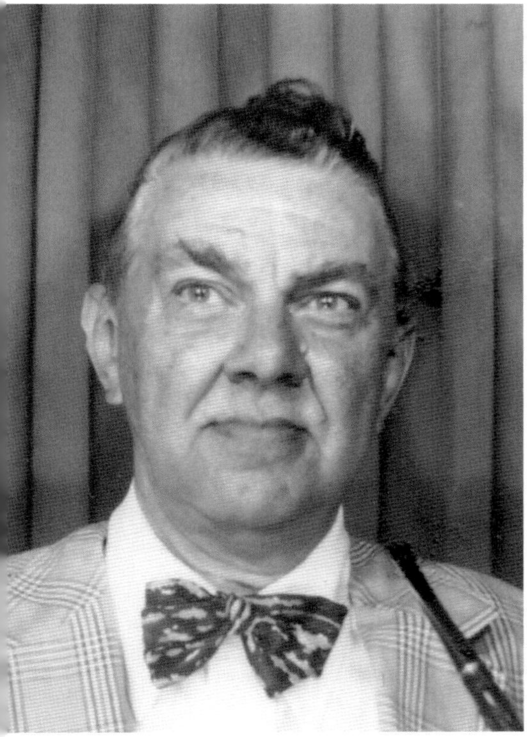

J. Owen Grundy

When he died at age 73 in 1985, J. Owen Grundy, who lived on Park Street in the Bergen Hill section of the city, left no void; his legacy continued in others he touched with his powerful passion. His towering presence can be felt in the work and advocacy of local descendant historians like Dennis Doran, Dr. Barbara Burns Petrick, Cynthia Harris, Dr. Hermann K. Platt, Randall Gabrielan, Ulana Zakalak, Patrick Shalhoub, Dr. Carmela A. Karnoutsous, Bob Leach, Dr. Joseph McLaughlin, and David Goodwin, all, like Grundy, championing the city's architectural patrimony and pounding the preservation pavement with their original research. Grundy was also a practicing preservationist, working closely with Ted Conrad, Morris Pesin, Audrey Zapp, Dr. Ethel Lawner, Jack Stokvis, and other titans to save threatened monuments and protect the urban environment, chairing the Municipal Historic Districts Commission, leading the Brownstone Revival Committee, and guiding the citizen-based Preservation and Restoration Association of Jersey City. A waterfront pier park at Exchange Place is named and dedicated in his honor. (Courtesy of the Jersey City Free Public Library.)

Dr. Barbara Burns Petrick

The list of academic and activist accomplishments of Dr. Barbara Burns Petrick, who stands in a historian class by herself, is awe-inspiring. A resident of the Jersey City Heights, where she helped found and organize the always-active Sgt. Anthony Park Neighborhood Association, Dr. Petrick is an authority on Jersey City–raised Mary Philbrook, the state's first woman attorney and advancer and fighter for equal rights and social improvements. A prominent scholar, Dr. Petrick has written and published important works, including *Mary Philbrook: The Radical Feminist in New Jersey* (1981, New Jersey Historical Commission) and *Church and School in the Immigrant City: A Social History of Public Education in Jersey City, 1830–1930* (2000, Upland Press). In 2010, Dr. Petrick was given the Jersey City Legend Award from the Jersey City Landmarks Conservancy "for her lifetime of scholarship in service to Jersey City and its history." (Courtesy of the Jersey City Free Public Library.)

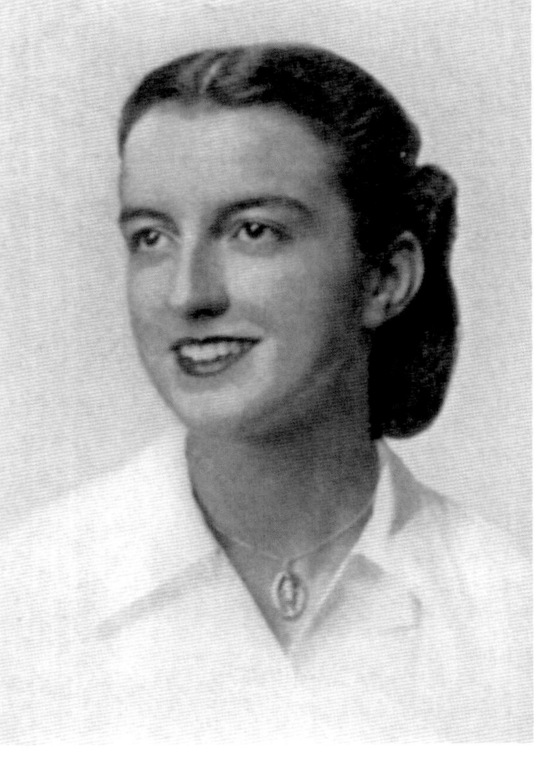

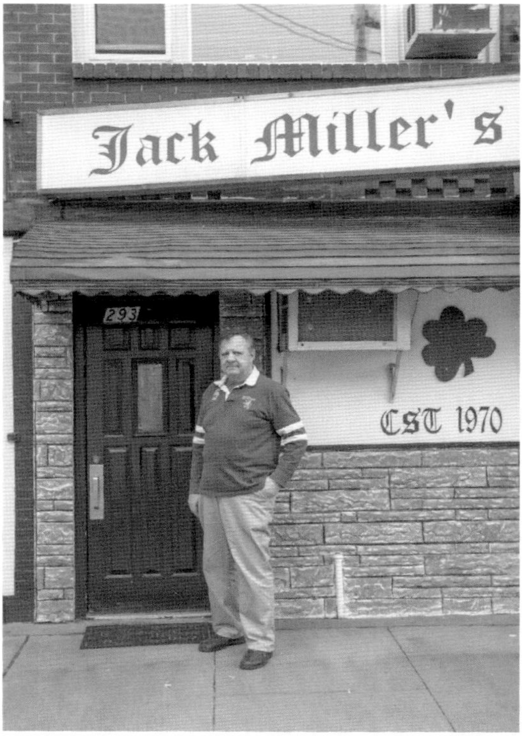

Jed Dimatteo

Jed Dimatteo is a carrier of extraordinary neighborhood memories perpetuated and pored over on a daily basis at the historic Jack Miller's pub right outside Journal Square. Who else can lay claim to a newsletter, *The Jedsey Journal*, that started in 1956 as distributed mimeographed copies and which continues today via the Internet? In Jed's eyes, childhood chums are as colossal as presidents, and neighborhood recollections are as integral as national holidays. "It's not about me," says Jed, pointing to the Jedsey Journal Hall of Fame photograph gallery that he put up in the pub. "It's about these people."

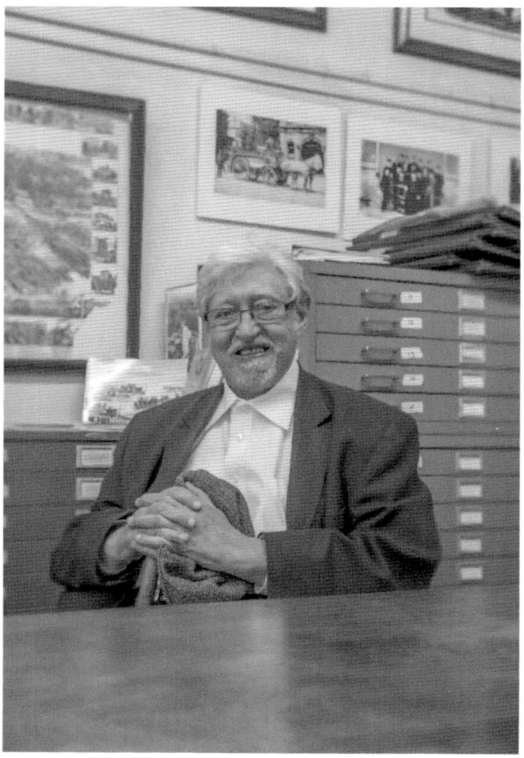

Bob Leach

Bob Leach is a special kind of historian. Fantastic municipal myths and "almost true" tales, as Bob calls his historical narratives, have defined his oral oeuvre. Over the years, Bob and the Jersey City Historical Project have brought out entertaining short story collections and illustrated chapbooks, including *Saloon Stories*, *The Frank Hague Picture Book*, and *Parade of the Shantytown Dead*. Bob is a folklorist filmmaker as well, working with local media interns to produce cable-ready documentaries, including *Eyes of St. Joseph* and *Invasion of the Reds: Mayor Frank Hague's War Against Radicals and Free Speech.*

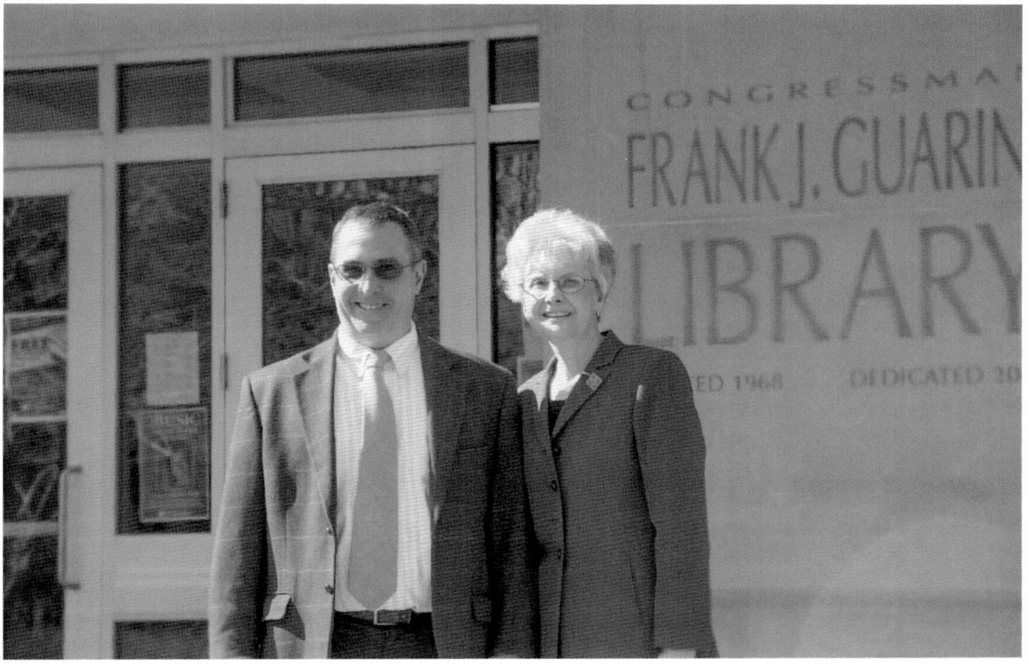

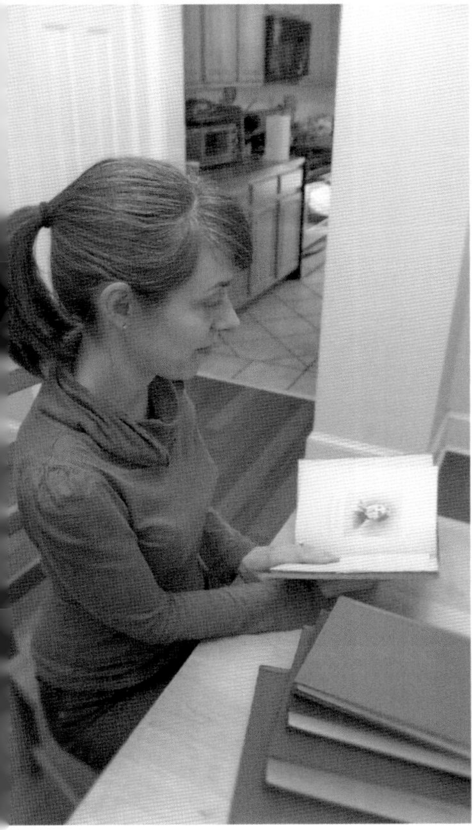

Dr. Carmela A. Karnoutsos and Patrick Shalhoub
Since 1999, Dr. Carmela A. Karnoutsos and Patrick Shalhoub have been the local historian duo to contend with. The two are the researchers, directors, and webmasters of *Jersey City: Past and Present*, a special digital history venture initiated, supported, and maintained by New Jersey City University, where Dr. Karnoutsos is professor emeritus of history and Shalhoub is the head librarian in the Periodicals and US Government Documents Department in the Congressman Frank J. Guarini Library. They continue to set new scholarship standards and offer easy public access to the city's historical compendiums. Visitors from around the world visit the site at www.historyofjerseycity.org to read over 200 alphabetized narratives, chronologies, and bibliographies related to local historical people, places, and institutions, from the American Can Company to Isaac Edge, Peter Henderson to Miss America Diner, and Prior's Mill to Peter Woodland.

Dr. Jennifer S. Furlong
One evening, while volunteering in the New Jersey Room on the third floor of the Jersey City Free Public Library on Jersey Avenue, Dr. Jennifer S. Furlong, a resident of the city's Lafayette neighborhood, came across a vertical file on Erminnie Smith (1836–1886), a world-famous 19th-century ethnologist, geologist, and founder, in 1876, of the Aesthetic Society of Jersey City, a cultural salon that Smith ran out of her Pacific Avenue parlor.

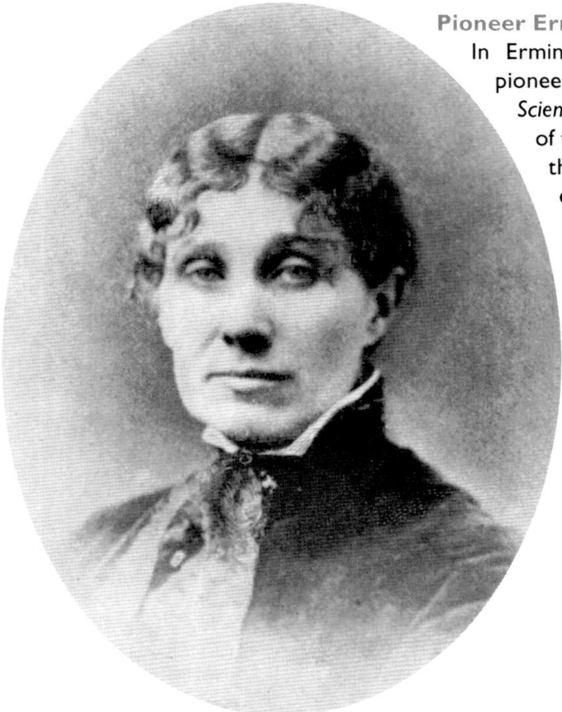

Pioneer Erminnie Smith

In Erminnie Smith, Dr. Furlong found an inspiring pioneer. She was the first woman to be published in *Science* and the first woman to become secretary of the male-dominated American Association for the Advancement of Science. Smith was also an expert on the Iroquois, with whom she lived and studied, fluently learning their tongues and customs; was a friend of invited Aesthetic Society guests Thomas Edison and Oscar Wilde; and was the namesake of a perpetual Vassar College geology scholarship. Through her ongoing scholarship on Smith, Dr. Furlong is introducing today's public to one of Jersey City's greatest citizens. (Courtesy of Dr. Jennifer S. Furlong.)

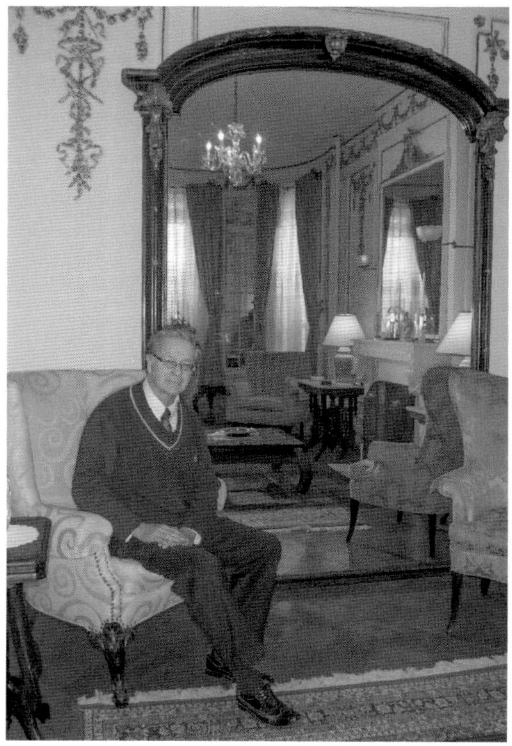

Dennis Doran

Like his mentor J. Owen Grundy (1912–1985), Dennis Doran has an uncanny ability to recall numerous names and dates without the use of notes. Dennis, a reporter for the *Jersey Journal* from 1970–1978 during the epochal political corruption cases of former mayor John V. Kenny and the infamous "Hudson Eight," leads popular architectural walking tours, which usually conclude at his Summit Avenue brownstone mansion, and gives history talks that draw crowds. A spirited voice in the current campaign to save the threatened St. John's Episcopal Church, Dennis, an active Jersey City Landmarks Conservancy board officer, believes that "roots are what make a community work. It's what makes life in our community worth living."

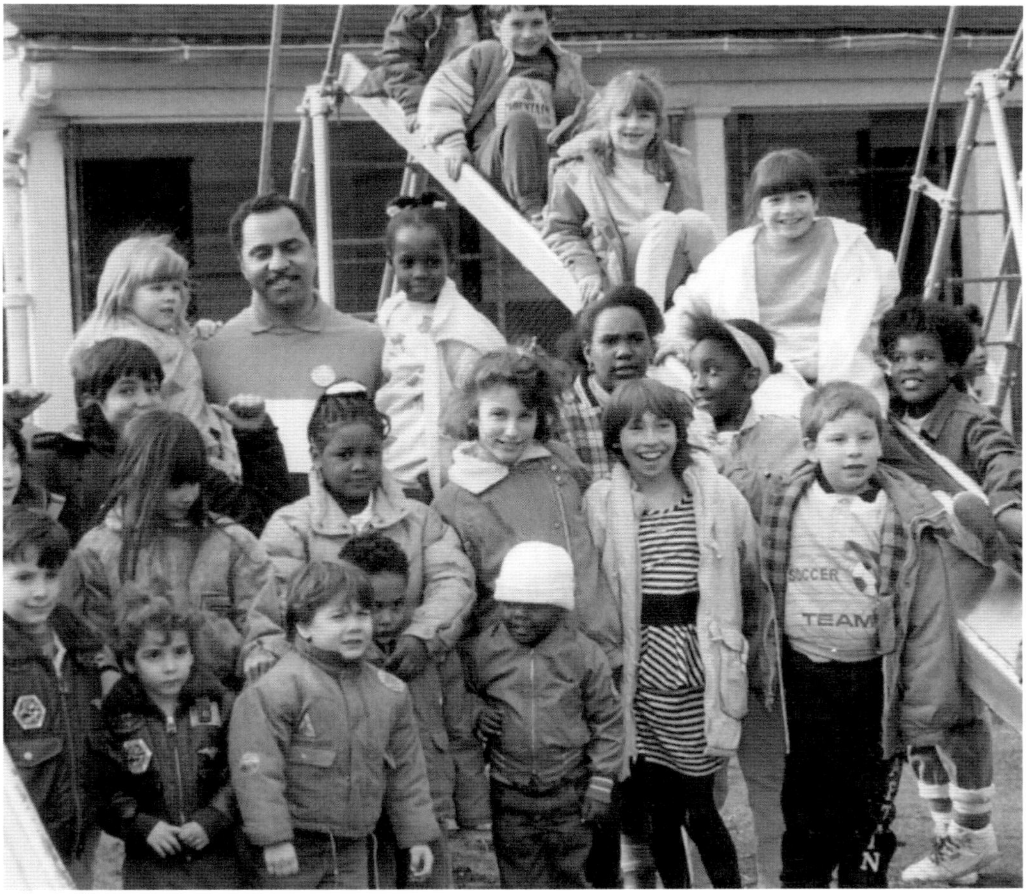

Mayor and State Senator Glenn D. Cunningham
Glenn D. Cunningham (1943–2004) was more than a mayor, a state senator, a city council president, a Hudson County freeholder, a US Marine, a police officer, and a US marshal. He was a historian. He was a down-in-the-microfilm-trenches type of researcher; a scholar who took to the streets to share stories with young citizens about Jersey City's role in the Underground Railroad; and a preservationist who helped save neighborhood monuments like Whitlock Cordage and Reservoir No. 3 when many claimed they could not be saved. Glenn's role as a city historian may have been his greatest civic role, which, perhaps, is why in 2012 Lafayette residents unveiled the Glenn D. Cunningham and Rev. Dr. Ercel F. Webb History Trail inside Rev. Dr. Ercel F. Webb Park, an arched-entrance lane that will feature neighborhood legends in bronze. (Courtesy of the Afro-American Historical Society Museum.)

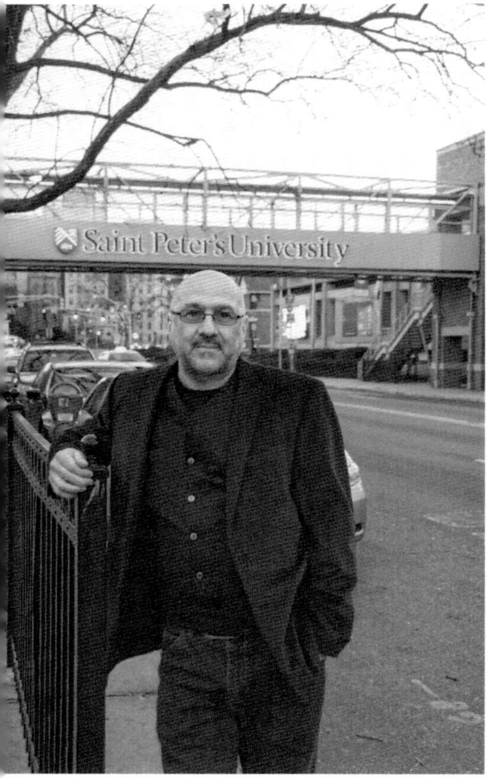

Dr. Joseph McLaughlin

What makes St. Peter's University's sociology and urban studies programs professor and local historian Dr. Joseph McLaughlin singular is that he practices the history he preaches. For his core and elective courses, including the Contemporary City; Urban Architecture and Design; and Urban Music, Jazz to Hip-Hop, he takes his students outside to local neighborhoods to feel the municipality's fabric, materiality, sounds, and pulse. "The city becomes the classroom," he says, and since 2006, he has been challenging students to look closely at the sociality, structurality, and sustainability of cities; to analyze how buildings and districts undergo a cycle of conversion and reinvention; and to conceive from their conclusions the ideal city. To demonstrate his own commitment to the university and its surrounding communities, Dr. McLaughlin, who holds a bachelor's of arts and a master's of arts from St. Peter's University and a doctorate of education from Seton Hall University, cowrote with Dr. Thomas Matteo an Arcadia Publishing book on the full history of the Jesuit university. "Teachers tell stories," he says, standing in front of the recently unveiled Glenwood Avenue–facing Mac Mahon Student Center, a stunning architectural addition to his city classroom.

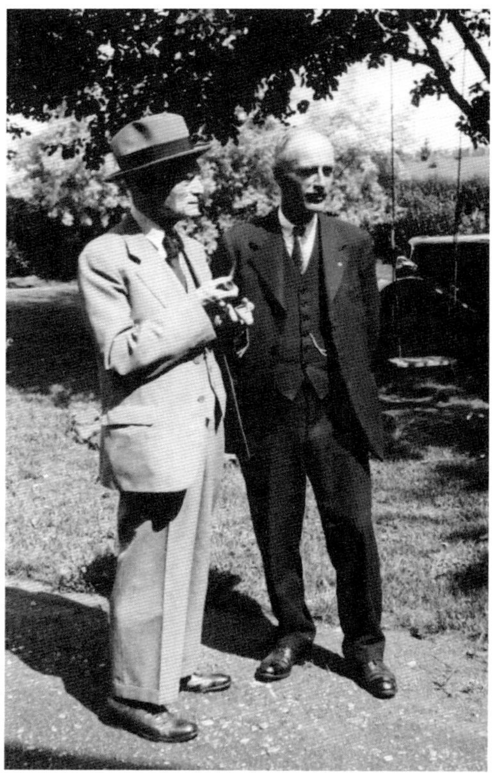

William H. Richardson

William H. Richardson (1864–1937, on left with hat) was Jersey City's first scholar to write for a local newspaper, enlightening a wide readership about forgotten municipal burghers, fables, and fabric. His papers, including pamphlets, compilations, profiles, features, appreciations, dedications, and architectural and aerial photography, are part of a special collection in the New Jersey Room of the Jersey City Free Public Library and reveal a historian of vernacular interests, prolific output, and an eclectic writing style. Among his best-known works are two chapters for the seminal publication *Jersey City of Today* and extensive news features for Bergen's 250th anniversary, both in 1910; an article in 1919 about the formation of the Lincoln Association of Jersey City; extended profiles starting in 1927 of Jersey City–born aeronaut Charles F. Durant (1805–1873); and, his crowning scholarly achievement in 1930, a full magazine section in the *Jersey Journal* for the Pavonia Tercentenary. (Courtesy of the Jersey City Free Public Library.)

Helene Stapinski

When Luc Sante, the renowned cultural and anthropological historian, observer of invisible cities, and author of the classic *Low Life*, told Helene Stapinski, his student at Columbia University, that she should write about her idiosyncratic childhood experience in Jersey City, she balked and battled against the thought. But he eventually convinced her that her family narrative of corner bar drunks, street swindlers, and numbers runners was material that great literature was built on. Helene, who used to write articles and a regular column for the *Jersey Journal* before going for her master's at Columbia, took a chance and captured not just a poignant chunk of her family biography but also of her city. From that inspired assignment came *Five-Finger Discount: A Crooked Family History*, a book-length epic published in 2001 by Random House. It was a sensation locally, though some took issue with Helene's depiction of degenerate city characters and near-omniscient citizens, especially the ever-beloved Mayor Frank Hague, and fanned outward to become a surprise national best seller during a period when the memoir form was not in vogue. For Helene, who writes regular features for the *New York Times* and other major publications, writing the book was "like an exorcism," a way to release her anger and come to terms with her municipal birthright. In fact, she now looks back and considers the book to be a living time capsule, an incorporeal inheritance that will be transferred to her children and descendants to come. (Below right, courtesy of Random House.)

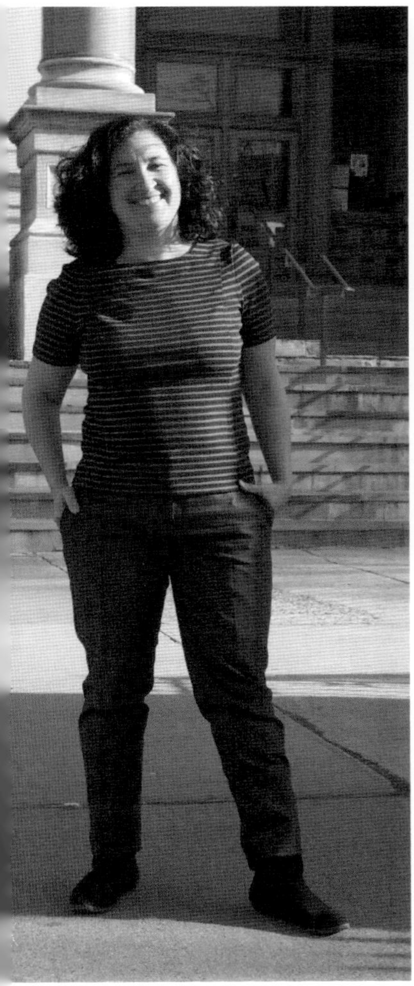

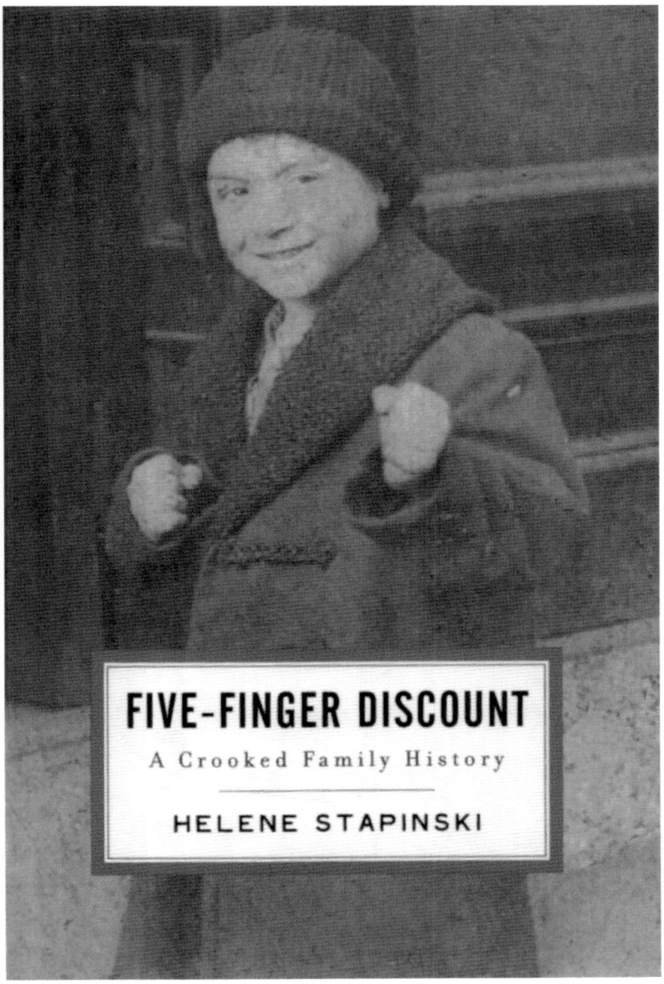

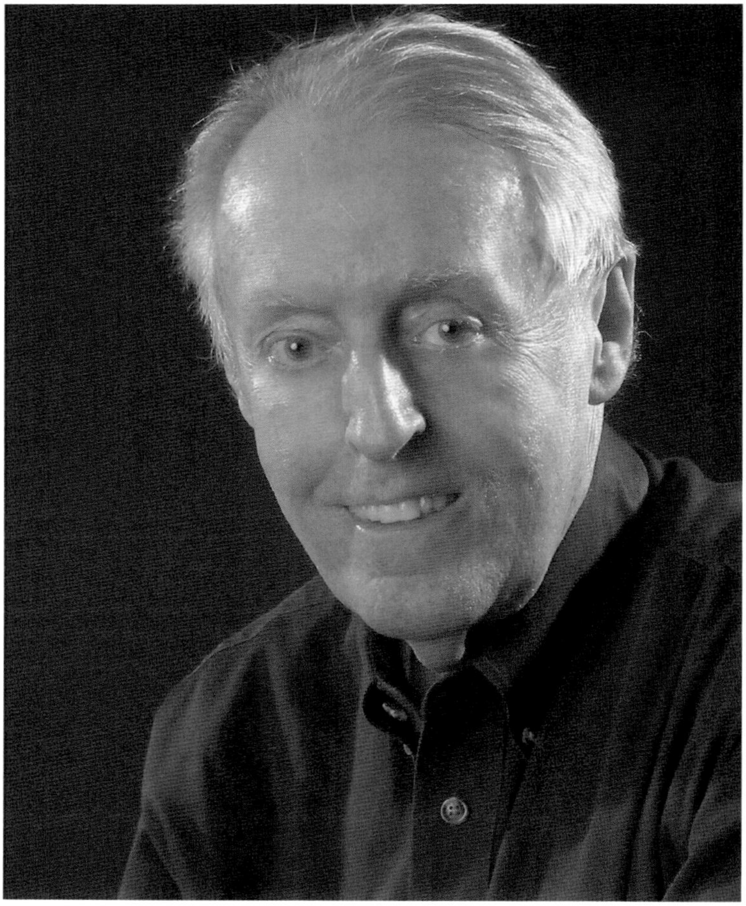

Thomas Fleming

"Jersey City is more than a city. It is a state of mind, especially if you grasp its history," says Thomas Fleming, one of America's greatest living historians and a proud Jersey City native. Tom, who grew up during the Depression in the strong Irish-American parish of St. Patrick, has come to understand and write about the city primarily through his father's political activities as the Sixth Ward Democratic leader under the spellbinding grip of Mayor Frank Hague (1876–1956). His father, Teddy Fleming, whose life he immortalized in *Mysteries of My Father: An Irish-American Memoir* (2005, Wiley), was the one who introduced him to Hague, a memory that looms like a great municipal mythology: "I met Mayor Frank Hague when I was seven years old. . . . The mayor, wearing a classic black derby, glared down at me as I had been scalping box seat tickets and shook my head, all but demolishing it. 'Your old man's a hell of a guy,' he growled. Thereafter, until I reached the age of 18 or so, he could do no wrong." After attending St. Peter's Preparatory School, where his teachers encouraged him to write, Tom would also compose two major short pieces about Hague, *Us Against Them* for New Jersey History and *I Am the Law* for American Heritage. It was inevitable, too, that Jersey City would enter his larger canon, which today includes exactly 50 fictional and nonfiction titles. *All Good Men* is a fictional depiction of the 1949 defeat of Hague's regime; succeeding novels like *The God of Love*, *King of the Hill*, and *Rulers of the City* "use the city and the state as a background," he says. In 2006, in great appreciation of his extraordinary oeuvre, Tom, famous for his other books about founding fathers and American military and political figures, was given the J. Owen Grundy History Award from the Jersey City Landmarks Conservancy. (Courtesy of Thomas Fleming.)

CHAPTER FIVE

Gather the Preservationists

To be a preservationist is to answer a higher civic calling. Preservationists—citizen activists who march for endangered buildings; property owners who proudly care for their historic homes; institutions that take the initiative to preserve, protect, and promote their neighborhood landmarks; materials scientists who develop and follow progressive practices for restoring and replicating architectural tissue; builders who prefer green-certified construction and technology when adaptively reusing or adding architectural additions to the original; developers of distinction who would rather rebuild and retain than demolish and destroy—respond to architecture in ways no one else does or no one else cares to.

Preservation, these practitioners all realize instinctually, is a no-brainer, especially in a distinct place like Jersey City, one of the most ancient municipalities in the country. There are no excuses in this age of historic preservation, they announce; it is a reaching modern movement toward the keeping of irreplaceable architectural keys. Jersey City, they know, offers a singular historicity, fabric, and framework; all of it is striking, unparalleled, and easily lost if not seized and sustained.

The city's preservation history, and the long road toward a continued practice, begins primarily in the civil rights era, when risings against wars, nuclear weapons, corruption, poverty, slum clearance programs, and the destruction of traditionalist architecture were all part of the country's racing pulse. The high-profile dismantling of Pennsylvania Station in New York City and the erasure of Louis Sullivan buildings in Chicago brought about preservation picket lines with the likes of Philip Johnson, Jane Jacobs, James Marston Fitch, Margot Gayle, Jacqueline Onassis, and Richard Nickel at the precarious front. In Jersey City, the Hudson County Board of Freeholders and a complacent city hall under Mayor Thomas Whelan called for the elimination of the Hudson County Courthouse, a spectacular 1910 Beaux-Arts beauty that was directly in the way of a blacktop parking lot for the newly minted Hudson County Hall of Records and Administration Building. Enter Ted Conrad and a fierce brigade of citizens, scholars, and college students; they were united and a force to be reckoned with.

The courthouse battle was actually preceded by two citizen campaigns that set the stage for everything else that followed. In the late 1950s, Morris Pesin, a local children's clothing store merchant in the McGinley Square shopping district, paddled with a *Jersey Journal* reporter from the blackened mudflat shores of Communipaw Cove to Liberty Island to prove that Jersey City's proximity to the national monument made it a pivotal symbolic link to the nation. Pesin's simple Homeric journey led to the vast transformation of a former rail kingdom into a state park that opened in 1976, unmatched in vista and vision. In the early 1960s, a virtual street fight to save majestic old-growth trees along the city's main boulevard broke out. Steered by Dr. Ethel Lawner, Audrey Zapp, and others, the campaign not only saved the trees, but also led to the formation of the Citizens Committee of Hudson County, a preservation and environmental advocacy organization that became the model for all future groups. And in the 1970s, visionary city planner Jack Stokvis and Italian Village steward Anthony Nicodemo partnered to revitalize an ancient immigrant neighborhood, creating along the way community pride.

From these primordial preservation models—from the passionate actions of a concerned citizenry—emerged the Friends of the Loew's in the late 1980s, with Colin Egan, Patty Giordan, and dozens of volunteers campaigning against the demolition of the 1929 movie palace in Journal Square; the Jersey City Landmarks Conservancy, formed in 1999 out of the Internet-powered fight to save the Hudson & Manhattan Railroad Powerhouse from being replaced with a tall tower; the Embankment Preservation Coalition, campaigning to preserve the Pennsylvania Railroad Harsimus Branch Embankment, a soaring stone trestle that stretches the length of Sixth Street in the downtown area and promises to be the High Line of Jersey City; Steve Latham and the Jersey City Reservoir Preservation Alliance, a Jersey City Heights group organized in the 2000s to stave off damaging development of the historic waterworks site; and Eileen Markenstein, who walked into an abandoned, neglected cemetery in 2008 and turned it overnight into a hip historic site that respects the buried and opens the gates to a caring audience.

Advocacy is just one part of the preservation legacy in Jersey City. Homeowners, institutions, and developers have taken up the bricks-and-mortar side of the field, carrying out hands-on restoration, adaptive reuse, and architectural addition projects. Over the last few years, Hope Susan Barett has tenderly restored the once-ruined 1906 Rudiger Mansion at the intersection of Manhattan and Summit Avenues, reincorporating original design elements and opening up soaring cathedral ceiling spaces. Ben LoPiccolo is transforming a decommissioned Civil War–era brick church building and a former Polish community hall into residential, retail, and cultural assets, all in an attempt to inject life into lifeless edifices so that communities can benefit. Butterfly Webb and Michael Rea are slowly saving a neglected brownstone in the city's elegant Bergen-Lafayette district so that their children may live history, not just hear about it.

Jersey City's preservation paragons, those who bravely gathered and demonstrated in those early days and those who now follow and carry on what has been handed down and taken to new levels, saved and continue to save the municipality's physical patrimony. Like the buildings they have literally held up high, they are of a civic greatness—a perpetual greatness.

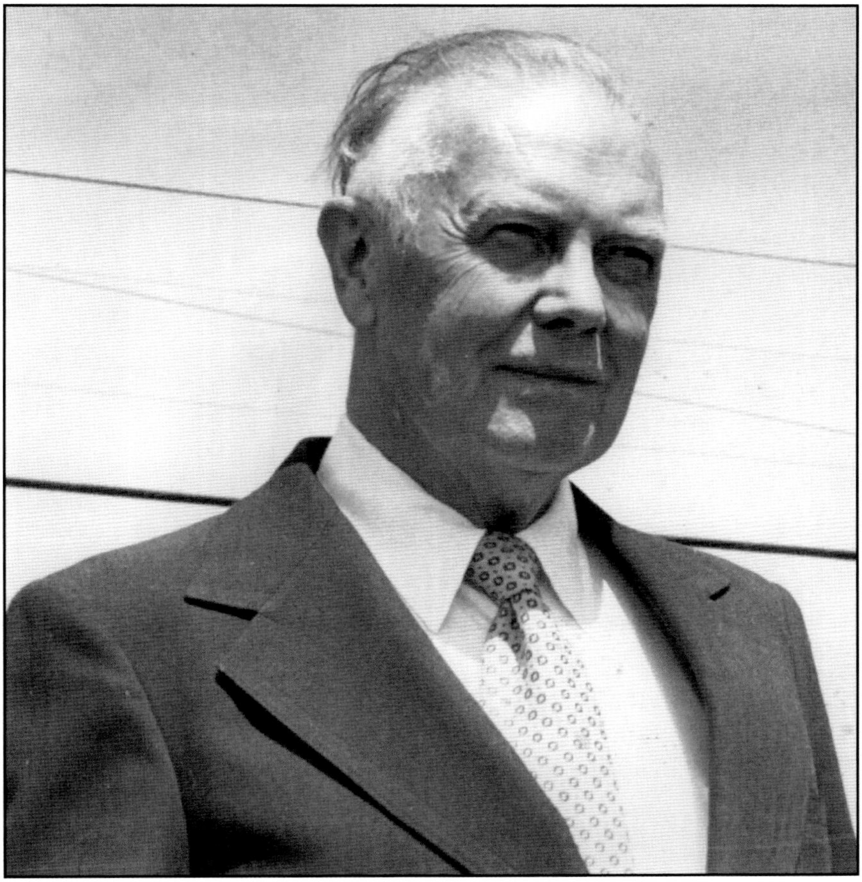

Theodore Conrad

Before he became a famous preservationist in the 1960s, Theodore Conrad (1910–1994) was a practicing architect and sought-after architectural model maker working out of a state-of-the-art studio on Ogden Avenue, in the Jersey City Heights, overlooking Hoboken rooftops and, beyond, the skyscrapers of Manhattan. Ted had a staff of assistants and apprentices who would sometimes work on his spacious front lawn, cutting out and assembling giant shapes and pieces of a plexi model that Ted had been commissioned to erect. But then, in 1966, Ted took note of the world of architecture shifting from the traditional to modernism. Old buildings were in the way of new styles and motives, and the Board of Chosen Freeholders and other governing bodies had announced plans to demolish the 1910 Hudson County Courthouse and replace it with a parking lot for new court facilities next door. Ted, having watched the demolition of Penn Station in New York, launched a public campaign by teaming up with local advocates Morris Pesin, Dr. Ethel Lawner, Audrey Zapp, state senator and later congressman Frank Guarini Jr., and other local civic giants. *New York Times* architectural historian and critic Ada Louise Huxtable (1921–2013) and esteemed historian Henry Hope Reed (1915–2013) voiced their opposition, turning the local battle into a national crusade. Ted and his spirited comrades persisted; obtained listing in the National Register of Historic Places, the first landmark designation for a Jersey City building; and guided the edifice through restoration. In the late 1980s and early 1990s, Ted, collaborating with a new generation of preservationists, helped steer the campaign to save the Loew's Jersey Theatre in Journal Square. Today, the Jersey City Landmarks Conservancy's Theodore Conrad Preservationist Award, given annually to a person or group that carries out a grassroots preservation campaign, keeps Ted's civic-minded memory alive. (Courtesy of Ruth and Doris Conrad.)

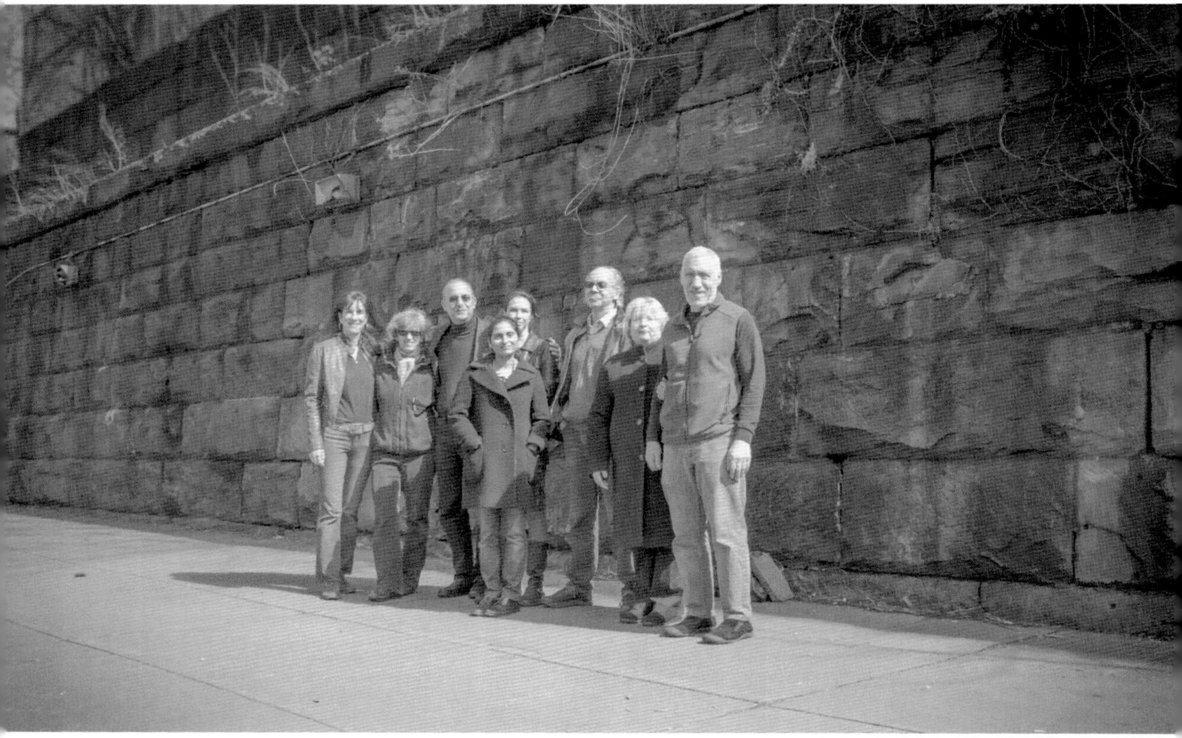

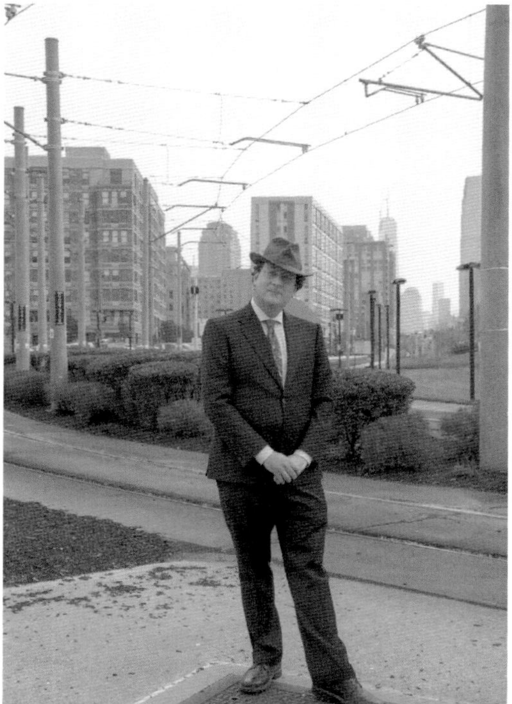

Joshua Parkhurst

As the former president of the Jersey City Landmarks Conservancy, Joshua Parkhurst knows all too well what it takes to be an active preservationist in the deepest of municipal trenches. Under his tenure, from 2005 to 2008, Joshua launched and led the campaign to raise awareness and protest the neglect and deterioration of St. John's Episcopal Church, a supreme 1871 Victorian Gothic stone edifice, designed by Jersey City architect J. Remsen Onderdonk (1840–1888). Joshua, a practicing Manhattan attorney, put countless hours into meetings with elected officials, community groups, and property owners; he made the case for the preservation and imaginative adaptive reuse of the building to media outlets; and, most compellingly, he invited the church's former rector, the Rev. Robert W. Castle Jr. (1929–2012), to return to Jersey City in loud vocal support of the group's valiant efforts. While the church building remains open to vandals and the elements, Joshua has demonstrated to other architectural advocates what is required professionally and personally to fight for defenseless community monuments.

Embankment Preservation Coalition (OPPOSITE PAGE)

The Embankment Preservation Coalition was formed in 1998 by local activists Maureen Crowley (second from right), Peter Delman, Richard James, Stephen and Joanne Gucciardo, Jennifer Meyer, and others to help preserve the c. 1902 Pennsylvania Railroad Harsimus Branch Embankment, known locally as the "Sixth Street Embankment," a soaring six-block-long masonry block freight rail trestle designed by renowned local engineer James J. Ferris (1860–1914). Since then, the group has worked hard to obtain landmark designation, preservation grants, and local appreciation for the site. Their vision is for the reuse of the embankment as a habitat-oriented park and destination on the East Coast Greenway, a walking trail from Maine to Florida. The Embankment has been compared to the High Line, a formerly abandoned viaduct in New York City that was transformed, with government and public support, into a world-class park.

Joe Hajcak

Joe Hajcak is a preservationist and does not even know it—he is one who seeks out collective municipal memories and brings them back to life with each visit and each gathering of friends and does not just keep them but hands them back to the community, refreshed and renewed. Every May, during National Preservation Month, Joe and his Lafayette neighborhood friends, Karen Darowski-Foerster, Barbara Gerzanich-McDermott, Susan Wal-Reingle, Kathy Wal, Judy Wal-Pugliese, Diane Przygocki-Nilson, Renee Wal-Stanfield, Billy Przygocki, Peter Hovick, Charles McGurk, and Geralyn Feniello-Coviello, return to the streets and stoops of their ancestry. Joining in on the Lafayette History Festival & Tour, Joe and his reunion partners follow and converse with architectural historian tour guides, stop at landmarks familiar to them as childhood beacons, and even chime in with personal anecdotes and animated images. Every year, without fail, Joe and his friends punctuate the event with unearthed photographs, black-and-white super-8mm home movies, drawings, and letters. After the event is over, the group gathers for dinner and drinks at a local eatery to reminisce about their days of learning, prayer, and confession at the Assumption Blessed Virgin Mary school and church; shopping at and supporting Lafayette mom-and-pops; playing in Lafayette Park (now the Rev. Dr. Ercel F. Webb Park); going to the neighborhood Provident Savings Bank with their parents to stare at the famous Ruth Wilcox mural of Washington Irving; riding the rattling buses across Pacific Avenue; and participating in novenas and street processions. "I think our Lafayette reunions will go on as long as we can make it," Joe says—a towering sentiment that goes to the core of the ancient neighborhood itself.

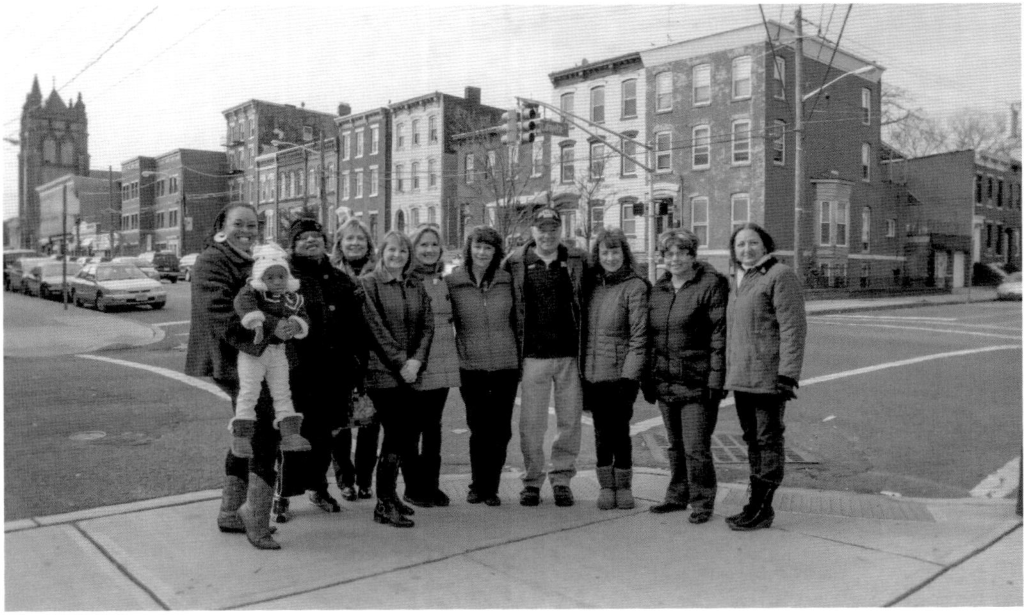

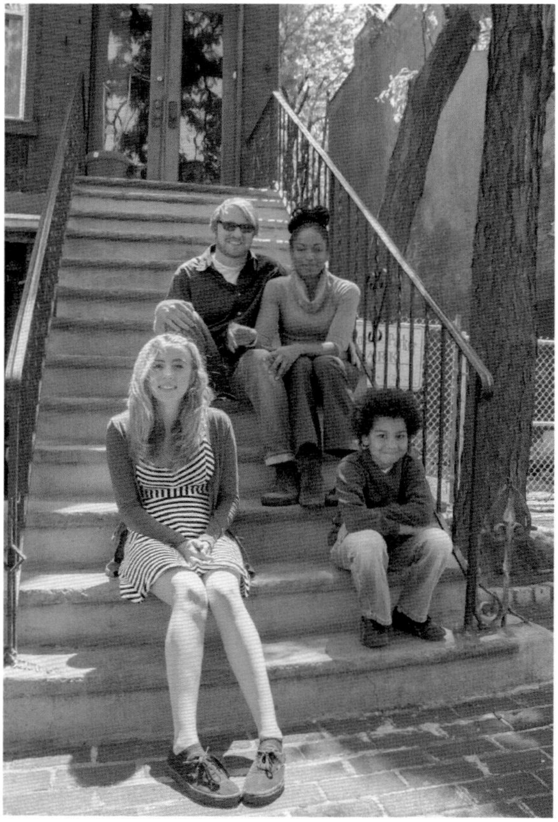

Butterfly Webb and Michael Rea

Butterfly Webb and Michael Rea, both longtime public school teachers in Jersey City, realized how special their c. 1890 town house on Madison Avenue, in the Bergen-Lafayette section of the city, was as soon as they pulled up to it in 2010. They had discovered a foreclosed property with enough structural and preservation problems to guarantee instant prospective-buyer refusal and flight. But Butterfly, who actually lived around the corner on Monticello Avenue when she was a child, and Michael, a self-trained renovation specialist, fell in love with the brownstone-trimmed building and knew right away what was possible; what it would take to heal and transform it into a special sanctum for their young children Ari, Pharaoh, and Taylor. By July 2011 they were moving in. "Our move was like a slow march to the promised land of the real," says Butterfly. "We were not expecting to find anything in mint condition. What we found was far more valuable." They were mesmerized by the "grassroots splendor of the property," the four floors of "splendid disaster," as Butterfly, a splendid writer, describes it. The restoration process, costly and pressing, brought out the dormant preservationists in the married couple. "I learned how to sand and finish floors, appreciate horsehair plaster walls, and the indomitable power of drafty dumbwaiters," says Butterfly. "Michael honed his painting skills from his stepfather, Skip, his ability to cut and refit moldings, kitchen cabinetry, and everything in between because he is just that talented—the pieces fell into place." Their inspiring efforts ended up being captured on HGTV's *Mom Caves*, and a full production crew took over the house for five full days, transforming the home and bringing back a long-missing Victorian atmosphere. While it is Butterfly's seminal voice that echoes throughout the beautifully preserved Madison Avenue house, it is the utterance of the great American novelist Toni Morrison, inscribed on the wall of Butterfly's new library designed and installed by host Beth Stern and the HGTV crew, that sagely speaks for the house's continuing history: "If there is a book you want to read but it hasn't been written yet, then you must write it."

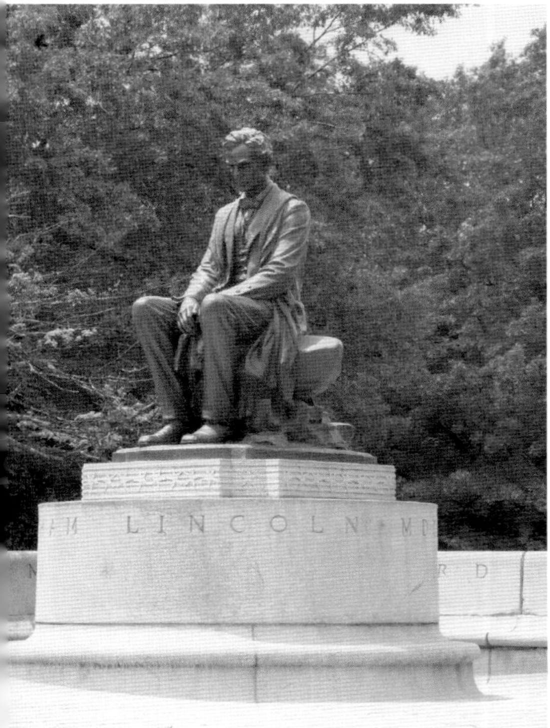

Lincoln Association of Jersey City
Founded in 1865 right after the assassination of Pres. Abraham Lincoln, the Lincoln Association of Jersey City, the oldest such organization in the country with its mission to maintain the President's memory, started a fundraising campaign in the late 1920s involving local school children, who collected enough nickels to build a permanent monument to the 16th president. In 1930, *Lincoln the Mystic*, designed by James Earle Fraser, was unveiled at the landscaped entrance to Lincoln Park, originally known as West Side Park when it was unveiled by landscape architects Daniel Langton and Charles Lowrie in 1905.

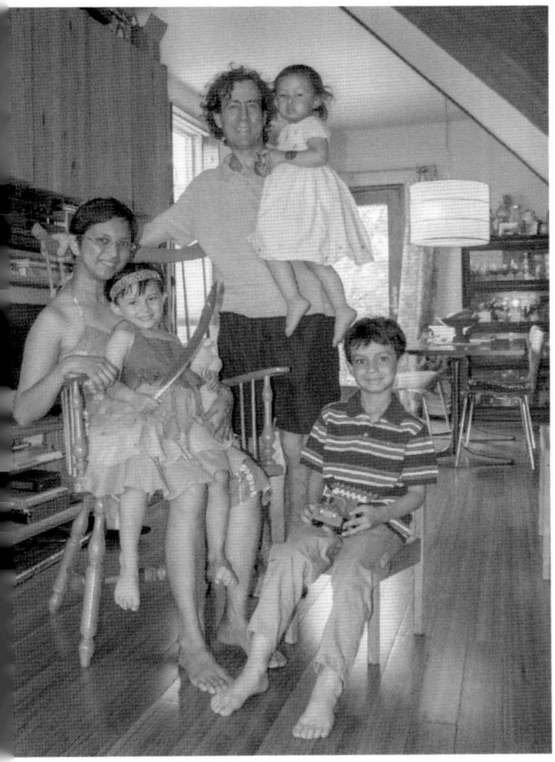

Lycel Villanueva and Miles Poindexter
When Lycel Villanueva and Miles Poindexter purchased their c. 1871 vernacular French Second Empire homestead in the Lafayette area, they knew the challenges. Miles had already restored a c. 1886 town house a few blocks away, and Lycel, an architect, had experience in historic preservation. The couple removed interior walls to allow more light and cross-ventilation and erected an exterior spiral staircase. "We'd like for our kids to develop a sense of respect for things that are old, historic," Lycel says. "There's a sense of place that grows with a house—and I'd like for them to be able to recognize that."

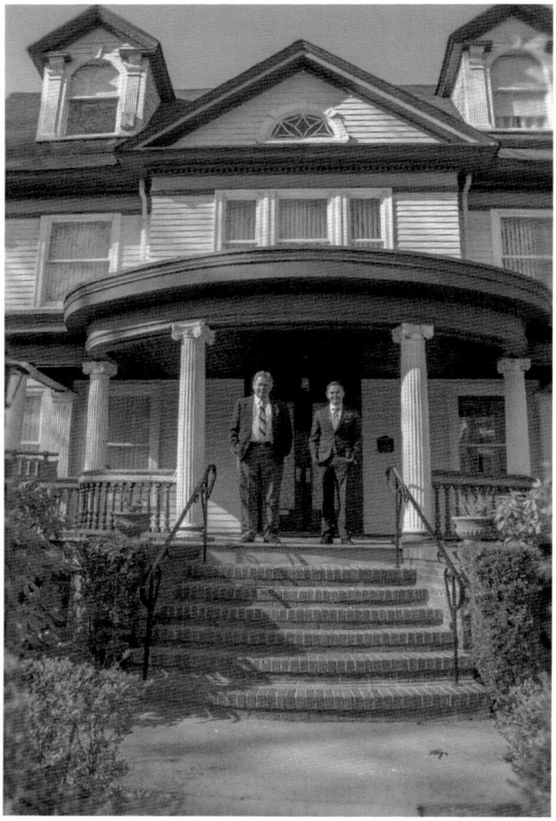

The Hallanans

John Hallanan Jr. and his son John Hallanan III are a father-and-son preservation powerhouse. Whenever they leave their tranquil Georgian Revival mansion on Gifford Avenue in the idyllic West Bergen section of the city, they enter a world of civic duty and deeds. In this inspiring partnership, the preservation of the entire community is paramount; volunteerism is a vocation; to do otherwise is to sink into communal complacency. They know about commitment; it is in their ancestry and in their maternal name of Muldoon, etched into a memorial stained-glass window inside St. Michael Church. Commissioned in 1898, the window evokes the effigy of seaman second class George A. Muldoon, who gave his life aboard the USS *Juneau* when it sank in 1942. This great sacrifice plays a part in the father and son's present pursuits. Collectively, they belong to and are active in over a dozen major local advocacy organizations, among them the Lincoln Association of Jersey City, Elks Lodge No. 211, the Knights of Columbus, the Society of the Friendly Sons of Saint Patrick of Hudson County, the Ancient Order of Hibernians, and the Hudson County Genealogical & Historical Society. John III, who clerked for a judge after graduating from Rutgers School of Law and has since been working in private and public practice, has been a commissioner on the Jersey City Historic Preservation Commission since 2007 and is the former president of the Jersey City Landmarks Conservancy, a position he treasured for its cornerstone of citizenship and conservation of fabric. During his leadership and lobbying efforts, the Bergen Monument, a bronze effigy of legendary director-general Peter Stuyvesant (c. 1612–1762) designed and erected between 1910 and 1913 by the world-renowned sculptor J. Massey Rhind (1860–1936), was restored by the city after being removed without permission in 2010. John's first foray into the wild world of preservation, however, occurred when he was just a kid climbing the podium stool to implore the city council to purchase the threatened Loew's Jersey Theatre from developers seeking demolition. That adolescent tenacity just may have saved the theater, but it most definitely spoke to the spirit of the Hallanan heart.

Paul and Eric Silverman

Paul and Eric Silverman (left and right, respectively) are builders with a community conscience, derived, no doubt, from their parents, who instilled in them traditional business fundamentals, principles, and virtues like honesty, hospitality, customer service, and concern. The brothers, whose development company, Silverman, can be traced to their father and grandfather's trucking and warehousing ventures starting in the 1930s, have for over 30 years been taking abandoned, dilapidated structures and breathing new life back into them—carefully, slowly, and with the participation of local talented architects, contractors, interior designers, craftspeople, and managers. Because of them, rows of neglected 19th-century tenements along Grove Street have been reinvigorated with new residences, offices, and storefront businesses; the historic fabric of a former lamp factory on Tenth Street has been resplendently retained and expertly restored; an entirely new, sensitively designed residential square has been planned and erected in the heart of the Hamilton Park Historic District; jobs have been generated; modern, sustainable construction practices have been implemented and certified. The brothers build and transform from the ground up, with the needs of the surrounding neighborhoods always coming first. Paul, the business mind, and Eric, the visualizer, have been told that the Hebrew word *zedekah*, which means being righteous and charitable, applies to them and to the actual developments they build.

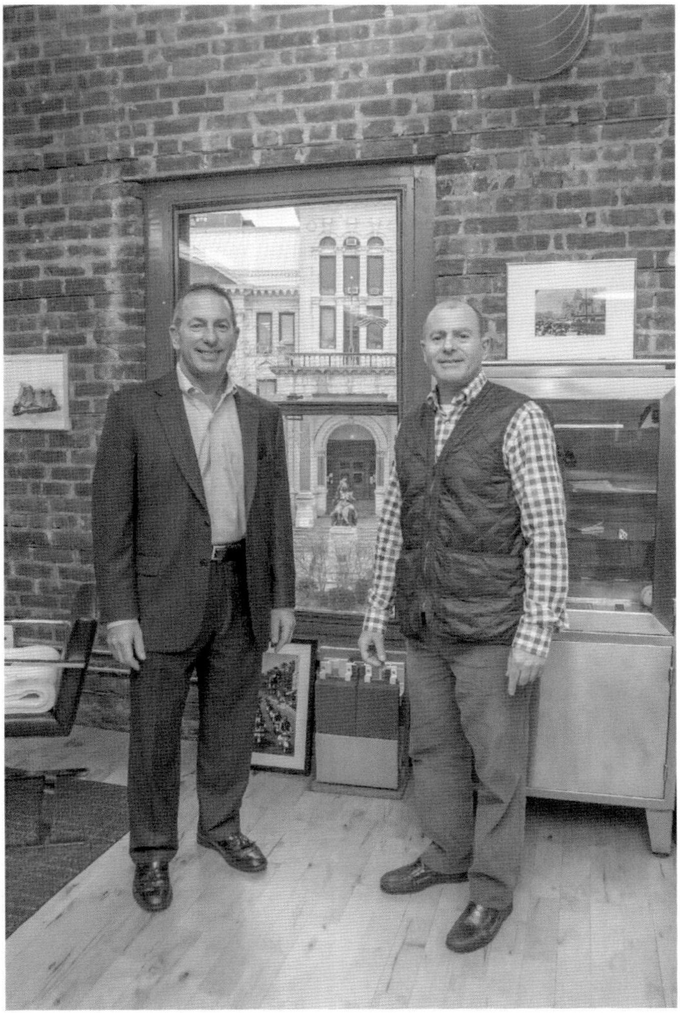

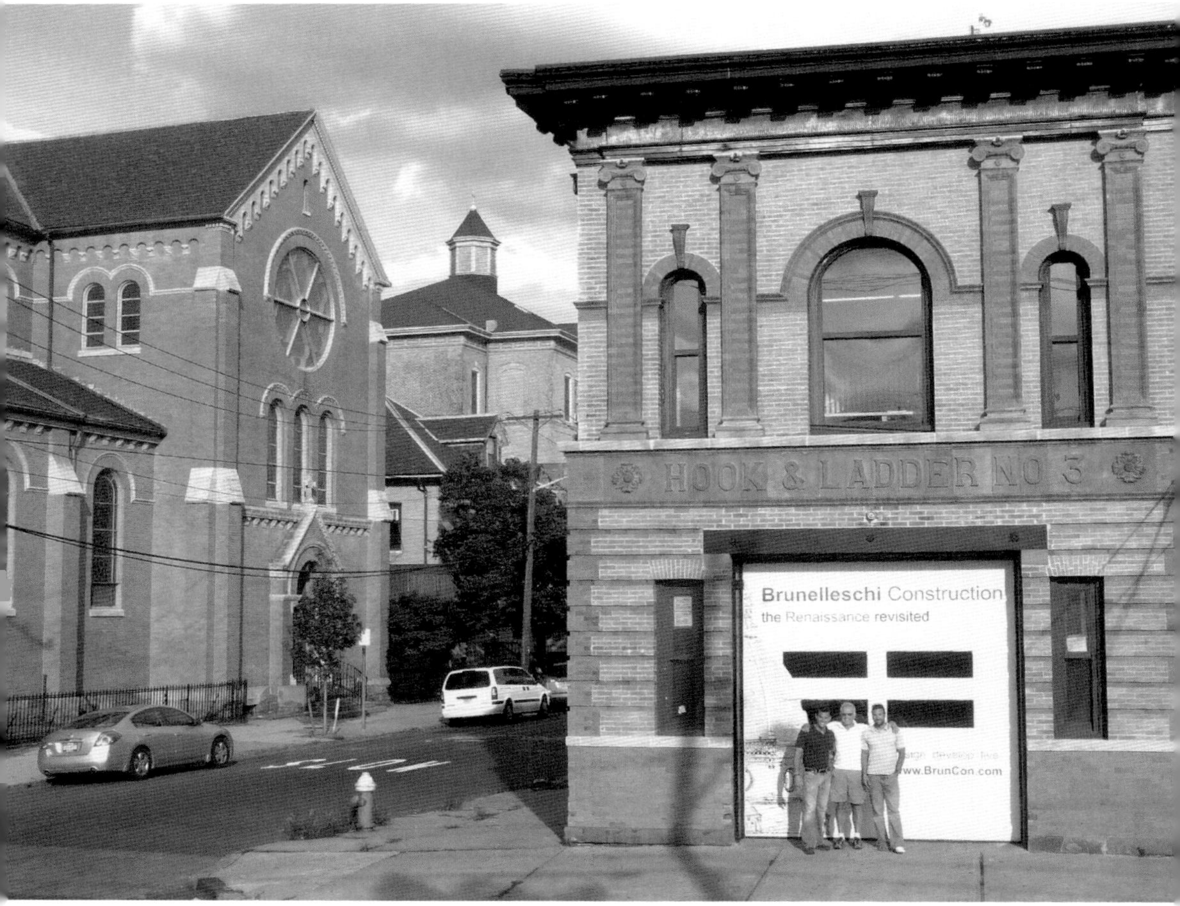

Brunelleschi Construction

For Alfonso Carrino, his son Anthony, and nephew John Colaneri, the recognition they have received for the pioneering preservation work carried out by their Jersey City contracting company, Brunelleschi Construction, has never been about the architectural awards or the HGTV fame. Their passion for hands-on construction and transforming historic buildings regarded as unsalvageable and cost prohibitive comes from a proud family tradition going back almost a century. The firm first came to the attention of the Jersey City Landmarks Conservancy, whose trustees took notice of and gave a special preservation award to their m650 Flats project, a former 1915 warehouse-turned-condominium. After further acknowledgement from the local press, the team, headquartered in a former 1896 firehouse in the Jersey City Heights, was suddenly on HGTV, showcasing its restorative talents to the nation in original programs like *Kitchen Cousins*, *Cousins on Call*, and *Cousins Undercover*, three huge hits for the network. But for Alfonso, Anthony, and John, commitment to the community is what ultimately matters. They demonstrated their commitment when Hurricane Sandy hit their hometown in 2012, and the family company, in a show of concern, offered neighbors free use of their generators. This same sense of public duty is reflected in their new show *Cousins Undercover*, where they focus on community heroes from around the country, helping, as John describes it, "those that have given up everything they have to help others. It could be a teacher, coach, police officer, or local resident that puts others before themselves." (Courtesy of Leon Yost.)

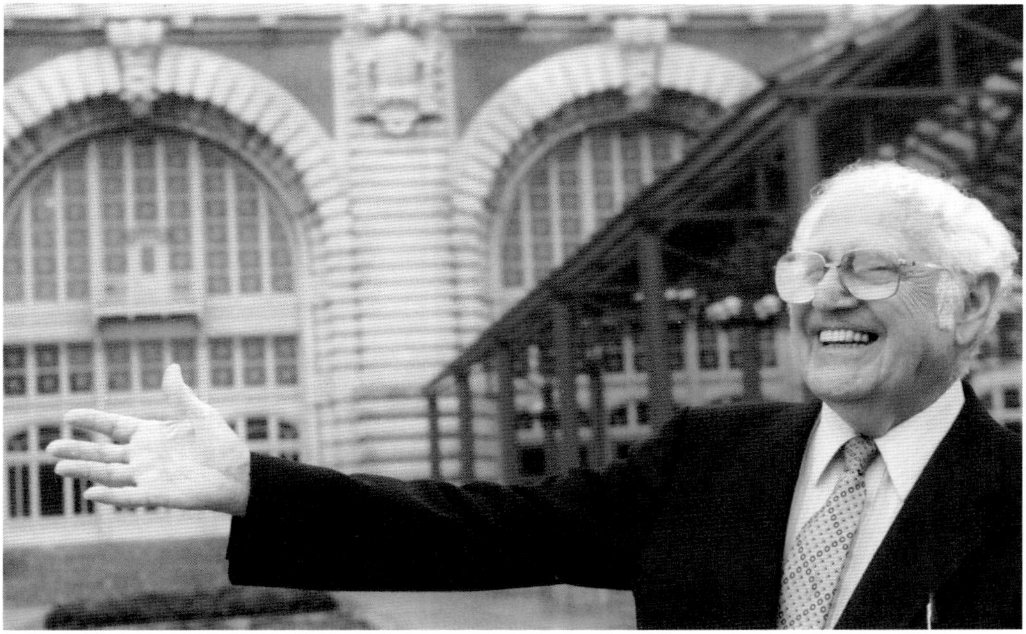

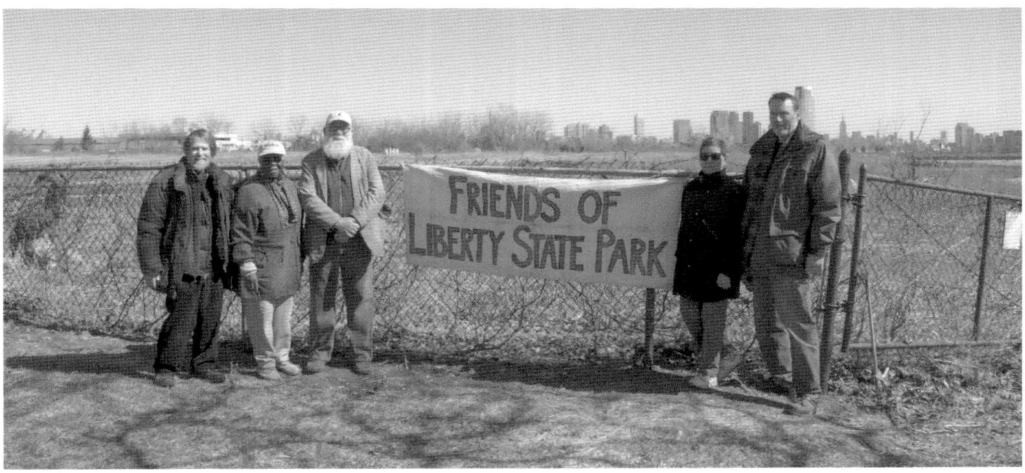

Morris Pesin

When, in 1958, lawyer and children's clothing store owner Morris Pesin (1911–1992) paddled, Odysseus-like, a small canoe from the Jersey City waterfront to Liberty Island, with a *Jersey Journal* reporter in tow, he wanted to show local officials, and the world, that the two shores were separated by only eight minutes worth of rowing. His vision to transform a derelict 700-acre swath of abandoned railroad land into a great public patriotic patrimony—Liberty State Park opened in 1976, the year of the country's bicentennial—is still heralded and an ongoing model for other environmental reclamation campaigns across the country. In 1988, Morris's wife, Ethel (1915–2013), son Sam, and fellow park stalwarts John Tichenor and Audrey Zapp (1925–2012) founded Friends of Liberty State Park, continuing the American dream that began almost 60 years ago. In 2013, a new footbridge, replacing one destroyed by Hurricane Sandy and providing an alternative access between the park and the Lafayette and downtown districts, was named the Ethel Pesin Memorial Bridge, a fitting honor for the entire Pesin family. (Morris Pesin photograph courtesy of Sam and Judy Pesin.)

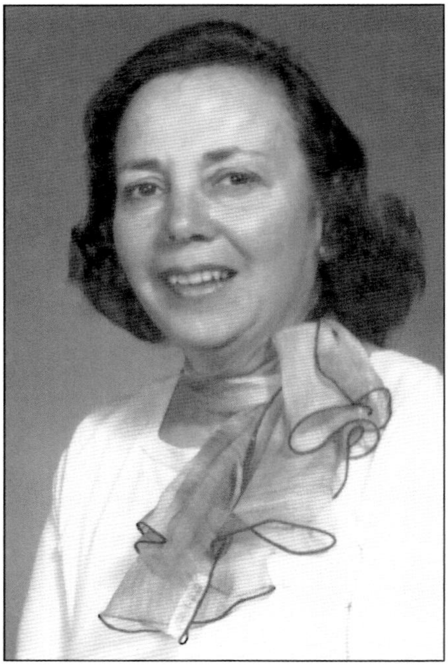

Dr. Ethel Lawner

Pity the anti-preservationist in Jersey City in the 1960s going up against Dr. Ethel Lawner (1922–2013). Government officials learned their lesson after sending work crews to cut down old-growth trees on Kennedy Boulevard. Dr. Lawner, joined by other advocates, publicly protested and declared: "There's going to be a hell of a commotion. The people here are used to being dictated to by the politicians, but now it's going to stop." The campaign prompted the formation of the Citizens Committee of Hudson County, which joined in the spirited battle to save the Hudson County Courthouse. (Courtesy of Sydne B. Marshall.)

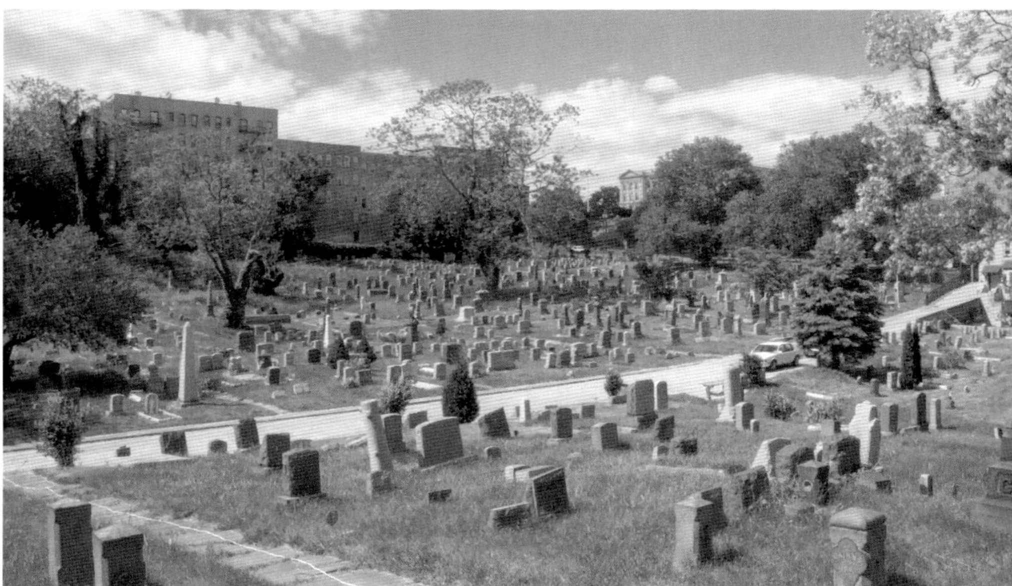

Eileen Markenstein

Were it not for Eileen Markenstein's efforts, starting in 2008, to rescue the Jersey City & Harsimus Cemetery from abandonment and neglect, the grounds, sloping down Newark Avenue, would still be an overgrown glade. Eileen proudly points out that the site was founded in 1829 as the state's first cemetery company and is the final resting place for soldiers from the Civil War to the War in Afghanistan. Eileen, joined by her husband, Aart, often sponsors special programs to help raise awareness, including Shakespearean productions, concerts, and volunteer days with waterfront office employees and local college, middle, and high school students.

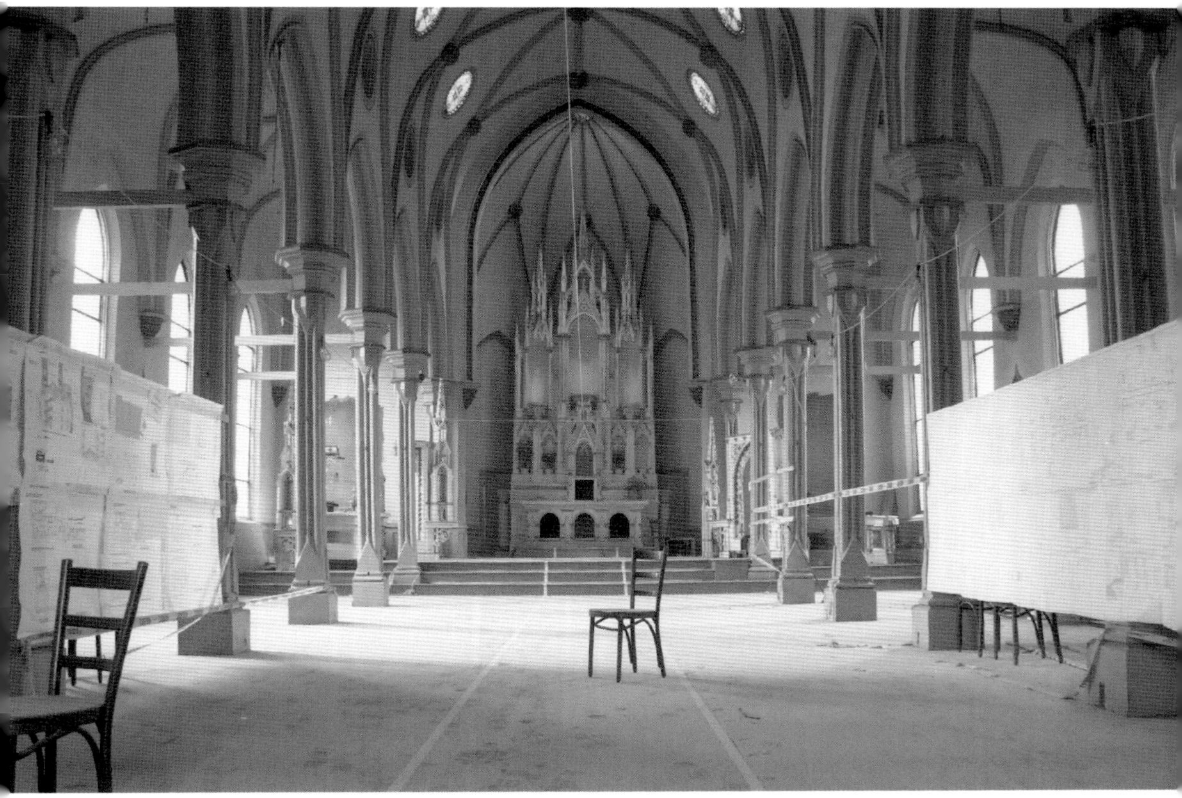

Ben LoPiccolo

Ben LoPiccolo is a real estate entrepreneur who approaches preservation projects differently. Instead of a complex and complete restoration program, which can sometimes strip the structure of its precious patina or architectural fabric, Ben prefers to let a historic building's imperfections—minute cracks, weathered exterior facings, missing tiles, soiled stone—remain as visual evidence that time has passed and architecture, like people, forms fissures and faults. In Boniface Lofts on First Street, Ben is converting the former St. Boniface Church (erected around 1864) into soaring-space condominiums with existing murals and stained glass left in place. At White Eagle Hall, erected in 1909–1910 as a social event space for St. Anthony Church, Ben will keep the levitating wraparound mezzanine, expose brick walls, retain tin ceilings, restore stained-glass skylights, and carry out simple repointing and masonry stabilization. With Boniface Lofts and White Eagle Hall, Ben, who comes from a proud Italian American family of construction craftsmen, will be pulling two pivotal monuments out of obscurity and putting them back into the community as living heritage destinations.

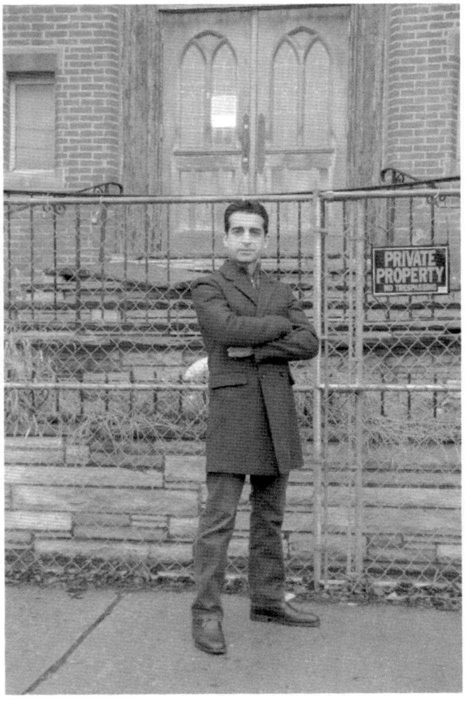

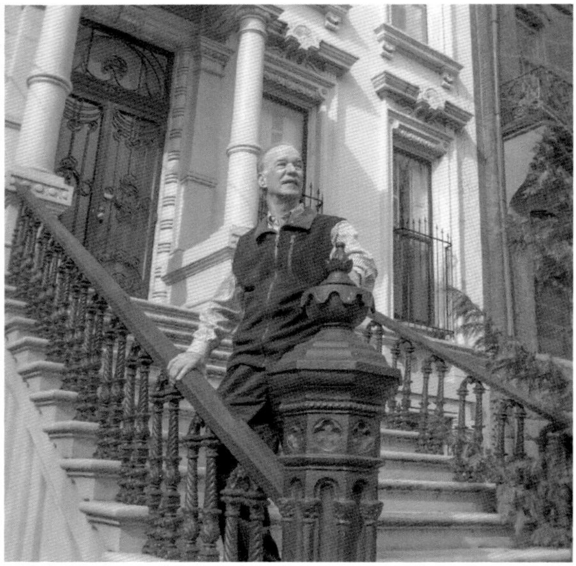

Jack Stokvis and Anthony Nicodemo

Almost 40 years have passed since Jack Stokvis (pictured) made preservation history in Jersey City, but with the recent bestowment upon him of the Jersey City Landmarks Conservancy's Jersey City Legend Award, his legacy as a visionary urban planner and preservationist has appeared at the municipal forefront where it belongs, amidst the gallery of civic greats. Jack was the head planner in the Jersey City Office of Planning under the Mayor Dr. Paul Jordan "reform" administration (1971–1977) and, working with community icons like Councilman Morris Pesin and architect Ted Conrad, helped launch revitalization projects and programs focused on architectural preservation and a high quality of life for all residents. In 1974, while attending an urban renewal conference in Manhattan, Jack watched a screening of *The Street of the Flower Boxes*, a documentary based on a children's book about how a New York City street laden with crime and decay is positively transformed by the introduction of flower planters. Jack, exasperated by Jersey City's abandoned brownstone districts, slums, and high-crime areas, slowly introduced his own Flower Box Program, attracting the help of community stalwarts Yvonne Balcer, Joe Duffy (1910–2001), and Anthony "Tony" Nicodemo (1936–2004). Local residents, including homeowners, merchants, and young students, ran with the initiative, sold hundreds of boxes, and gained national attention, including a major feature profile in *Reader's Digest*. Jack and Tony, a former high school and college basketball star, teacher at James J. Ferris High School, lifelong Second Street resident in the city's Italian Village neighborhood, and executive director of VITA (Village Italian Americans Take Action), became close friends and, over the next few years, took advantage of the sense of community that the flower boxes had generated so brilliantly. Tony and Jack recognized that the Italian Village, a roughly 20-block, late-19th-century Italian immigrant ward at the western boundary of the downtown area, was disappearing; old-timers were selling their generational homes for pittances; heritage businesses were shutting down; sewers and curbsides were enveloped by garbage; parks were being used by vagrants and addicts; and surrounding factories that had provided village residents with jobs were relocating to other states. Jack and Tony decided to carry out an 11th-hour campaign to save the neighborhood—a *risorgimento*, as Tony called it in Italian, a "resurgence." To them, the village was the city's premiere cultural neighborhood where residents and visitors could buy fresh foods from mom-and-pop storefronts, where street festivals and feasts brought neighbors together, and where the front stoop was the municipal altar. The duo convinced remaining merchants, residents, and church parishes to hold on; they sought the promise of modest funding from city officials and agencies; and they convinced art professors from local colleges, including Martin Holloway, to bring in volunteer students to help paint "Welcome to the Village—The World Lives Here!" murals and signs. Their campaign took hold and lasted into the early 1980s, but with Jack's departure for planning positions in other cities and, at the invitation of Pres. Ronald Reagan, in Washington, DC, at the Department of Housing and Urban Development, the village preservation effort lost its core. Tony, however, did not budge and remained on Second Street with his wife, Rosalie, and family; he kept at it and never lost hope for the neighborhood. Throughout the following decades, various independent groups emerged to provide support for the Italian Village in the pioneering spirit and devotion of the VITA group. Led by community activists Nicholas Sorrentino, Anthony Lambiase, Michele La Monica-Egar, Rob Crow, and Jim Ayers, the neighborhood that Jack and Tony worked tirelessly to save remains well protected to the present day.

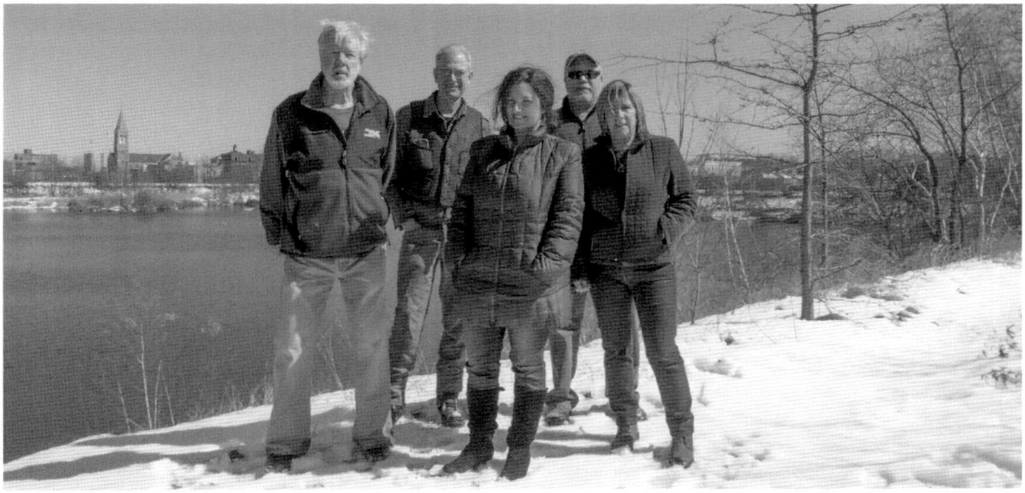

Steve Latham

In 2000, Steve Latham (second from left) and his children Hawk and Willow walked for the first time into Reservoir No. 3, a monumental water supply station erected in 1871–1880 to provide drinking water to surrounding municipalities and nearby Ellis Island. After he heard that city officials were planning to drain and demolish the site to make way for development, Steve sought the help of community activists and formed the Jersey City Reservoir Preservation Alliance. Through their efforts, Reservoir No. 3 was ultimately saved, listed in the National Register of Historic Places, and opened to the public for fishing, kayaking, and art activities.

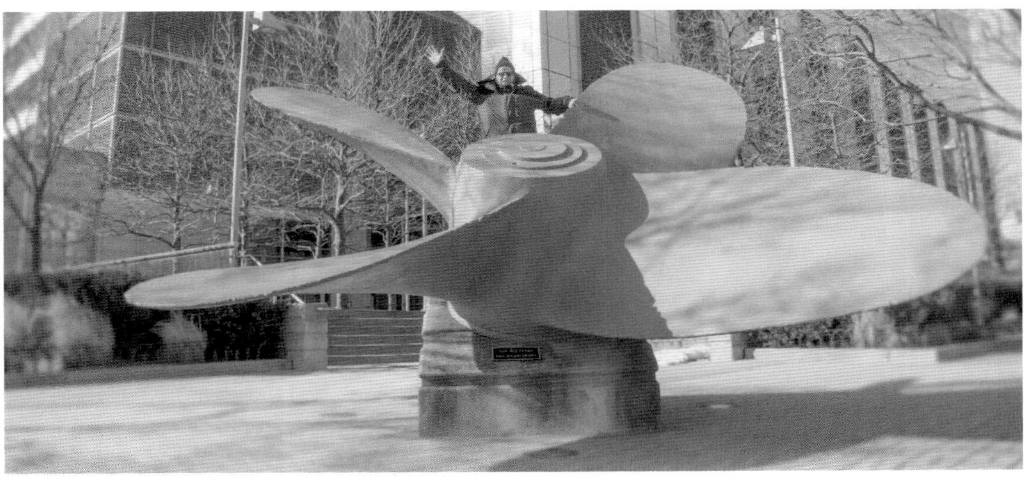

Leon Yost

Leon Yost is an all-in-one preservationist; he is a street activist, architectural historian, city planner, urban photographer, arts supporter, and advisor and mentor to community organizers. Yost served on the Jersey City Planning Board from 2001 to 2012, playing a pivotal role in the adoption and approval of LEED-certified construction methods and projects and even prompting developers to incorporate mammoth century-old merchant ship propellers into their public plazas. Yost is renowned nationally as a documentarian of prehistoric Native American petroglyphs; has produced full-color local history calendars since the 1990s; and, with Cynthia Harris, coauthored *Changing Jersey City: A History in Photographs* (Schiffer Books, 2009).

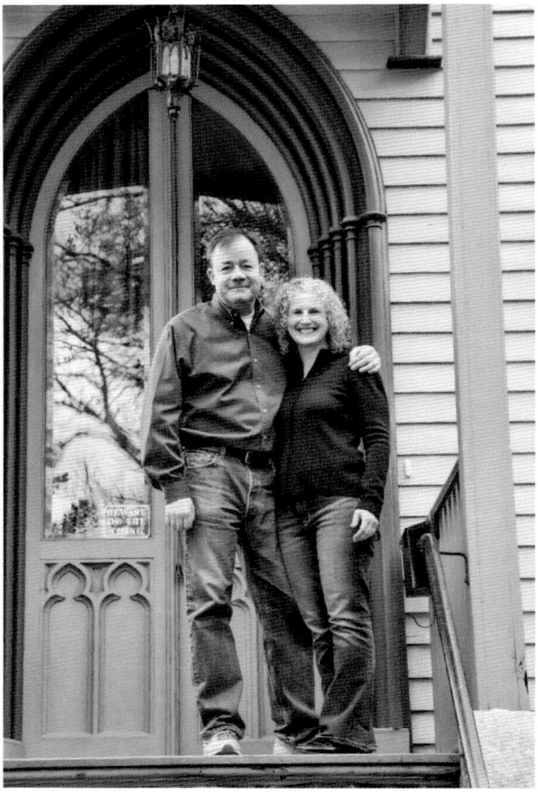

Carol Losos and Judson Weaver

Since 2006, Carol Losos and Judson Weaver have owned the only vernacular Gothic Revival house in Jersey City. Set far back from the Ogden Avenue sidewalk, their c. 1862 mansion was methodically restored and revived, including the repair of parlor pocket doors; the replication of missing moldings; the conservation of surviving clapboards; and the erection of a modernist addition propped up on stilts so as to maintain the property's historical layout and landscaping. At the conclusion of construction, the family buried a time capsule filled with found objects, coins, photographs, and a letter addressed to the owners of the future.

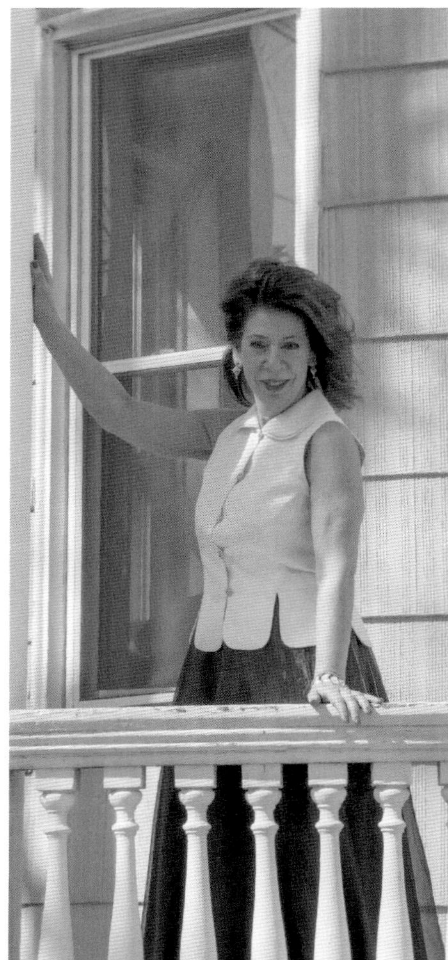

Hope Susan Barett

No one has shown more commitment to their historic home than Hope Susan Barett. When in 2005 she bought the stately 1906–1907 Joseph H. Rudiger Mansion, famous for its soaring exterior pillars and rotunda porch, high hedges, and electrified-eye sentinel owls, she found a dilapidated boardinghouse with missing moldings, fixtures, and fireplaces. From 2006 to the present, she has been painstakingly restoring original fabric, repurposing bricks and stained glass and importing red cedar fish-scale tiles for the facades, making the manse the architectural icon it used to be.

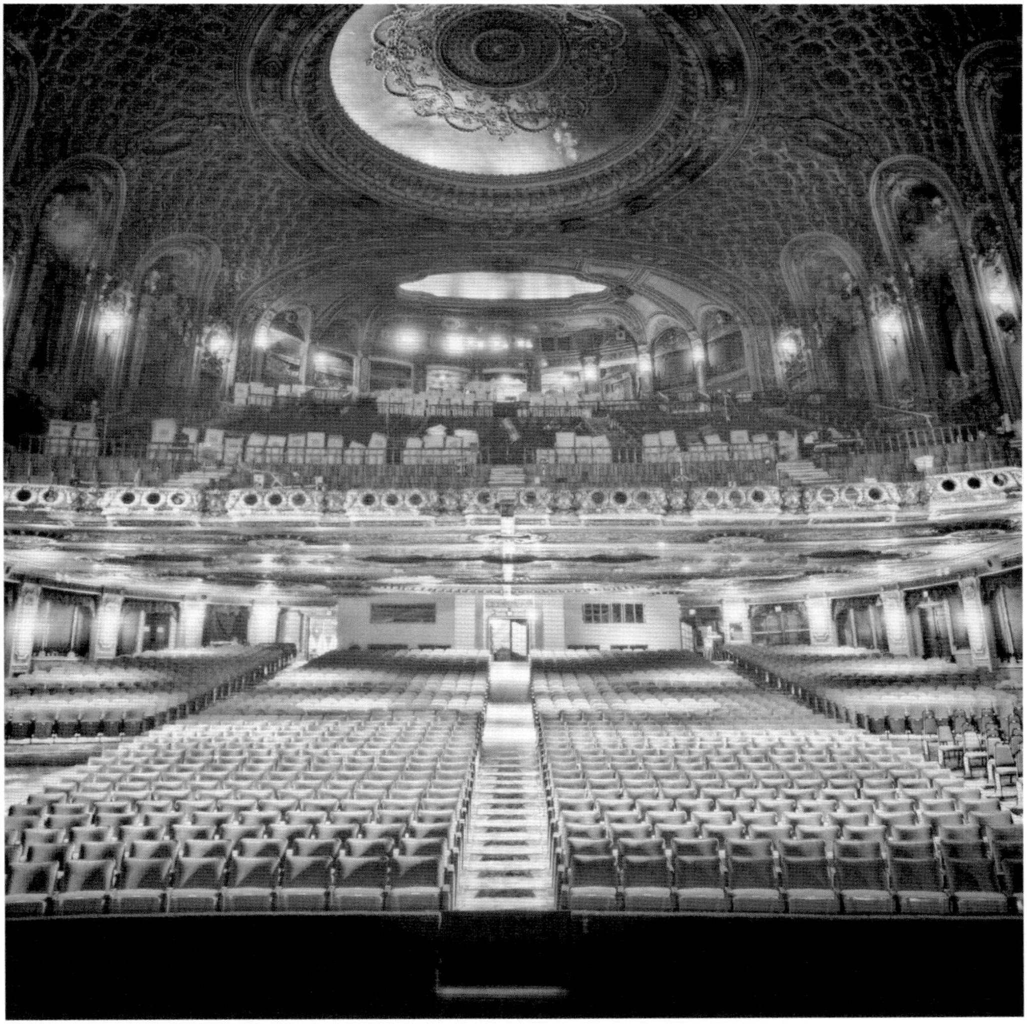

Friends of the Loew's

One day, in 1987, close friends Colin Egan and Walter Syrek were waiting in a car on Kennedy Boulevard, when, looking to their right, they took notice of the Loew's Jersey Theatre, the legendary movie palace that opened in 1929 and was now shuttered and slated for demolition. "It's a shame they are going to take that down without a fight," Colin commented. Walter, an architect, told him about a planning board meeting scheduled for the following week. When they went, they inadvertently ran into legendary preservationist Ted Conrad, who was virtually the lone attendee. From that moment, the campaign for the building was launched. Colin and Walter eventually met up with other like-minded Loew's advocates like Patty Giordan, forming the Save the Loew's Task Force as part of the Jersey City Historical & Preservation Association, an umbrella advocacy organization that Ted and other preservationists had been involved with. In spite of the cynicism coming from city hall and local developers who wanted to build an office tower on the site, Colin and his colleagues persevered, attending countless meetings, going to court to stop demolition permits from being released, lobbying city officials, and officially incorporating as the Friends of the Loew's. In 1993, pressured by intense public support and standing-room-only crowds, the city council voted to purchase the landmark movie palace and, with the Friends as managers and curators, convert it into a performing and cultural arts center.

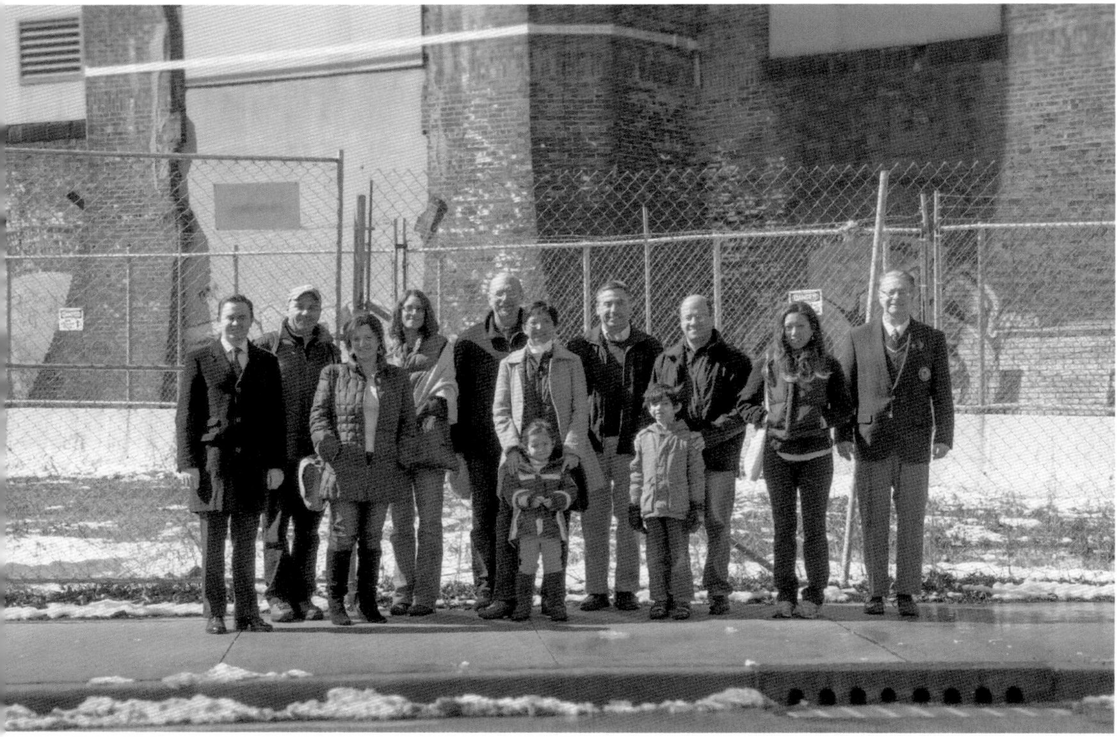

Jersey City Landmarks Conservancy

Established in 1999 by founding board members Charles Kessler, Dan Frohwirth, Joseph Cosenza, Rene Escobar, Joan Doherty-Lovero, and the Rev. Thomas Murphy, the Jersey City Landmarks Conservancy grew out of the battle to save the threatened Hudson & Manhattan Railroad Powerhouse. As the nonprofit organization started to take shape and gain recognition, other locals got involved, including past president Joshua Parkhurst and board members Mike Selender, Cynthia Hadjiyannis, Dan Levin, Lycel Villanueva, and Charlene Burke. From its inception, the conservancy has believed that public recognition must be bestowed upon those who preside over the city's physical and intrinsic patrimony. The annual JCLC Preservation Awards Ceremony, held every May during National Preservation Month, celebrates local preservation practitioners and heroes. Over the last dozen years, the group, through its website, e-mail subscriber list, and social network channels, has fought hard for the preservation and proper care of major landmarks like Reservoir No. 3, Whitlock Cordage, Holland Street, and St. John's Episcopal Church. Today, the conservancy is thriving under the leadership of board members Richelle Reyes, Dennis Doran, John Hallanan III, Dan Frohwirth, Norrice Raymaker, Andrew Doran, Lycel Villanueva, Justin Frohwirth, Dr. Rebecca Shapiro, and Dr. Jennifer S. Furlong. (Right, courtesy of Ed Mullen/Jersey City Landmarks Conservancy.)

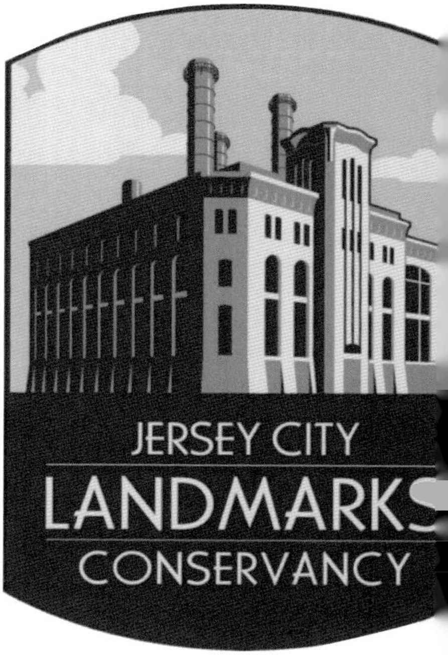

CHAPTER SIX

Architects Among Us

Architects, from the primordial to the postmodern, are conjoined by centuries, drawing their vertical visions from the same architectural well; unified intent, expression, and creativity are consistent and clear throughout time; originality is never lost. Architects who have called the city home—or have passed through, leaving their indelible structural signatures—have been a pivotal part of the municipal persona since the earliest days of settlement when architecture was manifested by the mason and the carpenter and when locally sourced materials, hand-hewn and tamed by hammer and chisel, added to the region's rich vernacularity and visual purity. The first Dutch homesteads in the hamlets of Communipaw, Pavonia, Harsimus, and Bergen Village were crafted out of ashlar sandstone blocks or earth-kilned yellow bricks; roofs were stepped with gables or sloped with straw skins; great gated gardens were fed by untainted brooks. No architectural elements were wasted. When houses were cleared from their lots, builders reused materials, creating new municipal entities and adding to the mystique and beauty of the age.

In the mid- to late 19th century, iron and steel construction advancements allowed architects to build boxier and taller. Electric saws and steam crane apparatuses, brought on by the genius engineers of industrial revolutions, allowed architects to be more precise, pronounced, and poignant in their facade proportions, rustications, and angularities. Colossal claddings could be hoisted high; sculptors and craftsmen could cut and shape more sophisticated woods, metals, and terra-cotta elements. Flamboyant Victorian and mansard-roofed manses, wrapped in verandas and porches and flanked by rear carriage houses; narrow-lotted cast-iron loft warehouses soldiered in symphonic rows; six-story-tall immigrant tenements stacked on slender streets; bulky Neoclassical civic buildings pinnacled inside dense city centers; sprawling parks landscaped with Rome-influenced fountains, piazzas, and pavilions—all appeared in and dramatically defined, street by added street, a flourishing Jersey City. Library Hall, erected in 1865 as the first municipal public meeting place in the short-lived Bergen City section; the Gothic-shadowed 1870s-era homesteads of Lafayette, set back and deepened by old forest tree-filled yards; the Thomas J. Stewart furniture warehouse on Erie Street and the New Jersey Title Guarantee & Trust Company Bank Building on Montgomery Street, two tour-de-forces of terra-cotta and brownstone ornamentation designed by local architect Herman Kreitler (1841–1915), were all reflections of their architectural time.

The 20th century brought bolder building opportunities for the architect in Jersey City. Verticality became the architectural rage; elevator bank engineering, steel cage construction, and mass-produced modular components pushed aside the need for small structures, largely replacing the arts-and-crafts mentality that had so mirrored the late 19th and early 20th centuries. Suddenly voluminous cooperative apartment buildings replaced firetrap tenements and wasted-space mansions; large school buildings enveloped overcrowded ramshackle schoolhouses. Ancillary cities within the mother city were created, as John T. Rowland Jr. and Christian Ziegler, Frank Hague's hand-picked architectural team during his long reign as mayor, demonstrated with their Depression-era Jersey City Medical Center campus. Local bank buildings, including the 1920–1922 First National Bank, a spectacular Spanish Renaissance edifice designed by British architect Alfred Charles Bossom, soared higher; department stores were cored through with deep showrooms and tinned ceilings; movie palaces replaced tiny vaudeville houses with vast dream-void interiors.

Starting in the early 1950s and coming to a high point in the 1970s, modernism afforded new architectural opportunities and lexicons. The 1950 Bethany Swedish Lutheran Church, designed by master Swedish architect Martin Hedmark (1896–1980), gave Jersey City its first Scandinavian landmark. Comparetto & Kenny's 1952 Hudson County Hall of Records and Administration Building introduced the commercial International-style tower, modeled after Gordon Bunshaft's seminal Lever House in Manhattan. In 1968, Ann Willis, one of Jersey City's few women architects, created a bold, absolutely original Brutalist edifice for Trinity United Methodist Church on Summit Avenue.

From the 1980s to today's green architecture movement, Jersey City has been at the very vanguard, with world and local architects dreaming up towers for a left-bank corridor facing off with New York City. At the edge of the main Jersey City waterfront, shining glass skyscrapers designed by Grad Associates, Cesar Pelli, Costas Kondylis, Gruzen Samton, DeWitt Tishman, and CetraRuddy are front-running the scene. Independent architects and smaller firms are not to be ignored; their work and commissions, in fact, are what make Jersey City's new or preserved architecture distinctive and exciting. Manny Naval and Debra David have taken historic preservation architecture to new heights; Lindemon Winckelmann Deupree Martin Russell & Associates, long established in Jersey City, creates infill architecture that is both traditionalist and thoroughly contemporary; and GRO Architects, a husband-and-wife team, has quickly become the city's most daring firm.

These architects' collective works are viewed with unwavering awe and celebrated in research, through preservation campaigns, and at their ground breakings and reveals. Architects are the greatest of civic philosophers, prescient planners of elevated skies, inventors of scaled cities, and poets who write verse in stone and steel. Jersey City is a city of architectural breakthroughs and monuments—some ancient, others instant—because of them.

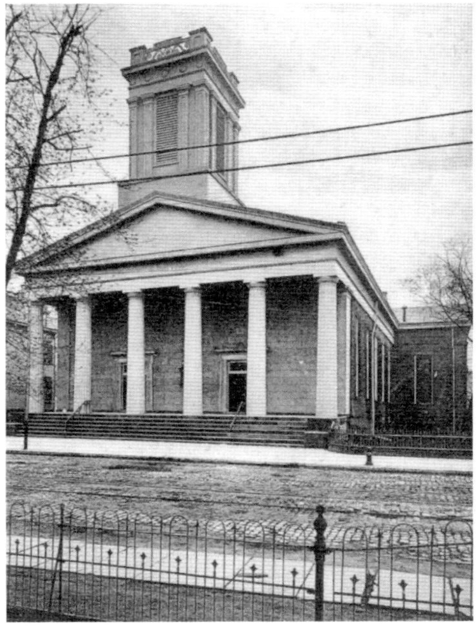

Andrew Clark and William H. Kirk

The first major architects to work in Jersey City were Andrew Clark, a prominent practitioner of the vernacular Greek Revival who designed many of the Paulus Hook brownstones on Grand and Sussex Streets, and William H. Kirk of Newark, a master mason who later became an influential state senator. From 1841 to 1842, Clark and Kirk worked with the centuries-old Dutch clans of the city to design a new Bergen Dutch Reformed Church, which is recognized as New Jersey's oldest religious institution, having been founded in 1662 after the establishment of Bergen Village. On Bergen Avenue, the two architects created an awesome Greek Revival temple, merged with the chiseled sandstone blocks and cornerstones salvaged from two earlier churches—a linked architectural lineage. Although no longer a Dutch congregation, the tall, heavy doors to this National Register–listed house of worship are open to a 21st-century public. (Collection of the Jersey City Landmarks Conservancy.)

John T. Rowland Jr.

John T. Rowland Jr. (1871–1945), pictured second from right, is Jersey City's greatest architect if only for his extraordinary output. His iconic buildings include Dickinson High School (1904; 1911); Jersey City Medical Center (1929–1941); and 2600 Hudson Boulevard (1922). Educated at Cornell, Rowland was Mayor Frank Hague's anointed architect, and when he died at the age of 73, Hague lamented: "I am greatly shocked by the untimely death of Mr. Rowland, who was one of my personal and dear friends. . . . My heartfelt sympathy is extended to his bereaved family." (Courtesy of the Jersey City Free Public Library.)

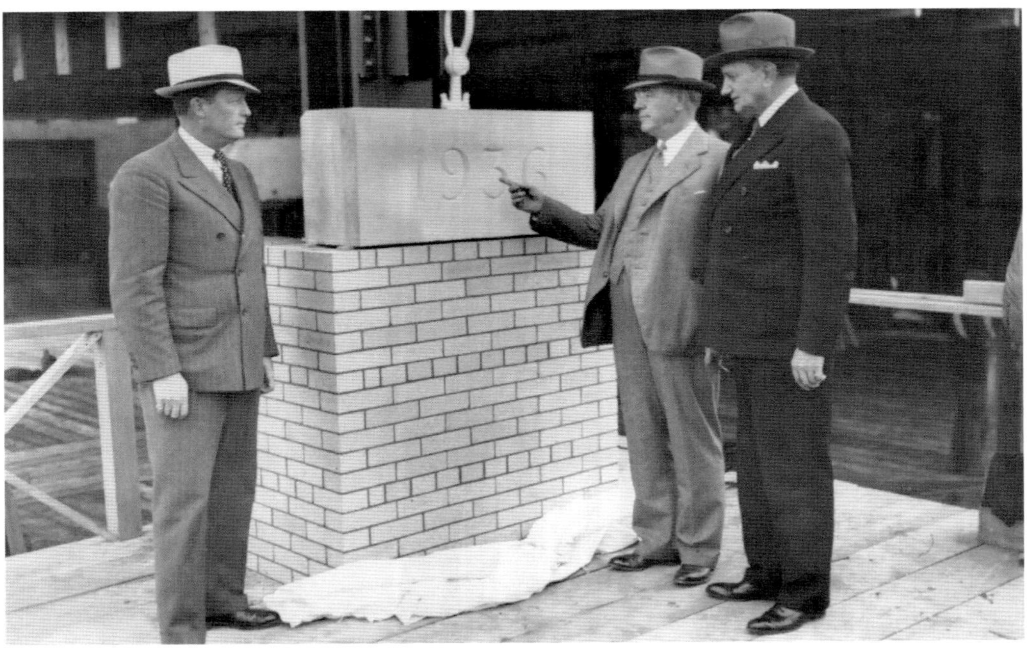

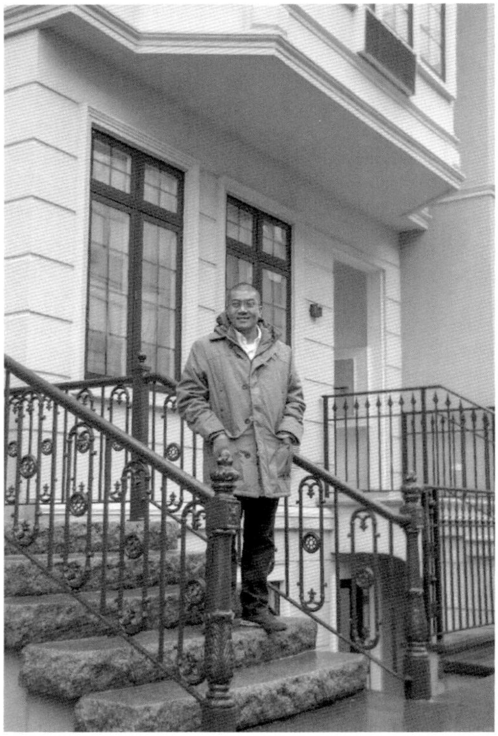

Emmanuel M. Naval

Emmanuel M. Naval may just be Jersey City's most gifted preservation architect; he is certainly its most prolific and hardworking. Like John T. Rowland Jr. a century before him, his touch can be seen everywhere. Contractors, construction code officials, city inspectors, tradespeople, engineers, and fellow architects, all know him well as the architect who is on site, clipboard, iPad, and folded plans in hand. Developers and homeowners alike seek his services because of his attention to detail, his willingness to work with clients on layout and program, and the way he makes them feel that their project is the only project that matters. This visible commitment comes, Manny explains, from his growing up in Jersey City surrounded by magical neighborhood monuments. There was no doubt, despite the lure and promise of a career as a classical concert pianist, that he would add to that constructed enchantment. Born in the Philippines, Manny came to Jersey City with his older sister Maria and his parents, who set out to establish their respective professions in engineering and medicine. Manny attended local schools before studying architecture at Vassar College, where he was mentored and inspired by the famous architect Jeh Vincent Johnson, and New Jersey Institute of Technology. The 1990s were dedicated to internships and foundational employment, working on housing, ecclesiastical, and transportation projects. In 2000, Manny began a 10-year sojourn at Inglese Architecture & Engineering, a respected local firm that introduced him to historic preservation, adaptive reuse, and traditionalist infill in and near historic districts. Manny's legacy at the firm is felt in such high-profile commissions as Liberty Harbor North, a new ultra-postmodern neighborhood along the downtown area's south waterfront; and Torico Ice Cream, a landmark Puerto-Rican business founded in 1968 by Pura and Peter Berrios. In 2010, Manny broke out on his own and founded Hampton Hill Architecture. His inspiration to do so not only came from his wife, Cora, but also from a recollection he had back in college—that the celebrated architect, designer, and theorist Aldo Rossi (1931–1997) practiced the form exclusively in his hometown. "By being a lifelong resident," Manny says, "he got what the city was about, and therefore it was natural for him to express that city," which is an extraordinary precedent for Manny's own vernacular vocation.

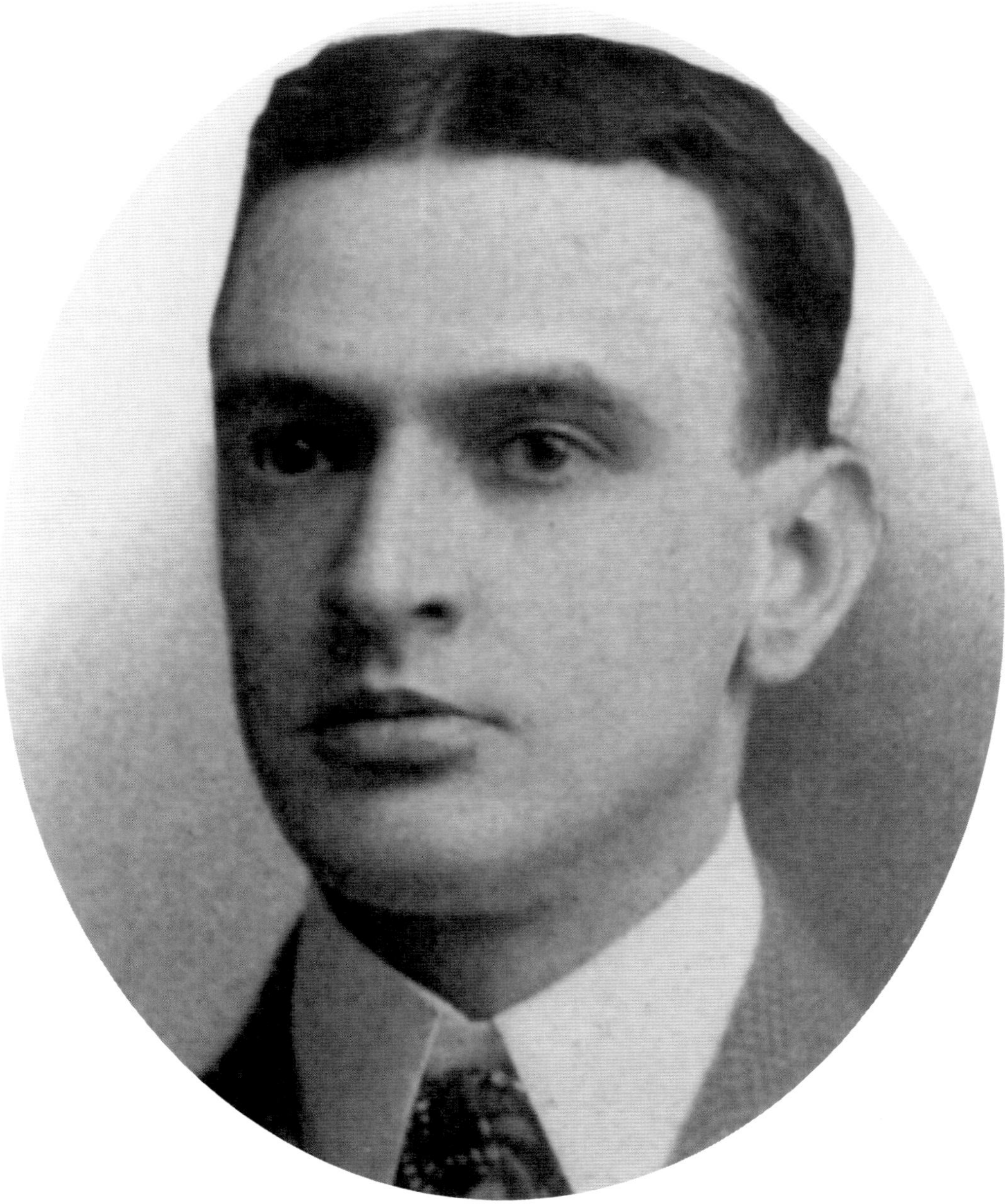

Hugh Roberts

Hugh Roberts (1867–1928) is the architect of the Hudson County Justice William J. Brennan Jr. Courthouse, Jersey City's supreme architectural monument and the soaring symbol of the city's preservation movement in the 1960s. Located on Newark Avenue in the commercial shadows of Journal Square and Five Corners, the granite and marble "temple of justice" eclipsed every other Beaux-Arts edifice in the city, and some architecture critics say the country, when it opened in 1910. Roberts's fame came with controversy, however—he was accused of overspending by several million dollars and faced a grand jury. Ultimately, he was found not guilty, but never worked in the same capacity again. (Courtesy of the Newark Public Library.)

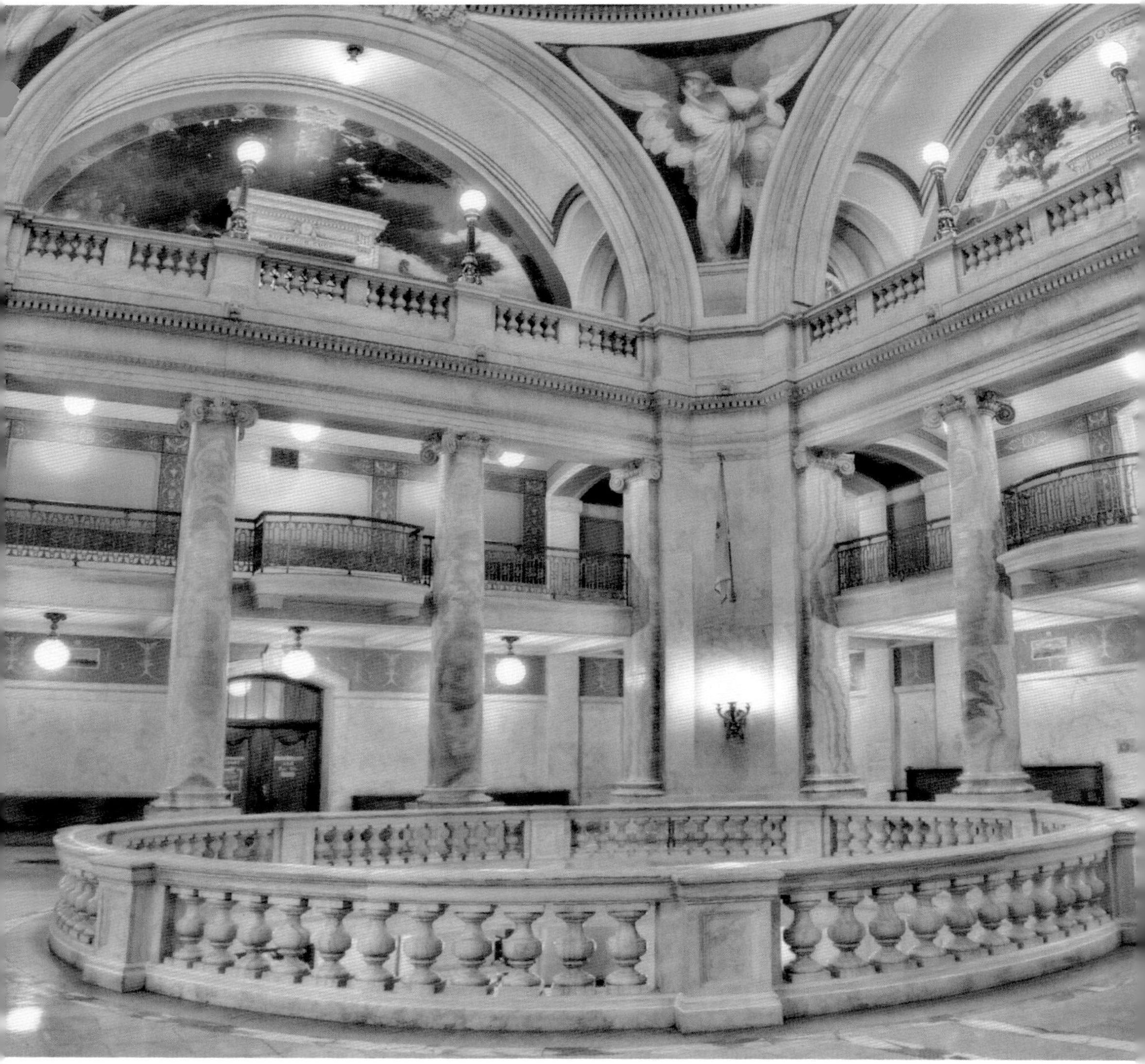

Old Masters
The Hudson County Justice William J. Brennan Jr. Courthouse is decorated with paintings by the greatest muralists working during the American Renaissance, including Edwin Howland Blashfield, Charles Yardley Turner, Kenyon Cox, Howard Pyle, and Francis David Millet, and Jersey City's own Vincent Aderente. Architect Roberts entrusted Millet, who supervised the decoration scheme, to surpass Cass Gilbert's Essex County Courthouse in nearby Newark—and many consider the Brennan Courthouse murals to be more supreme in scope and majesty.

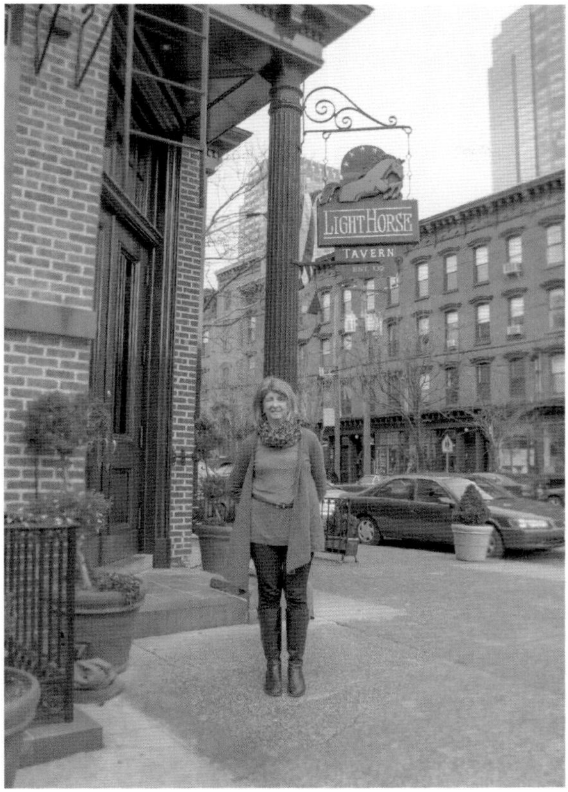

Debra David

Debra David came to architecture by way of the social sciences. At Purdue University, where she was pursuing a degree in child development and early childhood education, she worked on an assignment that required her to lay out classrooms for young learners. Later, while going for her master's in human development at Colorado State University, her thesis explored how the built environment affected the behavior of children. As she readied herself to work with architects in programming educational spaces, she decided that becoming an architect herself was the best course of action and a means of tapping into the teacher within. Her journey through architecture took her to numerous firms where she learned the architectural ropes. She was an early advocate of AutoCAD and computer-based drawing and planning and came to understand the vitality of adaptive reuse and gut-rehabilitation. After working for such firms as Soffes Wood and the Jersey City Heights–based Lee Levine Architects, Debra started her own firm, Debra David RA Architecture, right from her Hamilton Park apartment and, later, her home in Montclair. Almost immediately, and to her delight, her jobs entailed the puzzle-piecing-together and transformation of historic edifices. "My favorite type of project is a rundown, broken down, and falling down brick building built in the mid- to late 19th century," she says, "with bits and pieces of interior and exterior detailing still intact." Nowhere is this rehabilitation philosophy more on display than at Light Horse Tavern in the Paulus Hook Historic District. Owned by Ron Smith and Bill Gray, the popular tavern and restaurant is a former ramshackle 19th-century tenement built when Paulus Hook was known as "Gammontown," an Irish immigrant ward. Debra, in close collaboration with Ron and Bill, saved vital architectural fabric but introduced new and retro materials, arriving at a spectacular modern space with traditional touches. Proud of every project she tackles and the recipient of much-deserved recognition, including stints on the HGTV shows *ReZoned* and *You Live in What?*, Debra declares, "I want people to know that the sky is the limit with these old buildings—and you can work within zoning, planning, and historic preservation parameters to come up with something really special."

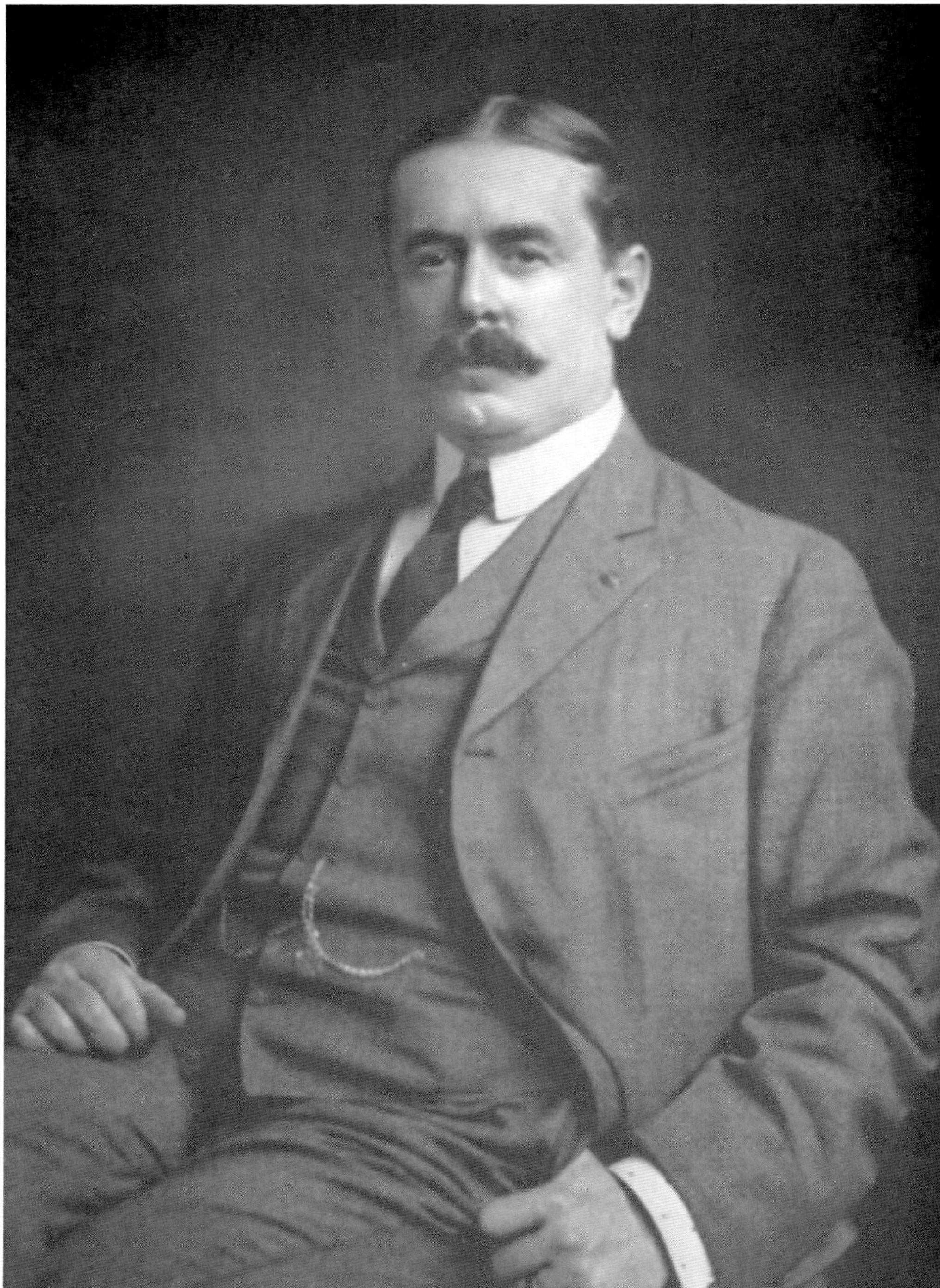

J. Hollis Wells

J. Hollis Wells (1864–1926) stands apart from his local architectural peers. He was the first to design a major American Renaissance–era edifice in Jersey City, and he was a national war hero. A graduate of Lehigh University, Wells's first commission in Jersey City on behalf of the New York City–based firm of Clinton & Russell was the Bergen and Lafayette Trust Company (1902–1903) at Monticello Avenue and Brinkerhoff Street in the Bergen Hill district. A mini Beaux-Arts masterwork of stunning solidity, the bank was built for the immigrant merchants of Monticello and Jackson avenues. Afterwards, Wells, a decorated colonel who rode side-by-side with Teddy Roosevelt and the Rough Riders in the 71st Regiment up San Juan Hill in Cuba during the Spanish-American War, designed the City Hospital (1905–1908) on a promontory on Baldwin Avenue and the Trust Company of New Jersey (below), a tall Neoclassical bank building erected in 1920–1922 in Journal Square. Nationally, Wells gained prominence for his 1906–1908 design of the Apthorp apartments on the Upper West Side of Manhattan; the Hotel Astor (1909–1910); and, his crowning architectural achievement, the Hudson & Manhattan Railroad Company's Hudson Terminal (1906–1909), a majestic Italian Renaissance twin-tower edifice that prefigured the World Trade Center towers by Minoru Yamasaki (1912–1986). (Left, courtesy of the Jersey City Free Public Library; below, courtesy of Avery Architectural & Fine Arts Library, Columbia University.)

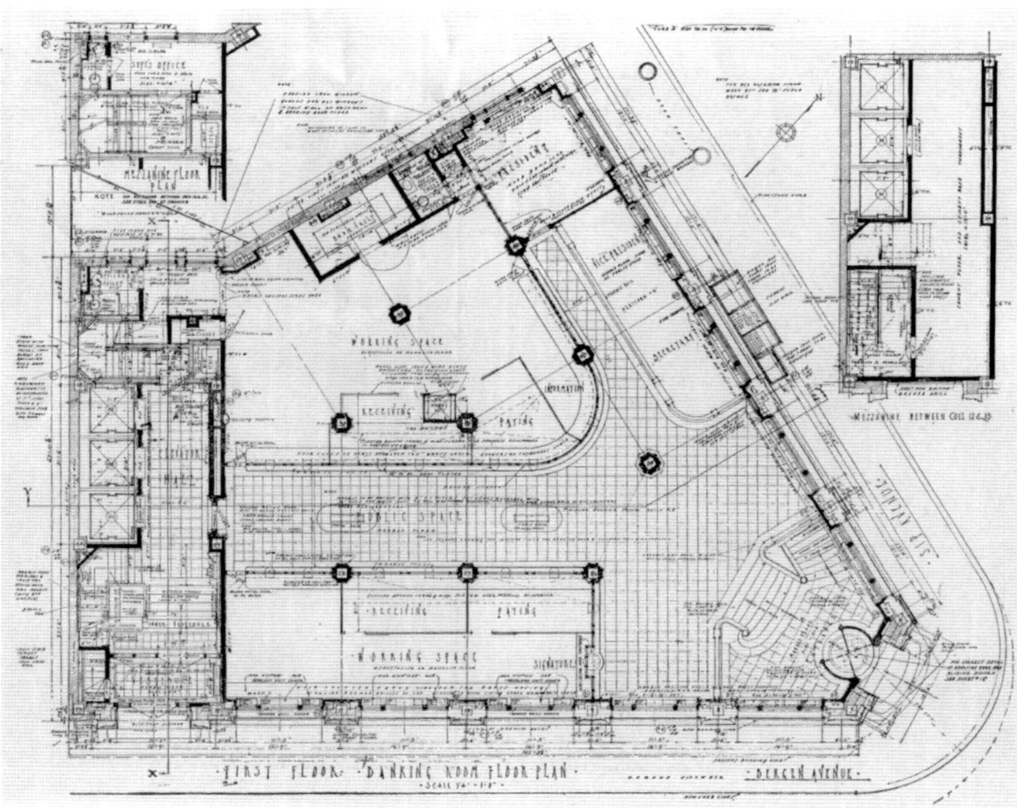

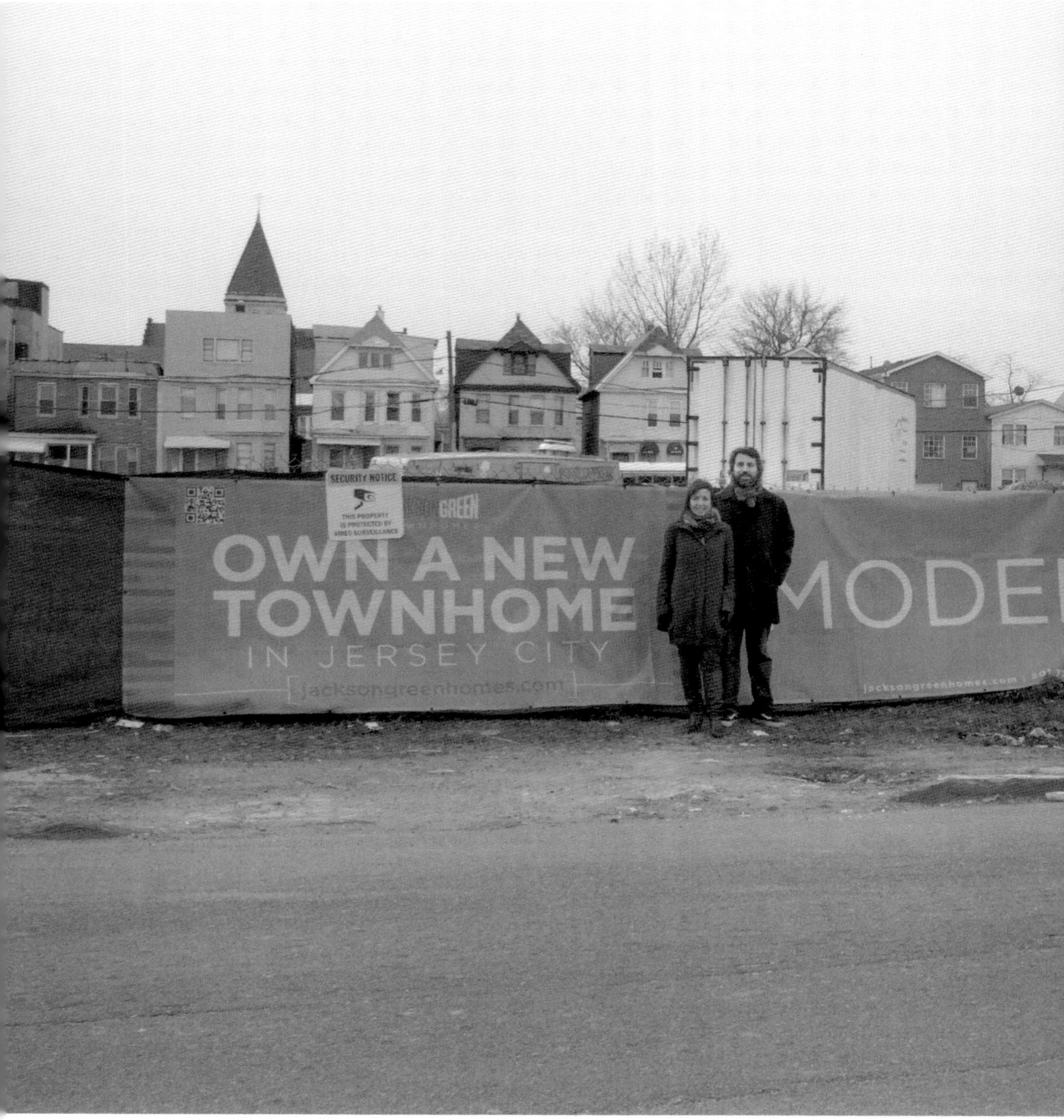

Nicole Robertson and Richard Garber

Nicole Robertson and Richard Garber, of GRO Architects, are architects who put the community and environment first. They conceive and bring to fruition public and private vernacular housing that is ultra-sustainable and adds directly to the rich architectural vocabulary and visual vitality of Jersey City's inner neighborhoods. Inventive and cutting-edge, the married architectural force has, since 2006, been gaining recognition and awards for their PREttyFAB "urban infill" energy efficient housing type, composed of prefabricated concrete panels and photovoltaic panels, and first manifested at 1 Minerva Street in the Bergen-Lafayette section of Jersey City. The house, sharply angled and pointed, perfectly exemplifies the architects' forward-thinking philosophy, which is grounded in digital design and fabrication and

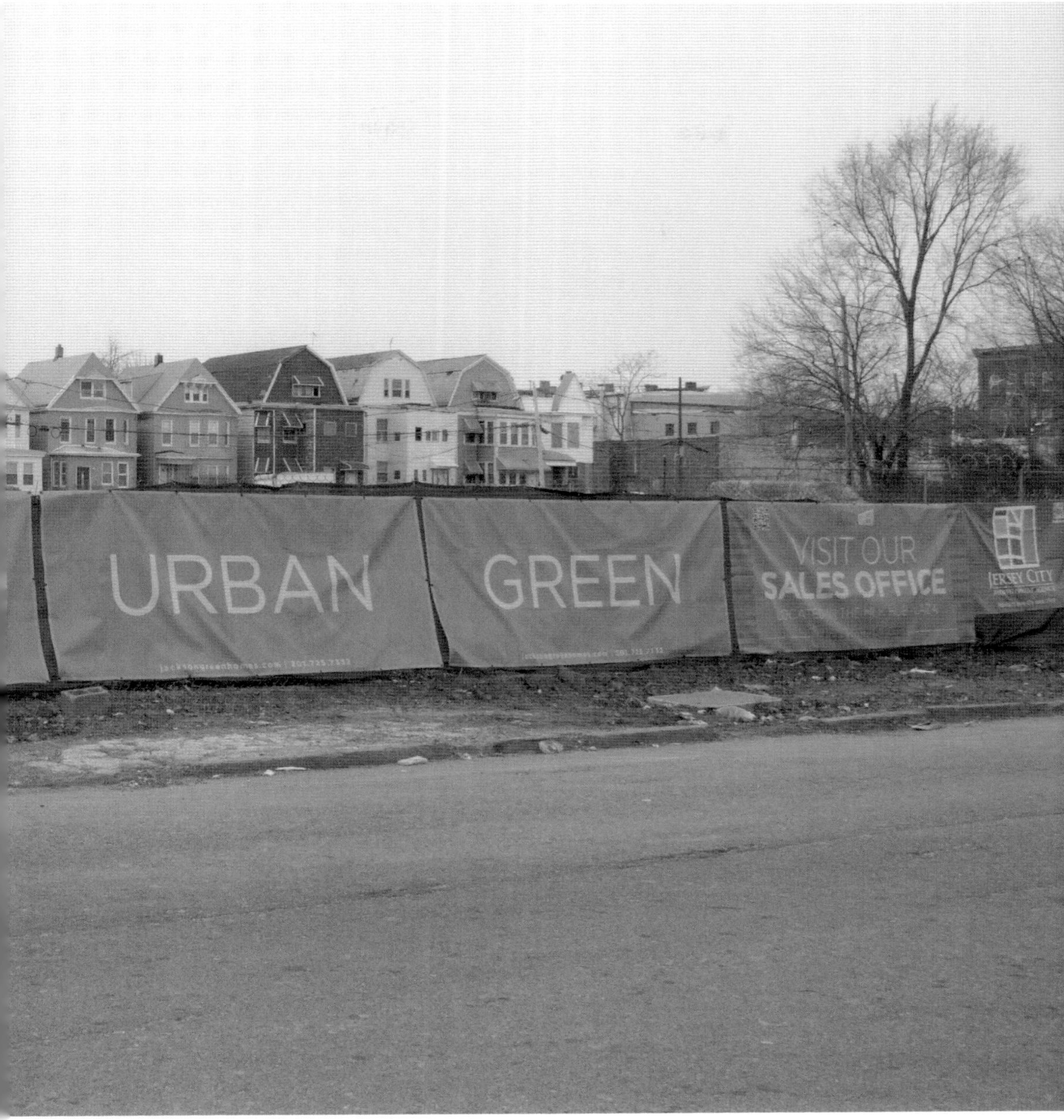

experiments with new and advanced materials and modular forms and pushes architecture to new technological heights. Their latest Jersey City project, Jackson Green—an affordable town house–style development that recently broke ground in the "Hub" section of the city, on Orient, Kearny, and Rose Avenues near Martin Luther King Drive—promises to be a crowning municipal achievement, with solar hot-water heaters, ECO lumber, and a Greensulate Jakob vertical steel cable trellis system that supports the growth of vegetation irrigated by rainwater collected from the roof. "We have become very interested in bringing innovative design to Jersey City," says Richard, an associate professor at New Jersey Institute of Technology in Newark, "seeing this city as a place for creative expression and sophisticated approaches to designing the urban environment."

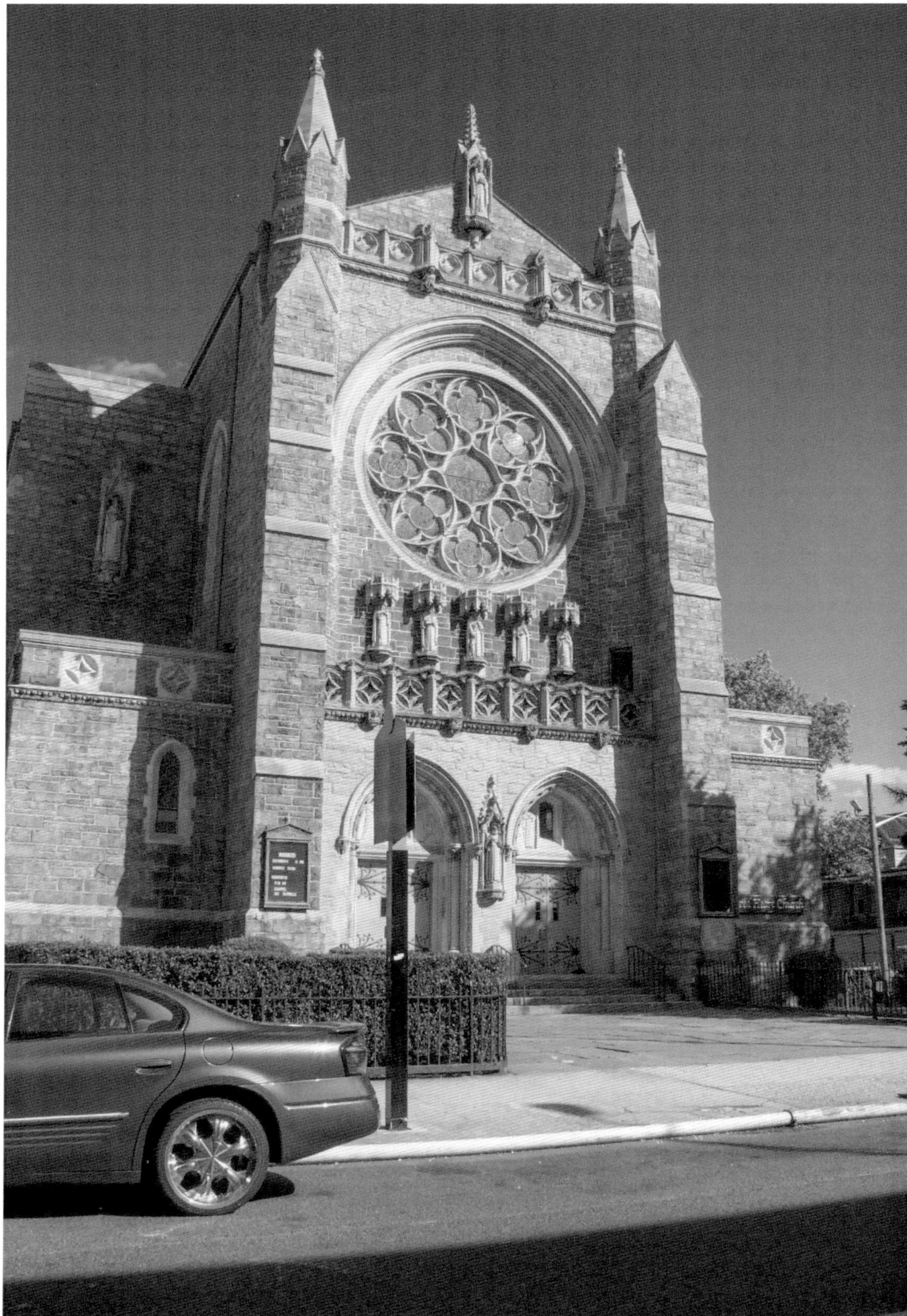

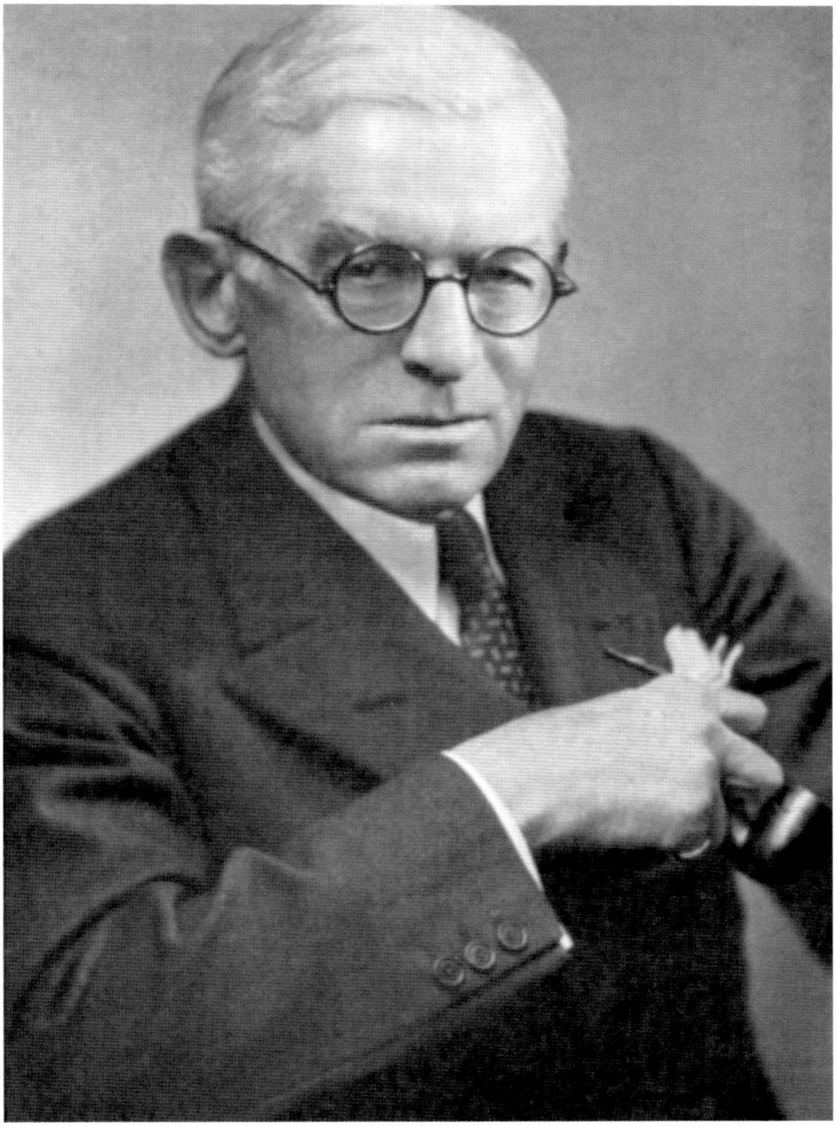

Ralph Adams Cram

In 1922, the eminent Boston architect Ralph Adams Cram (1863–1942), returning from his first sojourn in Spain, was hired by the Dominican Order of Friars of Jersey City's Sacred Heart parish to design a Spanish Gothic edifice that would rival and surpass St. Vincent Ferrer, the mother Dominican church in Manhattan erected a few years prior by Cram's former partner and nemesis, Bertram Grosvenor Goodhue (1869–1924). When completed in 1924, Sacred Heart was an instant Arts-and-Crafts masterwork with woodcarvings by Irving & Casson; chapel tiles by Mary Chase Perry; wrought-iron screens by Samuel Yellin; and a rose window by 18-year-old Harry Wright Goodhue. After 80 years of serving the Greenville community, Sacred Heart's doors were closed in 2005; its future remains uncertain. (Courtesy of the Jersey City Landmarks Conservancy.)

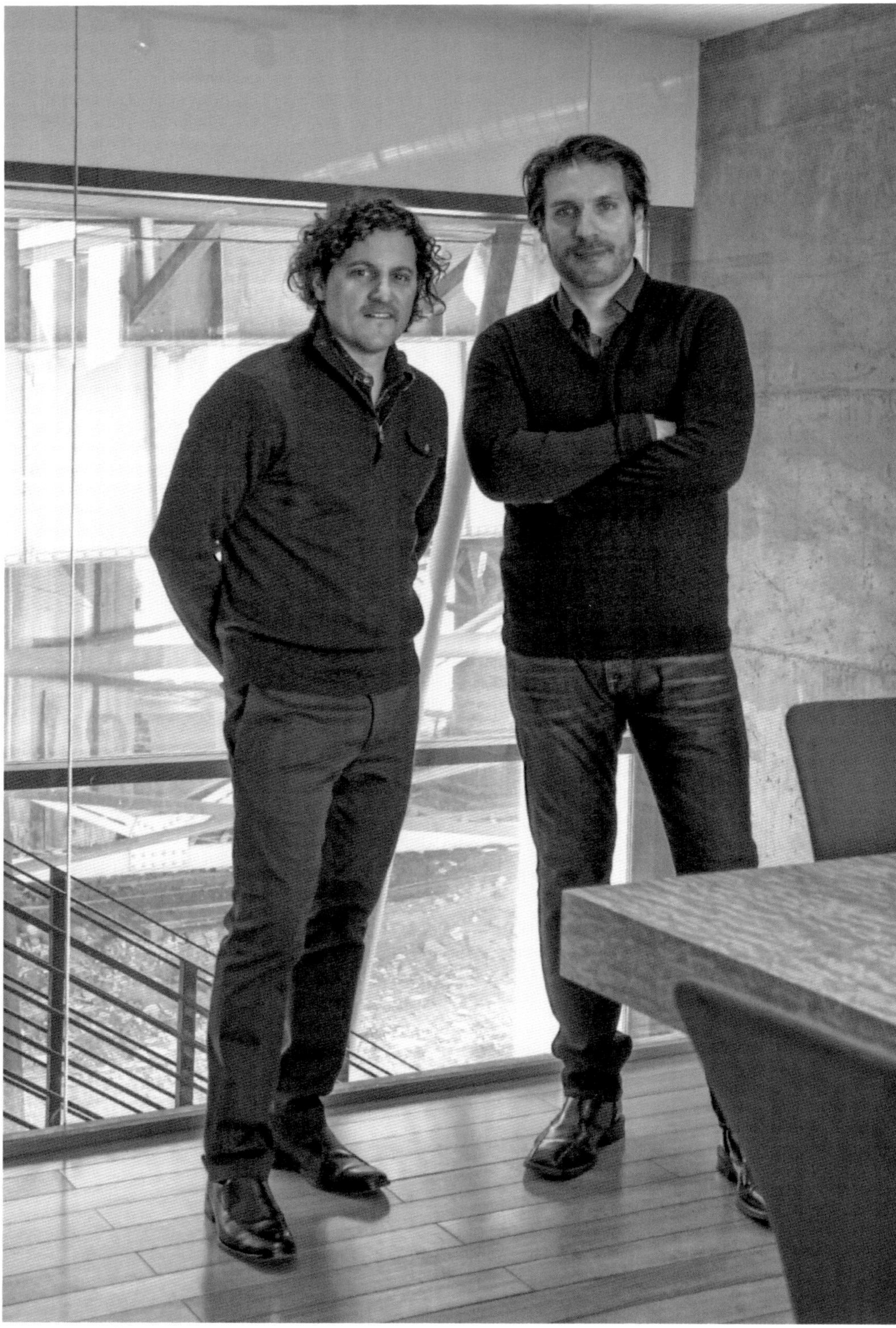

Minervini Vandermark Architecture

The collection of buildings that preservationists will be defending a century from now as important vernacular postmodernist architecture comes from Minervini Vandermark Architecture. The firm's structures are original, well-crafted works that are easily identifiable by and imprinted with their trademark use of earthen-hued envelopes; terra-cotta-like bricks; soaring glass; and canting and tilting smooth steel skins. Their Jersey City commissions include WALDO Lofts, a 12-story, 82-unit residential tower on Second Street with tall Romanesque windows and dark redbrick facades inspired by the nearby Hudson & Manhattan Railroad Powerhouse; m650 Flats, a former industrial warehouse on Montgomery Street sensitively transformed by the firm into an imposing edifice of ancient fabric and modern materials; and Library Hall (below), built in 1865 as a library, city hall, post office, and community center. Founded in 2000 in a small basement apartment by principals Frank J. Minervini and Anthony C. Vandermark (opposite, right to left), the firm, now headquartered in spacious quarters on Fourteenth Street in Hoboken, is currently working with Brunelleschi Construction on reinventing a former Erie Street telephone building designed by Rudolph L. Daus (1854–1916) and erected in 1891–1892.

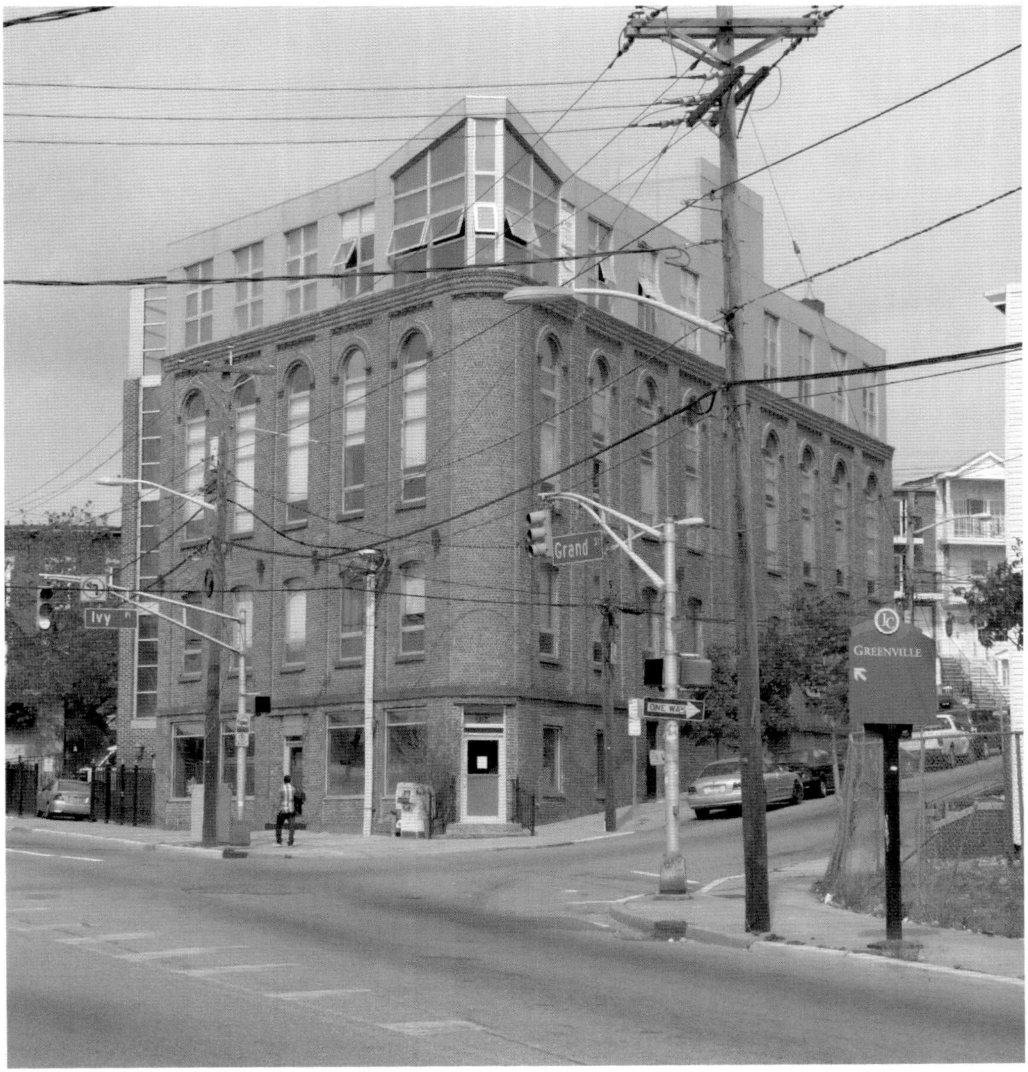

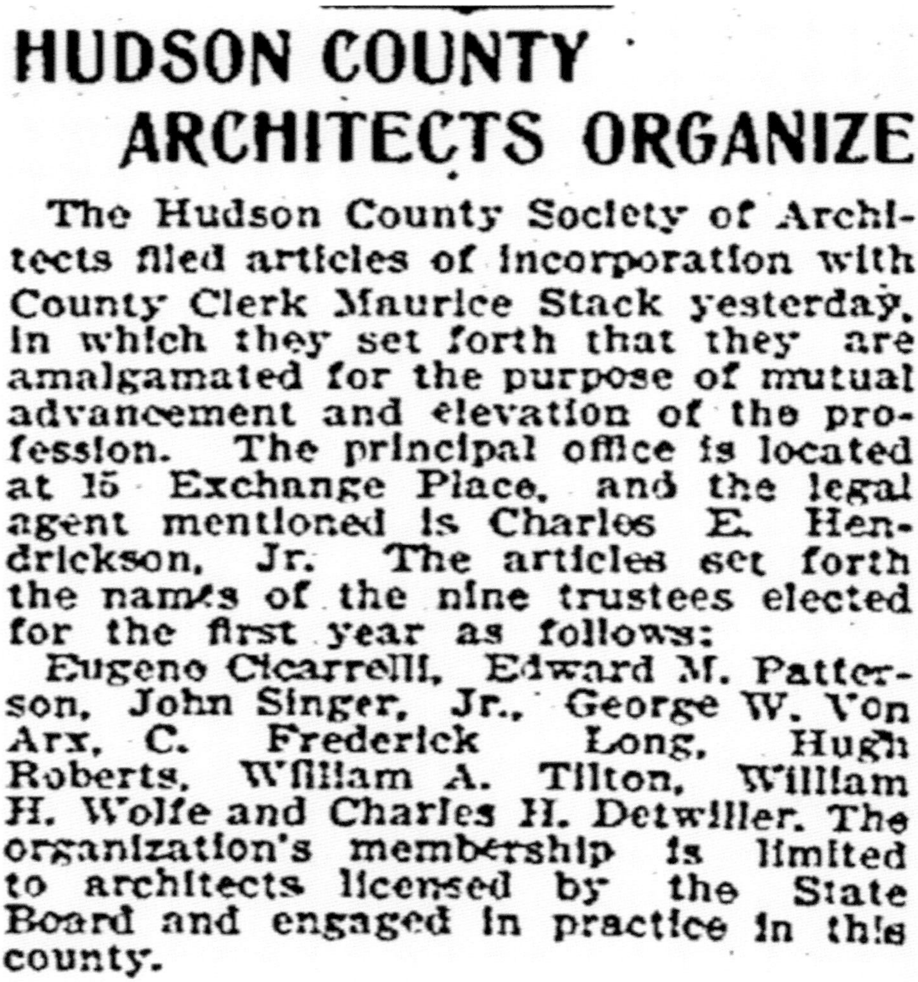

HUDSON COUNTY ARCHITECTS ORGANIZE

The Hudson County Society of Architects filed articles of incorporation with County Clerk Maurice Stack yesterday, in which they set forth that they are amalgamated for the purpose of mutual advancement and elevation of the profession. The principal office is located at 15 Exchange Place, and the legal agent mentioned is Charles E. Hendrickson, Jr. The articles set forth the names of the nine trustees elected for the first year as follows:

Eugeno Cicarrelli, Edward M. Patterson, John Singer, Jr., George W. Von Arx, C. Frederick Long, Hugh Roberts, William A. Tilton, William H. Wolfe and Charles H. Detwiller. The organization's membership is limited to architects licensed by the State Board and engaged in practice in this county.

Hudson County Society of Architects

Though forgotten today, the Hudson County Society of Architects was incorporated in 1904 as an offshoot of the Newark-based New Jersey Society of Architects, the forerunner to the New Jersey Chapter of the American Institute of Architects that still exists today, and was "amalgamated for the purpose of mutual advancement and elevation of the profession." Its mission—to assist Jersey City and Hudson County architects in obtaining commissions and becoming aware of design opportunities; to ensure fair and untainted design competitions and bidding processes; to establish rigorous architectural licensure requirements, examinations, and pay scales; to demand superior design and construction standards; to create a strict code of architectural ethics and expectations; and to help write and legislatively pass tenement house laws in order to prevent conflagration and loss of life—was ambitious and visionary. The first officers were primarily prominent Jersey City architects, including George Von Arx, Charles Frederick Long, Hugh Roberts, and Charles H. Detwiller. Located at 15 Exchange Place, the organization soon swelled to a membership of 50, representing almost all registered local architects. Municipal officials, the public, and visitors took notice of the high-quality construction methods and stylized designs of the building stock that was appearing mostly after the group's formation; they were solid, beautiful structures that would last and become, years later, celebrated landmarks. (Collection of the Jersey City Landmarks Conservancy.)

Thomas E. Ogorzalek and Cecilia S. deLeon

Thomas E. Ogorzalek and Cecilia S. deLeon are true community architects. Property owners in the Van Vorst Park Historic District for over 20 years and principals since 2004 in their own architecture practice, Continuum Design Studio LLC, they both have been active and long-term trustees and commissioners on community boards and historic district commissions. In their capacity as civic stewards, they have acted as architectural advisors to city agencies and developers to ensure sensitive, appropriate development. As partners of a progressive architecture firm, they are, as Cecilia states, "interested in utilizing design as an agent of positive change and improving the quality of life for people and the environment through design innovation. An underlying thread running through the practice is the research and application of emerging materials and technologies that perpetuate environmentally sustainable systems. In doing so it aspires to develop a conscientious design approach enabling a healthier global environment." But Continuum is also, in Tom's words, "a teaching office" that hires student interns in an effort to "enable future architects." Tom would know about teaching architecture; he has been an award-winning university lecturer in the College of Architecture and Design at New Jersey Institute of Technology in Newark since 2000, where he currently instructs upper-level design studios, special topics seminars, and independent studies. From the classroom of knowledge to the atelier of architecture, Tom and Cecilia inspire emerging visionaries who are destined, like them, to become integral to the community they live and work in.

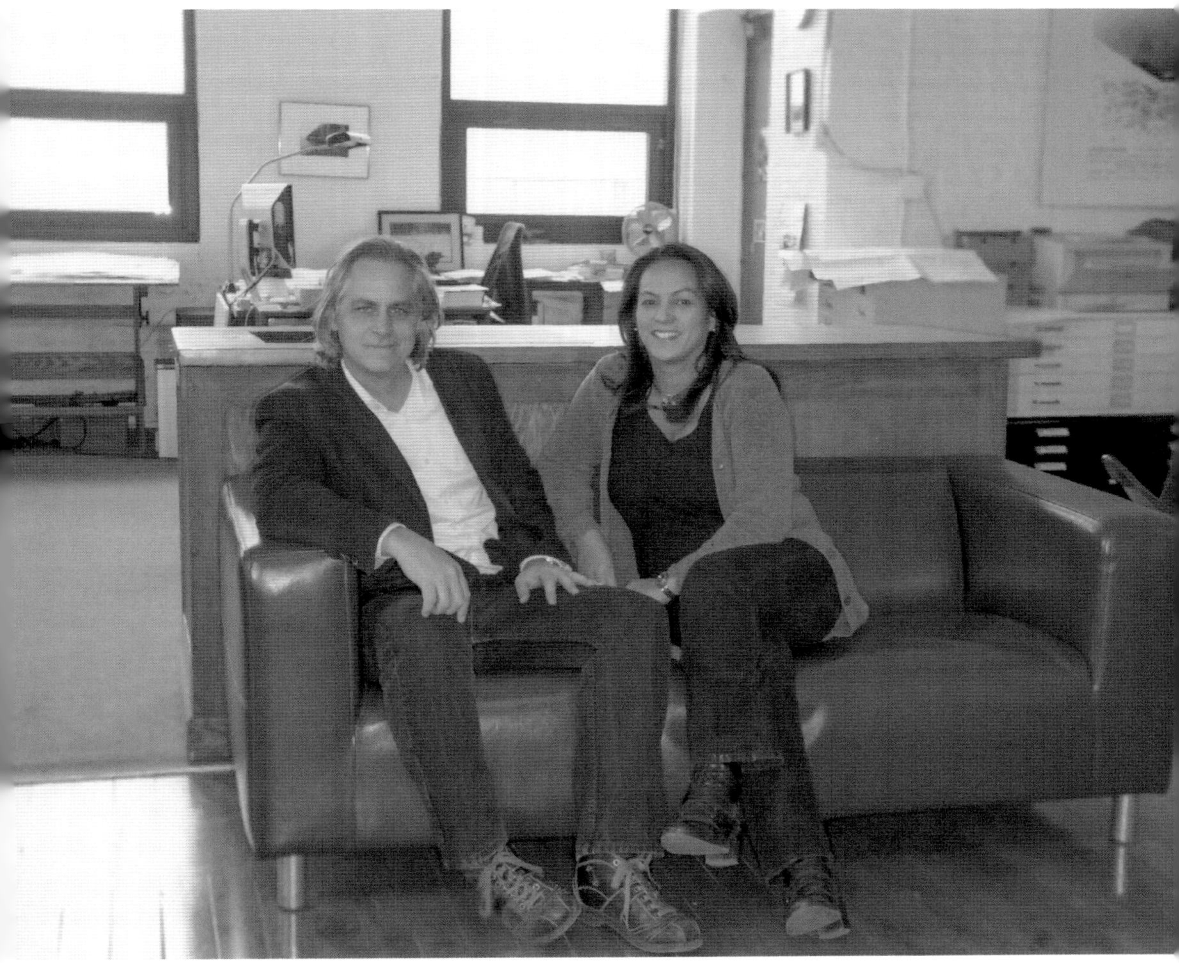

Alfred Charles Bossom

Amazingly, Jersey City is in possession of two buildings designed by Alfred Charles Bossom (1881–1965), one of the most important British architects of the 20th century, proponent of the skyscraper form, author of seminal architectural texts, and distinguished member of Parliament. Educated in England at Regent Street Polytechnic and the Royal Academy of Arts, Bossom came to the United States in 1903 to practice architecture, specializing at first in Neoclassical residences. Working from offices at 680 Fifth Avenue in New York, Bossom turned toward skyscraper engineering and design and became a specialist in tall bank building construction. An interpreter of Italian and Spanish Renaissance Revival forms, Bossom also incorporated Pre-Columbian Mayan motifs into his work, presaging the Art Deco movement. In Jersey City, at the apex of his career, Bossom designed the First National Bank (1920–1922) at Exchange Place and the Greenville Bank and Trust Company (1923–1924) at Ocean and Lembeck Avenues in the Greenville section. At 10 stories, the First National Bank was, when dedicated, the tallest building in Jersey City, beating out the adjacent George B. Post–designed Commercial Trust Company (erected in 1898–1900 as the city's first commercial skyscraper) by one flight. The Greenville Bank and Trust Company, while significantly smaller, is nonetheless a visually powerful vernacular Neo-Greek-stylized edifice roughly 50 feet in height. Aside from the practice of architecture, Bossom was a great scholar and supporter of new motives and emerging architects. In 1926, he curated the first exhibition devoted to the "American skyscraper as a work of art" in New York City, featuring the futuristic renderings of Hugh Ferris and the early structures of Emery Roth, and he wrote seminal texts on architectural history and theory, including *An Architectural Pilgrimage in Old Mexico* (1924) and *Building to the Skies: The Romance of the Skyscraper* (1934). (Courtesy of Avery Architectural & Fine Arts Library, Columbia University.)

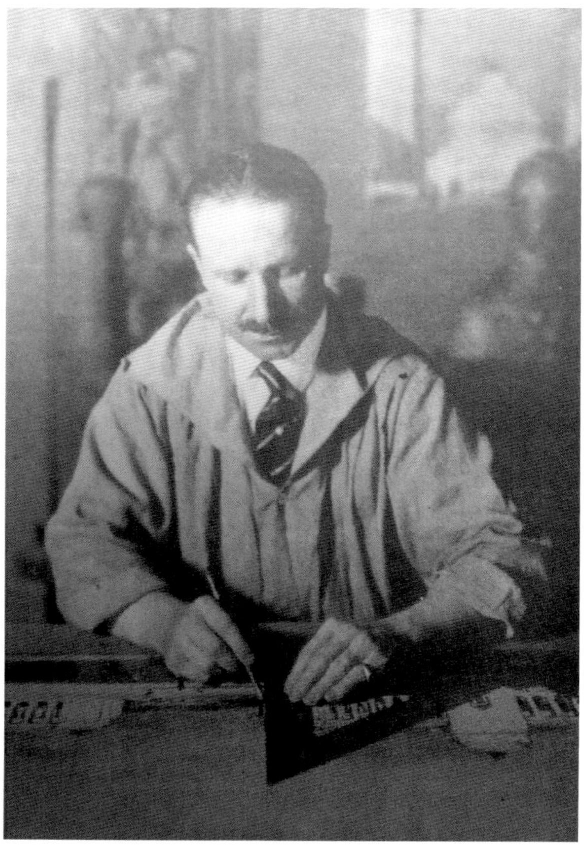

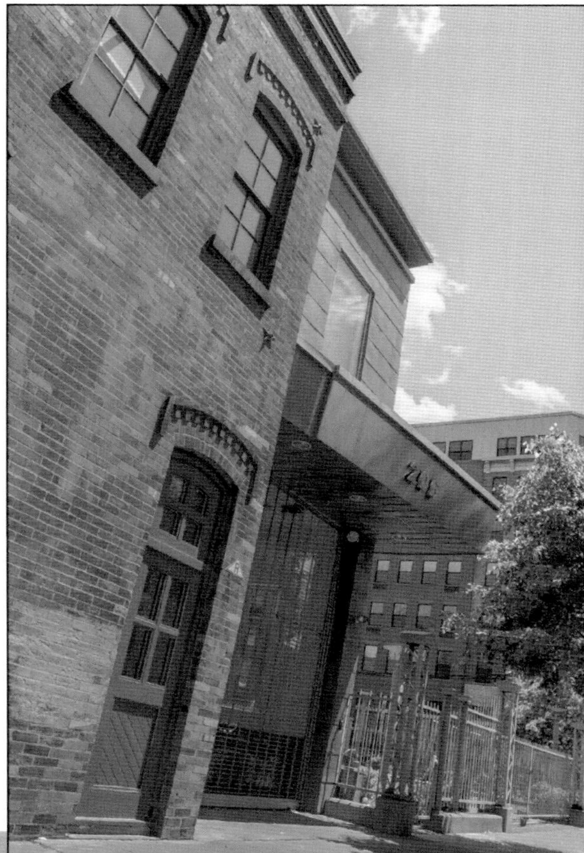

Ron Russell

When Jersey City native Ron Russell (below, rear center), who attended Dickinson High School, became an esteemed local architect, and served as a leading commissioner and architectural voice of reason on the Jersey City Historic Preservation Commission, was named a principal at the architectural firm of Lindemon Winckelmann Deupree Martin Russell & Associates (LWDMR), he knew he was joining the firm that pioneered local historic preservation. In 1986, the former Dixon Ticonderoga pencil factory complex stretching along Railroad Avenue (now Christopher Columbus Drive) was, with LWDMR's vision, transformed in phases into 475 market-rate residential units, the first residential adaptive reuse project of a large-scale industrial building in the city. Since that momentous preservation commission, the firm has gone on to preserve other pivotal structures like the former Koven Stove Works (now The Cliffs residences) on Paterson Plank Road and the c. 1888 Brinkmann & Hauck Wheelwrights warehouse (right) for the new Bel Fuse headquarters in Paulus Hook.

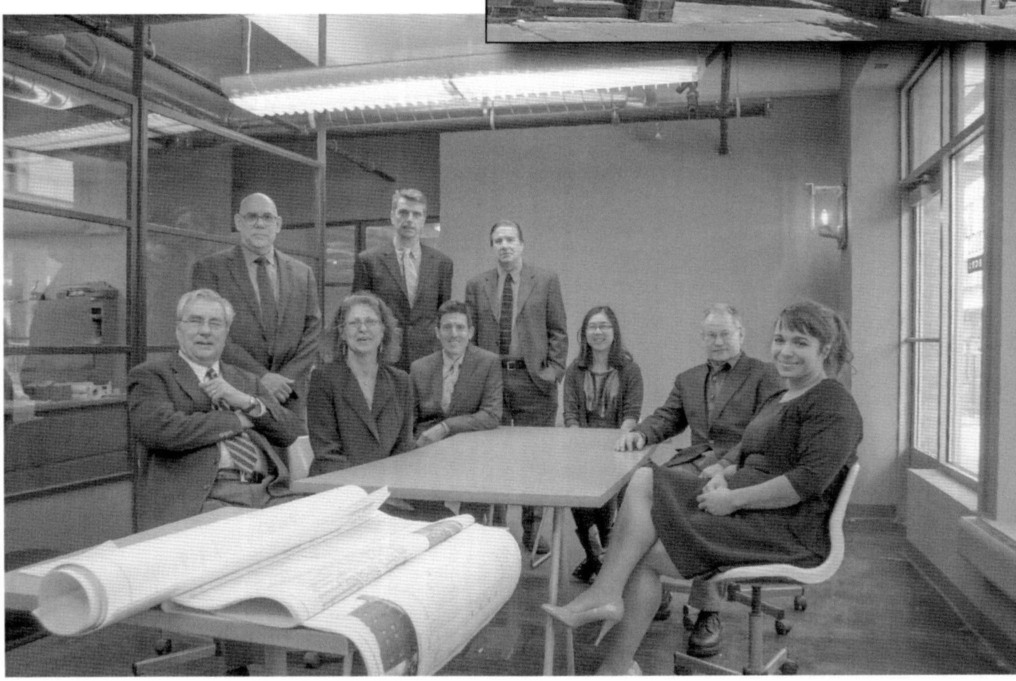

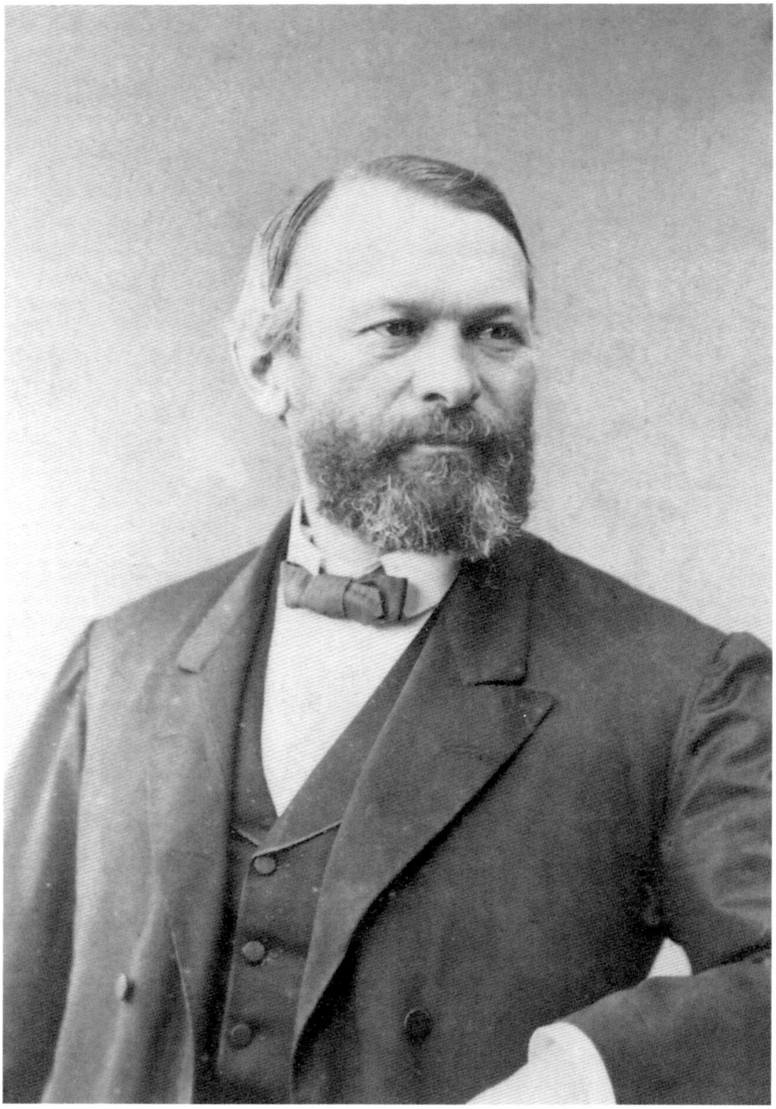

Detlef Lienau

Jersey City's first star architect was Detlef Lienau. Born in Denmark in 1818, Lienau studied construction craft and carpentry in Germany before apprenticing in the studio of the great French architect Henri Labrouste. Lienau abruptly left Europe in 1848 and sailed for America, settling in Van Vorst Township, which is now part of Jersey City's Harsimus Cove Historic District. In 1850, he drafted the plans for Grace Church at Second and Erie Streets. His design scheme was a stunning synthesis of the German and English rural Gothic, with picturesque elements of the early Romanesque—the first reference of its kind in America. Unveiled in 1853, the church hosted the wedding of Lienau and Catherine Van Giesen Booraem of the influential and wealthy Van Vorst family. Lienau, who resided in Jersey City up to 1886, a year before his death in Manhattan due to typhoid fever, was recognized as a true original; he introduced the French mansard roof into the American vernacular, a result of his experience in Paris, and he was one of the original charter members of the American Institute of Architects, an institution that continues to this day. (Courtesy of Michel Lanneau.)

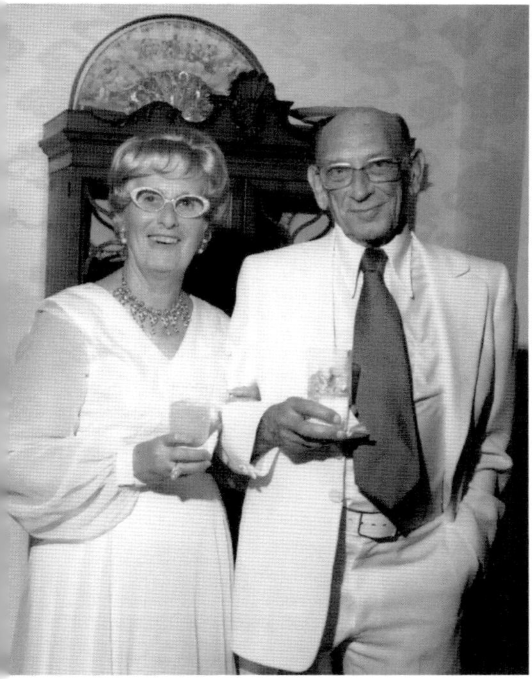

George Siegler

George Siegler (1895–1978) is a local engineering success story. Raised in Jersey City by Newark Avenue clothing store merchants, Siegler was a star student at the prestigious Steven's Institute of Technology in Hoboken, graduating in 1917 with a mechanical engineering degree. As a World War I army soldier, he achieved the rank of lieutenant, and later, he was founder, in 1927, of the George Siegler Company, an engineering firm specializing in monumental construction. He was also a participant in the building of the Holland Tunnel, the most lucrative and prominent engineering project in the world. Siegler, whose headquarters were located at 26 Journal Square, worked on major projects where architecture and engineering crossed paths. For the Holland Tunnel project and later the Lincoln Tunnel, he helped Norwegian architect Erling Owre express the mechanical moderne design of the vehicular system's ventilation towers. Other major engineering undertakings over the decades included the Marion Gardens housing project; Public School No. 38; Hudson Cinema, designed by the Jersey City firm of Comparetto & Kenny; and the Jewish Hospital (below), an awesome Brutalist structure designed in collaboration with Joseph Blumenkronz & Associates. "Everywhere, for all the world to see," an illustrated company brochure from the early 1970s states, "are the lasting monuments to a builder's integrity and ability." (Archival photographs courtesy of Judith J. Mender.)

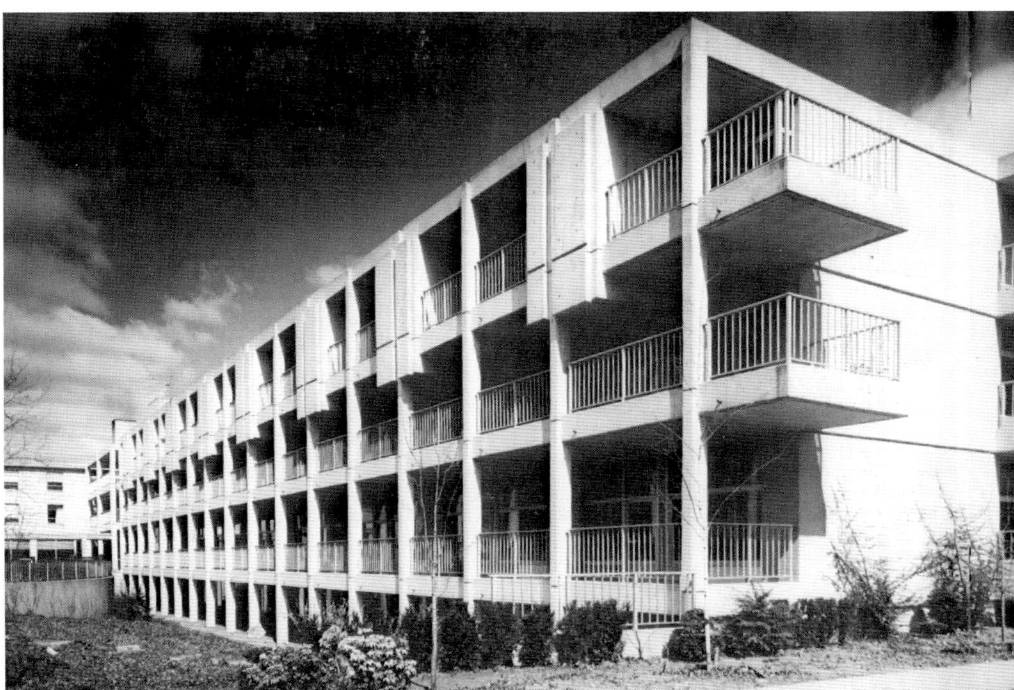

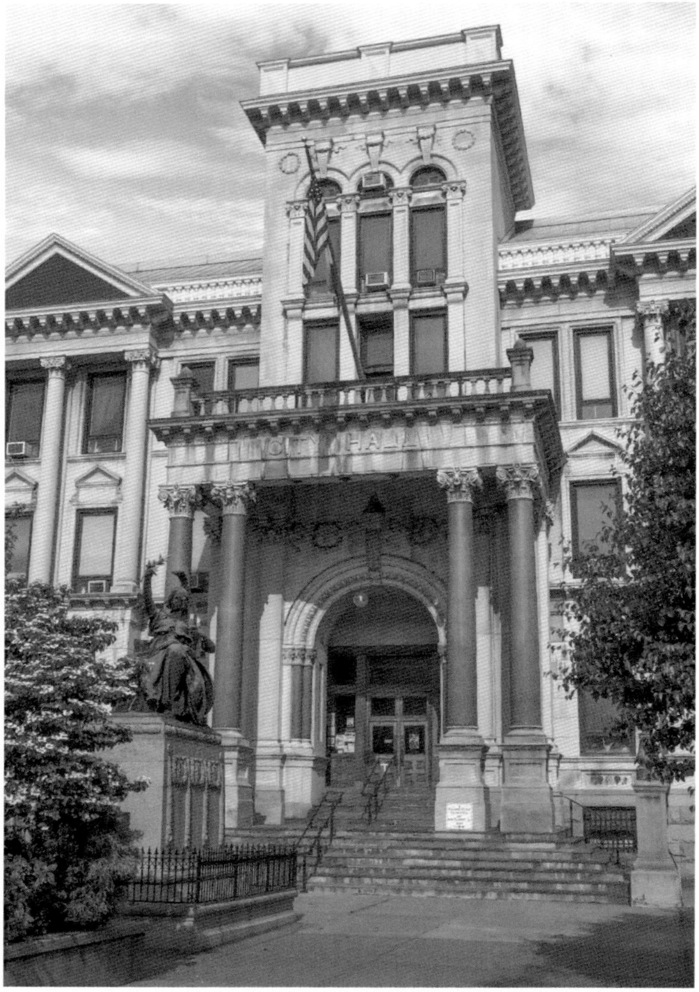

Lewis H. Broome

Lewis H. Broome (1849–1927) must be placed at the top of the Parthenon of Jersey City architects for his sheer output and resilience. Over a 50-year span, Broome, a veteran of the Civil War, dotted the city with significant buildings that stand as considerable monuments today, starting in 1870 with the steeple-cresting Bergen Baptist Church (now Salem Baptist Church) at Madison and Clinton Avenues. For nearly two decades, he designed every municipal building type—the tenement tower, the brooding brownstone, the multistoried stable, and the leisure lyceum—until he stumbled upon his supreme architectural métier, the legislative temple. In 1885, a massive fire destroyed the New Jersey State House in Trenton; a statewide competition was held, and Broome, who submitted plans calling for a combination Neoclassical-and-Victorian front facade and dome, won, instantly becoming the state's most renowned and envied architect. When the competition for a new municipal hall in Jersey City was held in 1892, he easily obtained first place, beating out serious upstarts like Hugh Roberts and Charles H. Detwiller. But Broome's success was short lived. Not long after the new city hall was completed in 1897, the architect was accused of substandard construction. The charges were eventually dropped, but Broome, struggling to fend off younger architects with progressive ideas, dropped out of the architectural limelight and worked on small commissions from a city hall office. Still, his career was long and prosperous; he held the respect of his peers and kept working into the 1920s.

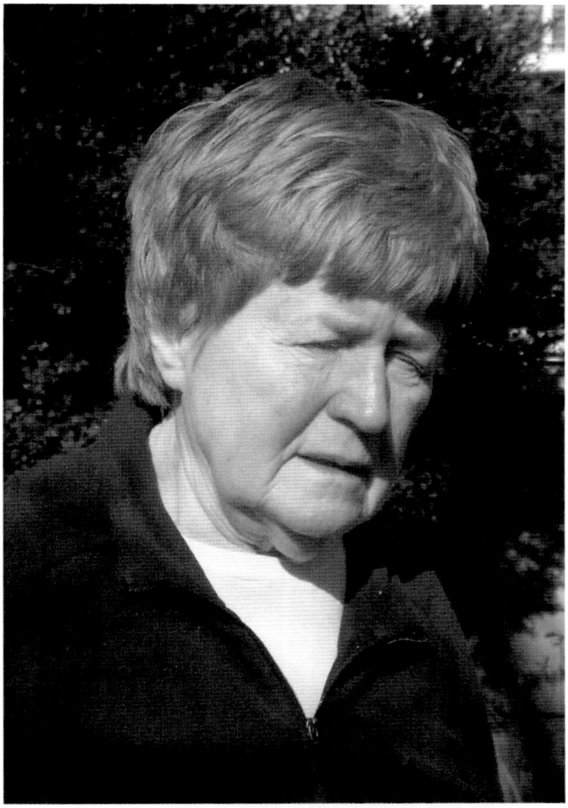

Ann Willis

Ann Willis (1935–2009) has the distinction of being Jersey City's first woman architect on equal, if not greater, par with her male-domineering architect counterparts. One of the first two women architects to be admitted into the New Jersey Chapter of the American Institute of Architects, Willis was one of the most creative local modernist architects of the 1960s. Her reputation and genius rests on a single building designed and erected from 1967 to 1969, which still stops passersby, 45 years later, in their tracks—Trinity United Methodist Church. The church is located at the southwest corner of Summit Avenue and Bowers Street in the Jersey City Heights. Still considered revolutionary for its shocking sculptural concrete form, bold exterior Brutalist materiality, and inner spatial beauty, Trinity retains most of Willis's features, including a suspended wood-paneled organ loft that seems to unfold in sheer space and a colossal poured-in-place concrete retaining wall over 80 feet high. (Architectural elevation courtesy of Ann Willis.)

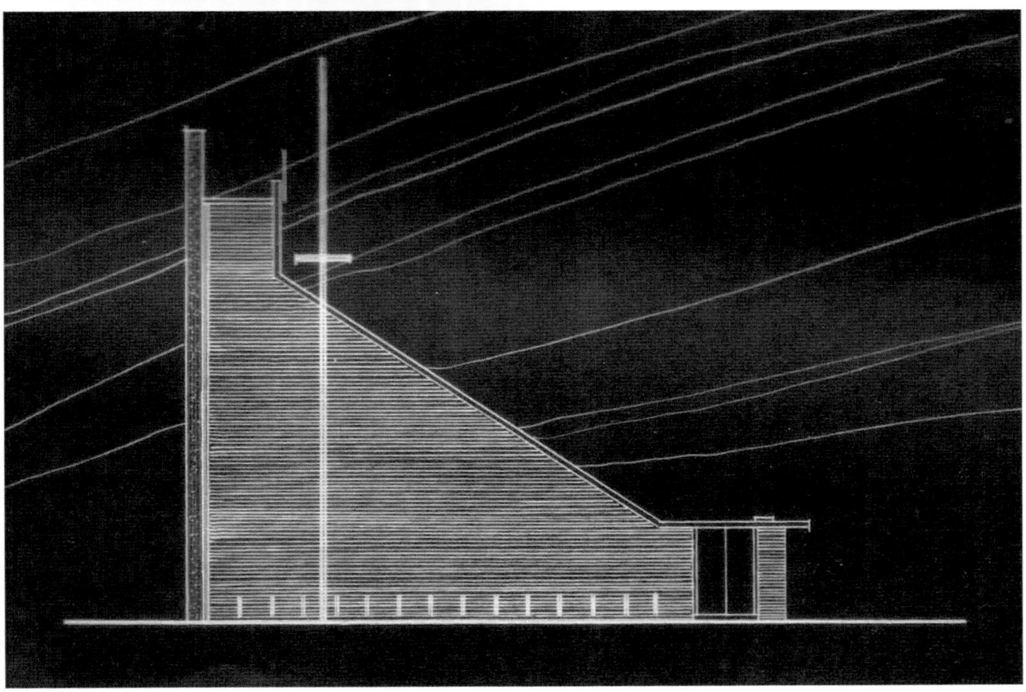

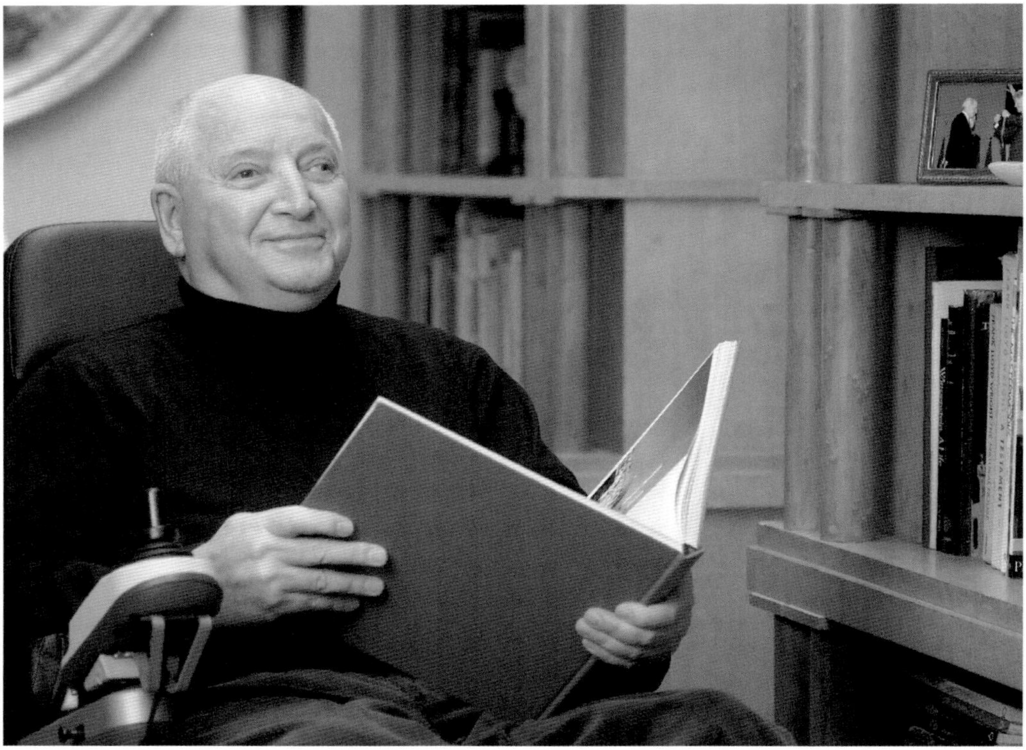

Michael Graves

Although based in Princeton, Michael Graves, the legendary American architect, painter, professor, lecturer, writer, and designer of popular consumer products for Target, has touched and transformed Jersey City forever. Two major works by the heralded master stand at two opposite ends of the city: the Environmental Education Center (1982–1983), located in the precise center of Liberty State Park amidst the rocky banks of the Hudson River; and the George Karnoutsos Arts & Sciences Hall (2002–2006) at the northern campus of New Jersey City University bounded by Kennedy Boulevard and Culver, West Side, and Audubon Avenues. For the entire Liberty State Park commission—single edifice, landscaped grounds, and lobby mural—Graves looked to the park's bounty of marshes, mudflats, industrial ruins, and "indigenous park structures built of exposed heavy timber construction." But the site is more sophisticated, and mysterious, than is suggested. An elegant vessel of instantly perceived lattice arches and trellises, the cedar and stucco-sided building—one of Jersey City's greatest postmodern monuments—is approachable from two sides and is marked by intimate walks and lanes through crossing colonnades. A few steps south of the central entrance are meandering paths leading visitors to a forested, idyllic region, punctuated every few feet by pavilions that were originally supposed to be pinnacled with windmills, a sustainable element decades ahead of its time. Inside, side exhibition rooms flank a long main auditorium with exposed beams and rafters. A mural painted by Graves depicting the industrial landscapes of Jersey City was part of the original plan, but it was removed at some point and relocated to Trenton. At New Jersey City University's main quadrangle, Graves erected a watercolor-like edifice for undergraduate study, but, unlike the university's adjacent 1960s- and 1970s-era halls and administration buildings, the building packs a visceral architectural power with its massing of colossal portico columns, modular precast concrete wall sections, a bracketed pyramidal tower, quaint courtyard loggias, and a subdued interior rotunda lit by natural and artificial light sources. While Graves's two Jersey City buildings are literally years and miles apart, they stand—as all architects secretly know about their creations—as one ephemeral entity, one municipal monument. (Portrait and architectural sketch courtesy of Michael Graves & Associates.)

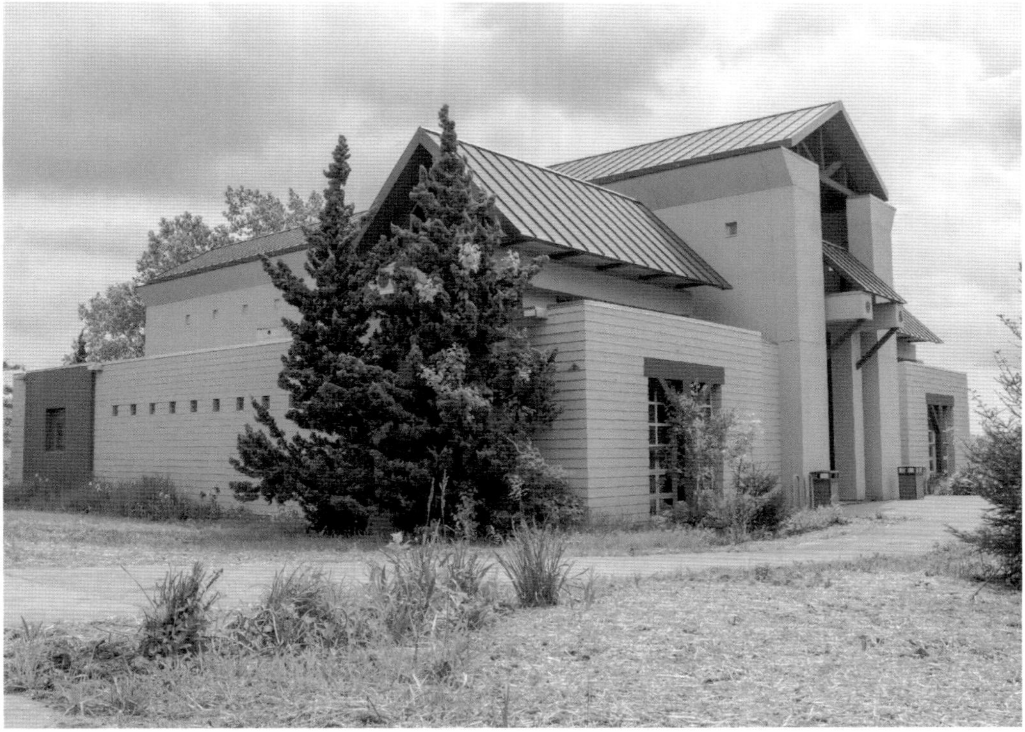

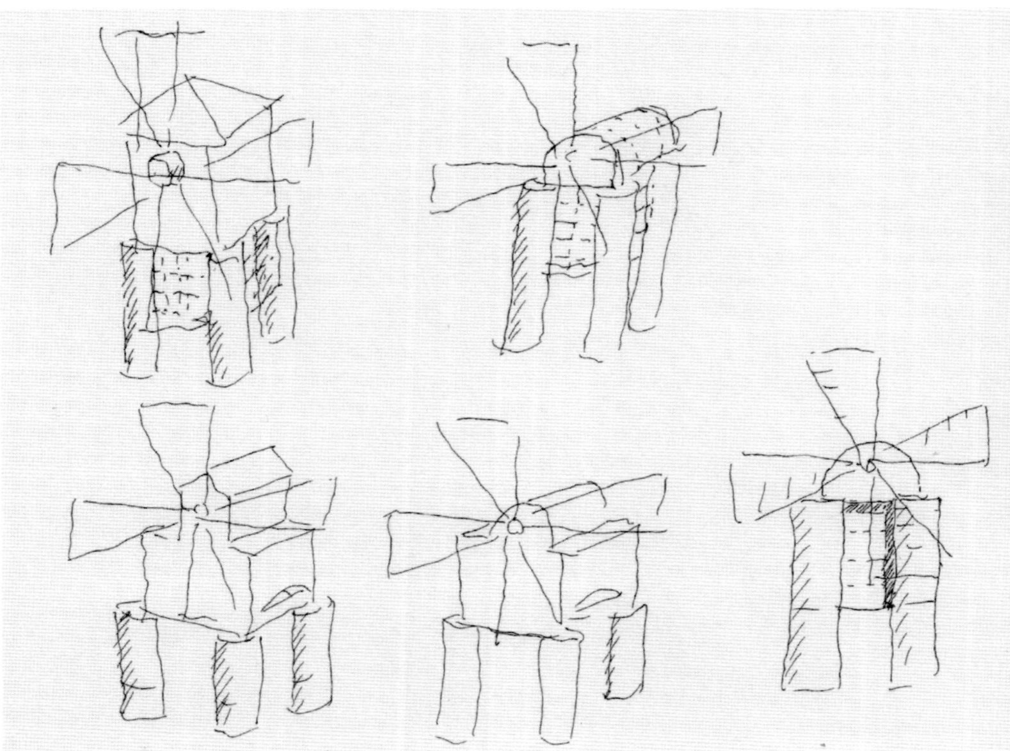

INDEX

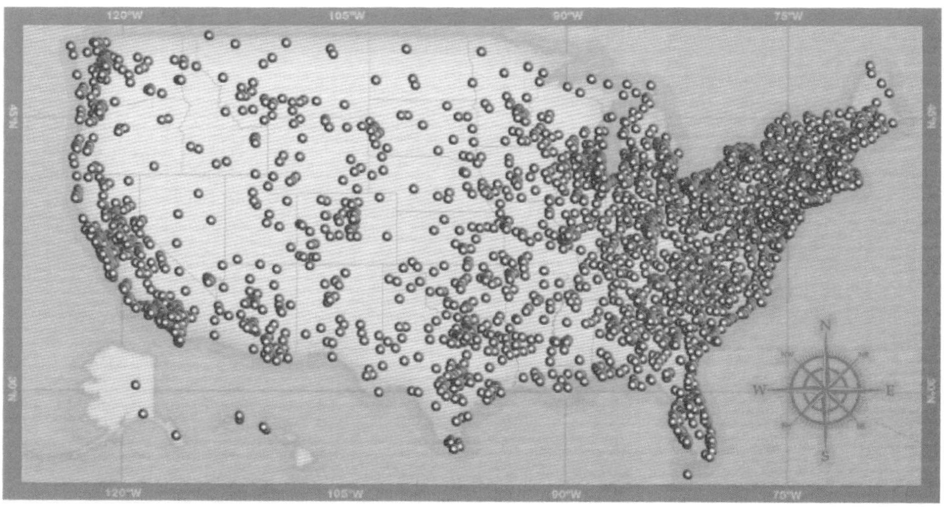